MATHS IN ACTION

Kevin Lamont

MATHEMATICS

Preparation for Assessment

Mathematics 1(H), 2(H), 3(H)
and Statistics (H)

E.C.K Mullan
K. Nisbet
R. Riddiough
R.D. Howat

Nelson

Nelson
Delta Place
27 Bath Road
Cheltenham
Glos GL53 7TH
United Kingdom

This edition first published by Nelson 2000

ISBN 0-17-431-540-6
9 8 7 6 5 4 3 2
04 03 02 01 00

Typeset by Upstream, London
Printed in Scotland

Contents

Preface

This book has been written to complement *Higher Mathematics* and *Statistics for Higher Mathematics* in the *Maths in Action* series. It provides additional practice exercises and assessment questions for all four units of Higher Mathematics.

Its structure follows the Learning Outcomes and Performance Criteria (PC) set out in the Higher Still Arrangements. It offers exercises to prepare students for Unit Assessment and Course Assessment.

Each unit contains the following elements:

• Preparation for Unit Assessment
There is an exercise for each Performance Criterion, which works around the specific content matter of the PC in the realisation that some candidates will be doing these exercises as a remedial loop. The exercises go beyond the PC in the knowledge that it is always good practice to go a bit further than is required by minimum assessment. Reminder notes are appropriately placed to serve as quick revision aids for students.

• Unit Assessment Tests
At the end of each Learning Outcome, a short test has been constructed in which each PC is tested in a very basic manner similar to that of the official instruments of assessment. As a general rule, however, each PC is tested twice. These tests will provide evidence of minimum C grade competence.

• Preparation for Course Assessment
These are questions which go beyond minimum competency, providing opportunities for extended response. They are often contextualised questions similar to those found in course assessment. Exercising the integration of knowledge and skills is essential. The questions, which are loosely associated with a particular Learning Outcome, allow this to happen. The Course Assessment Tests provide A/B grade evidence.

At the end of the book two specimen papers have been constructed to give students a thorough preparation for their final examination.

The contents of the book can be used in a variety of ways.
• The Unit Assessment Tests can be issued as homework with the Preparation for Unit Assessment pages acting as follow-up remedial exercises.
• Subsequent to an unsuccessful official Unit Assessment Test, the Preparation for Unit Assessment pages can be used for remediation, while the Preparation for Course Assessment pages can be used by successful candidates for reinforcement.
• Prior to Prelim exams or the Final course exam, the contents provide a well structured bank of questions for revision. Used for this purpose, the structure of the book itself will assist in the timetabling of the revision.

This book provides a wealth of high quality practice, reinforcement and revision exercises which will help students achieve success in their examinations.

Mathematics 1 (H) Contents

Preparation for Unit Assessment

OUTCOME 1a
Determine the equation of a straight line given two points on the line or one point and the gradient

1 Find the equation of the line through the given point with the given gradient:

   a (2, 5); 2   **b** (1, 3); –3   **c** (0, 5); 3

   d (4, 0); 5   **e** (–1, 4); –2   **f** (–3, –5); –4

   g (1, 3); $\frac{1}{2}$ **h** (–2, –1); $-\frac{1}{2}$ **i** (2, 6); $\frac{2}{3}$

> **Reminder**
> The line, with gradient m, which passes through the point (a, b) has equation
> $$y - b = m(x - a)$$

2 Three lines with gradients 2, –3 and $\frac{1}{2}$ each pass through (3, –1).
  Find their equations.

3 Calculate the gradient of the line passing through the points:

   a A(1, 5) and B(3, 7)

   b K(1, 8) and L(8, 1)

   c E(3, 7) and F(1, –1)

   d C(–2, 0) and D(0, 4)

   e G(2, –3) and H(4 ,–4)

   f M(3, –1) and N(–2, 1)

> **Reminder**
> The gradient of the line joining $A(x_A, y_A)$ and $B(x_B, y_B)$ is
> $$m_{AB} = \frac{y_B - y_A}{x_B - x_A}$$

4 Find the equation of the line passing through:

   a S(2, 7) and T(1, 5)

   b A(5, 1) and B(3, 7)

   c E(–3, 2) and F(0, –1)

   d C(–1, –3) and D(–2, –1)

   e G(–3, 3) and H(–1, 2)

   f K(–7, 3) and L(–4, 1)

> **Reminder**
> To find the equation of the line passing through two points, first find the gradient.

5

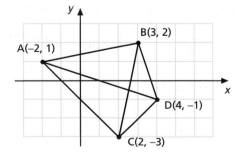

Using the information in the diagram, find the equation of:

   a AB   **b** BD   **c** BC

   d DC   **e** AC   **f** AD

6 Using the points A(–1, 3), B(2, 4), C(–3, –2) and D(1, –5), find the equations of:

   a AC   **b** AB   **c** BD   **d** CD   **e** AD   **f** BC

Preparation for Unit Assessment

OUTCOME 1b
Find the gradient of a straight line using m = tan θ

Reminder	Example 1	Example 2
The gradient of a straight line can be calculated using $m = \tan\theta$ where θ is the angle the line makes with the positive direction of the x-axis.	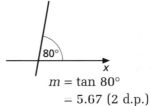 $m = \tan 80°$ $= 5.67$ (2 d.p.)	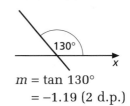 $m = \tan 130°$ $= -1.19$ (2 d.p.)

1 Find the gradient of each line, giving your answers to 3 significant figures where necessary (scales on the axes are equal):

a 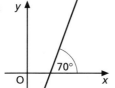 b 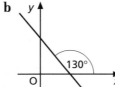 c 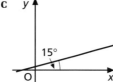 d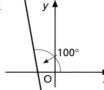

2 Find the gradient of the following lines (to 3 significant figures where necessary). The scales are equal on the axes.

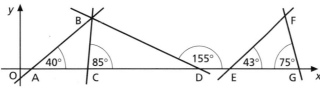

  a AB   b BC   c BD   d EF   e FG (careful)

Reminder		
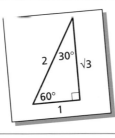	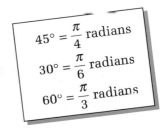	$45° = \dfrac{\pi}{4}$ radians $30° = \dfrac{\pi}{6}$ radians $60° = \dfrac{\pi}{3}$ radians

3 Find the *exact* value of the gradient of each line.

a 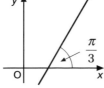 b 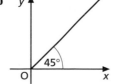 c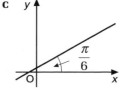

Preparation for Unit Assessment

OUTCOME 1c
Find the equation of a line parallel to and perpendicular to a given line

1 Find the gradient of each line:

a $y = 3x - 2$ **b** $y = -2x$

c $y = \frac{1}{2}x + 3$ **d** $y = 4$

e $y + 4x = 6$ **f** $3x - y = 2$

g $5x + y = 7$ **h** $2y = 4x + 3$

i $3y = 9x - 2$ **j** $2y = x + 4$

k $3y = 2x - 1$ **l** $2y - 4x = 7$

Reminder

When the equation of a line is written in the form $y = mx + c$ then m is the gradient

Reminder

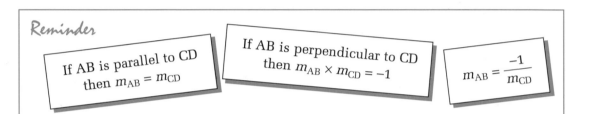

If AB is parallel to CD then $m_{AB} = m_{CD}$

If AB is perpendicular to CD then $m_{AB} \times m_{CD} = -1$

$m_{AB} = \dfrac{-1}{m_{CD}}$

2 Give the gradient of a line (**i**) parallel (**ii**) perpendicular to the given line:

a $y = 2x - 1$ **b** $y = \frac{1}{2}x + 2$ **c** $y = -3$

d $y = -x - 1$ **e** $y = x$ **f** $y = -4x + 2$

g $3y - 6x = 2$ **h** $3y + x = 2$ **i** $2y + 3x = 1$

3 Find the equation of a line passing through the given point that is parallel to the given line:

a $(1, 2); y = 2x + 1$ **b** $(-1, 3); y = -x + 2$ **c** $(3, -2); y = 3$

d $(-2, -1); y = -3x + 1$ **e** $(4, 2); y - 2x = 1$ **f** $(-3, 1); y - 5x = 2$

4 Find the equation of a line passing through the given point that is perpendicular to the given line:

a $(1, 2); y = x + 1$ **b** $(1, 5); y = 2x + 3$ **c** $(1, 2); y = 4$

d $(2, 0); y = -2x + 1$ **e** $(3, 12); y - 3x = 2$ **f** $(0, 0); 2y - x = 1$

5 Find the equation of:

a PQ

b RS

c TV

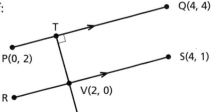

Q(4, 4)

T

P(0, 2)

S(4, 1)

V(2, 0)

R

Outcome 1 Assessment

1 P and Q are the points (2, 4) and (−1, −5) respectively. Calculate the equation of the line which passes through P and Q.

2 AB has a gradient of −4. A is point (2, −3). Work out the equation of the line AB and express it in the form $y = mx + c$.

3 Calculate the gradient of PQ in each diagram.

a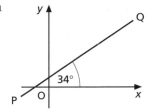

b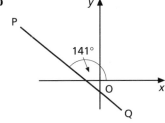

4 Work out the equation of the line passing through (1, 1)
  a parallel to
  b perpendicular to
  the line with equation $y + 2x = 4$.

5 Work out the equation of
  a TK
  b KG
  given the information in the diagram.

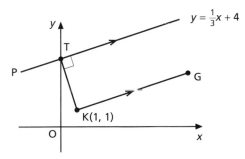

Preparation for Unit Assessment

OUTCOME 2a
Sketch and identify related graphs and functions

Reminder

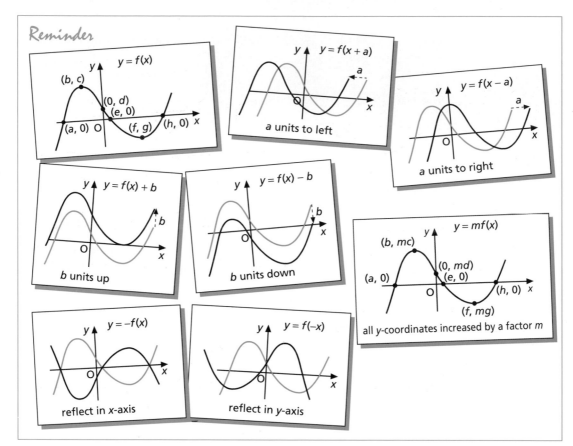

1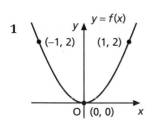

Use the graph of $y = f(x)$ to help you sketch:

a $y = f(x + 1)$ **b** $y = f(x - 1)$ **c** $y = -f(x)$

d $y = f(-x)$ **e** $y = \frac{1}{2}f(x)$ **f** $y = f(x) + 1$

2 Given $y = g(x)$:

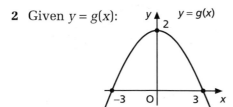

sketch the graphs: **a** $y = g(x + 2)$
b $y = g(x - 3)$ **c** $y = 3g(x)$
d $y = -g(x)$ **e** $y = g(x) - 1$

3 Given $y = f(x)$:

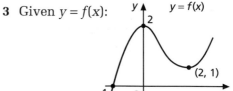

sketch the graphs: **a** $y = -f(x)$
b $y = f(x - 1)$ **c** $y = f(x + 2)$
d $y = 2f(x)$ **e** $y = f(x) - 2$

Preparation for Unit Assessment

OUTCOME 2a
Sketch and identify related graphs and functions (trigonometry)

Reminder

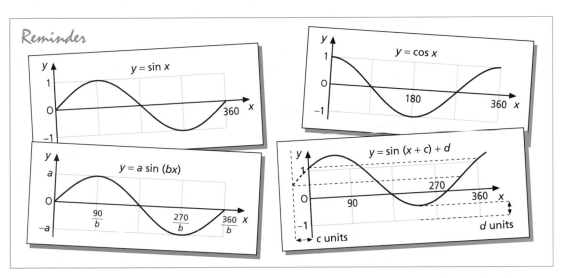

1   Each of the following graphs has an equation of the form $y = a \sin (bx + c) + d$.
    Work out the equation in each case.

a
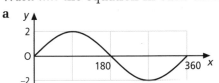

b
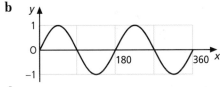

c
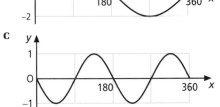

d
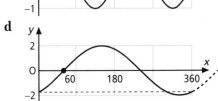

2   Each of the following graphs has an equation of the form $y = a \cos (bx + c) + d$.
    Work out the equation in each case.

a
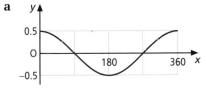

b
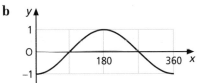

c
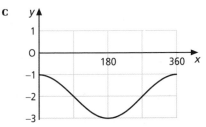

d
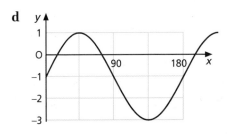

Preparation for Unit Assessment

OUTCOME 2b
Identify exponential and logarithmic graphs

Reminder

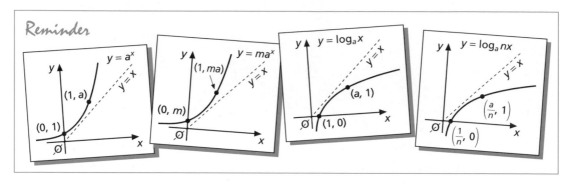

1 Sketch the graph of each function. On your graph mark the coordinates of a point
   (i) to the left of (ii) on (iii) to the right of the y-axis.
   a $y = 3^x$ **b** $y = 5^x$ **c** $y = 10^x$ **d** $y = 6^x$

2 The equation for each graph is of the form $y = a^x$. In each case state the value of the
   constant a.

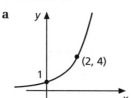

a (2, 4)   **b** (−1, 0.25)   **c** (1, 3)

3 The equation for each graph is of the form $y = ma^x$. In each case state the value of:
   (i) the constant m (examine the y-axis)
   (ii) the constant a (examine the given point).

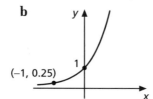
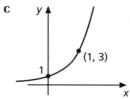

a (1, 6)   **b** (1, 12)   **c** (1, −5)

4 Sketch the following graphs showing clearly the x-axis intercept and marking the
   coordinates of one other point on the graph:
   a $y = \log_6 x$ **b** $y = \log_{10} x$ **c** $y = \log_2 x$ **d** $y = \log_4 x$ **e** $y = \log_9 x$

5 State the equation of each graph. (Its form has been given.)

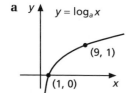
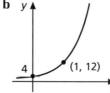
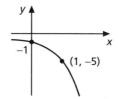
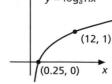

a $y = \log_a x$, (9, 1), (1, 0)
b $y = \log_a x$, (4, 1), (1, 0)
c $y = \log_a nx$, (1, 1), (0.5, 0)
d $y = \log_a nx$, (12, 1), (0.25, 0)

Preparation for Unit Assessment

OUTCOME 2c
Find the composite functions of the form f(g(x)), given f(x) and g(x)

Example

$$f(x) = 2x^2 + 3x + 4, g(x) = 2x + 1$$

$$f(g(x)) = f(2x + 1)$$
$$= 2(\ldots)^2 + 3(\ldots) + 4$$
$$= 2(2x + 1)^2 + 3(2x + 1) + 4$$
$$= 2(4x^2 + 4x + 1) + 6x + 3 + 4$$
$$= 8x^2 + 14x + 9$$

$$g(f(x)) = g(2x^2 + 3x + 4)$$
$$= 2(\ldots) + 1$$
$$= 2(2x^2 + 3x + 4) + 1$$
$$= (4x^2 + 6x + 8) + 1$$
$$= 4x^2 + 6x + 9$$

---

1 **a** Replace A by $x + 1$ and simplify: **(i)** 2A   **(ii)** A^2 **(iii)** A + 3   **(iv)** 2A − 3
   b Replace B by x^2:   **(i)** 3B   **(ii)** B − 1   **(iii)** 4B + 1   **(iv)** $\frac{1}{2}$B
   c Replace E by $2x − 4$:   **(i)** E^2 **(ii)** 2E − 4   **(iii)** $\frac{1}{2}$E   **(iv)** 3 + E

2 Find expressions for:
   a $f(x + 1)$ where   **(i)** $f(x) = x^2$ **(ii)** $f(x) = x − 2$ **(iii)** $f(x) = 3x$
   b $g(2x)$ where   **(i)** $g(x) = 5 − x$ **(ii)** $g(x) = x + 1$ **(iii)** $g(x) = x^2$
   c $f(x − 1)$ where   **(i)** $f(x) = x^2$ **(ii)** $f(x) = \sqrt{x}$ **(iii)** $f(x) = x + 1$

3 Obtain an expression for **(i)** $f(g(x))$ and **(ii)** $g(f(x))$ where:
   a $f(x) = x + 2, g(x) = 2x$ **b** $f(x) = x^2, g(x) = x − 1$
   c $f(x) = \sqrt{x}, g(x) = x + 1$ **d** $f(x) = \sin x, g(x) = 2x$
   e $f(x) = 1 − x, g(x) = 2x$ **f** $f(x) = 3x, g(x) = \cos x$

4 Functions g, h and k are defined on suitable domains by $g(x) = \frac{1}{2}x$, $h(x) = x^2$ and
   $k(x) = 2x + 4$. Find:
   a $g(k(x))$ **b** $k(g(x))$ **c** $h(k(x))$
   d $k(h(x))$ **e** $k(k(x))$ **f** $g(h(x))$
   g $h(h(x))$ **h** $g(g(x))$ **i** $h(g(x))$

5 For each pair of functions f and g find an expression for
   (i) $f(f(x))$ **(ii)** $f(g(x))$ **(iii)** $g(f(x))$ **(iv)** $g(g(x))$
   a $f(x) = x + 4, g(x) = 3x$ **b** $f(x) = x − 5, g(x) = 2x$
   c $f(x) = 2x, g(x) = 1 − x$ **d** $f(x) = x^2, g(x) = x + 2$

Outcome 2 Assessment

1 This is the graph of $y = f(x)$ near the origin.
   a Draw a graph of $y = -f(x)$
   b Sketch **(i)** $y = f(x - 3)$ **(ii)** $y = 4 + f(x)$

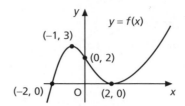

2 Here is a graph of $y = \sin x$ and two related functions. State the equations of the two related functions.

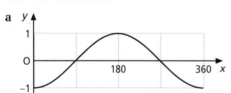

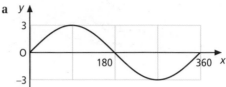

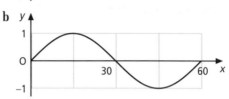

3 Here are the graphs of two functions related to $y = \cos x$. State the equations of the two functions.

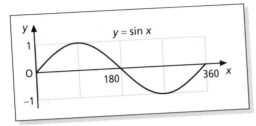

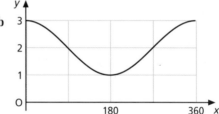

4 **a** Write down the equation of the graph of this exponential function in the form $y = a^x$
   b Write down the equation of its inverse function.

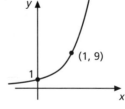

5

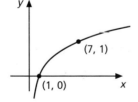

Write down the equation of the graph of this logarithmic function.

6 **a** Two functions are defined by $f(x) = x^2$ and $g(x) = 3x - 1$.
    Obtain an expression for $f(g(x))$.
   b Functions p and q are defined on suitable domains by $p(x) = \cos x$ and $q(x) = \dfrac{1}{x}$.
    Obtain an expression for **(i)** $p(q(x))$ **(ii)** $q(p(x))$.

Preparation for Unit Assessment

OUTCOME 3a

Differentiate a function reducible to a sum of powers of x

Reminder

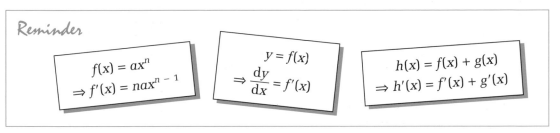

$$f(x) = ax^n$$
$$\Rightarrow f'(x) = nax^{n-1}$$

$$y = f(x)$$
$$\Rightarrow \frac{dy}{dx} = f'(x)$$

$$h(x) = f(x) + g(x)$$
$$\Rightarrow h'(x) = f'(x) + g'(x)$$

1 Differentiate: **a** $4x^3$ **b** x **c** $2x - 3$ **d** $2x^2 + 2x + 6$

2 Find $\dfrac{dy}{dx}$:

  a $y = x^3 - x^{-2}$ **b** $y = x + x^{-1}$ **c** $y = 3x - x^{-1}$ **d** $y = 5x^2 - x^{-3}$

3 Write each of these in the form ax^n then differentiate:

  a $\dfrac{1}{x^2}$ **b** $\dfrac{3}{x}$ **c** $\dfrac{1}{x^3}$ **d** $\dfrac{-3}{x^4}$ **e** $-\dfrac{2}{3x^2}$ **f** $\dfrac{1}{4x}$ **g** $\dfrac{2}{3x}$

4 Find $f'(x)$:

  a $f(x) = \sqrt{x}$ **b** $f(x) = 3\sqrt{x}$ **c** $f(x) = -2\sqrt{x}$ **d** $f(x) = \dfrac{1}{\sqrt{x}}$

  e $f(x) = -\dfrac{4}{\sqrt{x}}$ **f** $f(x) = -\dfrac{4}{3\sqrt{x}}$

5 Differentiate:

  a $(x + 1)^2$ **b** $(2x - 1)^2$ **c** $(x + 1)(x - 3)$ **d** $x^2(x - 1)$

  e $3(x - 1)^2$ **f** $2(x - 1)(x + 4)$ **g** $-(x - 3)^2$ **h** $(3x - 2)^2$

6 Find $\dfrac{dy}{dx}$:

  a $y = 3x - \dfrac{1}{x}$ **b** $y = x^2 + \dfrac{2}{x}$ **c** $y = \sqrt{x} + 3x$ **d** $y = \dfrac{3}{x} - \sqrt{x}$

  e $y = \dfrac{x}{2} + x^2$ **f** $y = 2\sqrt{x} - \dfrac{x}{3}$ **g** $y = \dfrac{x^2}{5} - 3\sqrt{x}$ **h** $y = \dfrac{1}{\sqrt{x}} + \sqrt{x}$

7 Find $g'(x)$:

  a $g(x) = \dfrac{x + 1}{x^2}$ **b** $g(x) = \dfrac{x^2 - 1}{x}$ **c** $g(x) = \dfrac{2x + 3}{x^3}$ **d** $g(x) = \dfrac{5 - 3x}{x}$

  e $g(x) = \dfrac{3x^2 + x}{x}$ **f** $g(x) = \dfrac{4 - x^2}{2x}$ **g** $g(x) = \dfrac{x + 1}{\sqrt{x}}$ **h** $g(x) = \dfrac{2x - 1}{\sqrt{x}}$

  i $g(x) = \dfrac{\sqrt{x} + 3x}{x}$ **j** $g(x) = \dfrac{x^2 - 2\sqrt{x}}{x}$

Preparation for Unit Assessment

OUTCOME 3b
Determine the gradient of a tangent to a curve by differentiation

1 a $f(x) = x^2$. Find the values of:
   (i) $f'(3)$ (ii) $f'(0)$ (iii) $f'(-2)$

> **Reminder**
>
> The gradient of the curve $y = f(x)$ at $x = a$ is given by $f'(a)$.

   b $f(x) = 3x^2 - x$. Find the values of:
   (i) $f'(2)$ (ii) $f'(-1)$ (iii) $f'\left(\frac{1}{2}\right)$

   c $f(x) = (x + 1)(x - 1)$. Find the values of: (i) $f'(10)$ (ii) $f'\left(-\frac{1}{2}\right)$ (iii) $f'(-3)$

2 Find the gradient of the curve:
   a $y = x^3$ at $x = 2$
   b $y = 4x^2$ at $x = -1$
   c $y = x^2 - x$ at $x = 1$
   d $y = 2x - x^2$ at $x = -2$
   e $y = 3 - x^3$ at $x = 3$
   f $y = 4x^2 - 2x + 3$ at $x = 5$
   g $y = 5(x^2 - 2x)$ at $x = -1$
   h $y = (x + 3)(x - 3)$ at $x = 2$
   i $y = (2x + 1)^2$ at $x = -2$

3 In each case find the gradient of the tangent drawn to the curve at the given point:

   a
   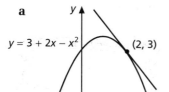

   b
   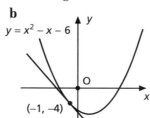

   c
   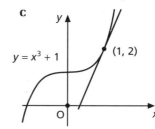

   d
   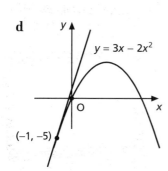

   e
   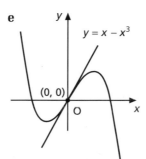

   f
   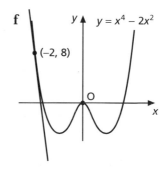

4 Find the gradient of the tangent drawn to the curve:
   a $y = x(x + 2)$ at the point $(-2, 0)$
   b $y = 5x(1 - x)$ at the point $(2, -10)$
   c $y = (2x + 1)(x - 1)$ at the point $\left(\frac{1}{2}, -1\right)$
   d $y = \sqrt{x}$ at the point $(4, 2)$
   e $y = \dfrac{4}{\sqrt{x}}$ at the point $(1, 4)$

Preparation for Unit Assessment

OUTCOME 3c
Determine the coordinates of the stationary points on a curve and justify their nature using differentiation

Reminder

If $f'(x) > 0$ then $f(x)$ is strictly increasing.
If $f'(x) < 0$ then $f(x)$ is strictly decreasing.
If $f'(x) = 0$ then $f(x)$ is stationary.

Studying the value of $f'(x)$ to the left and right of a stationary point helps you determine its nature.

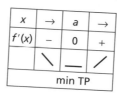

x	$\rightarrow$	a	$\rightarrow$
$f'(x)$	$+$	0	$-$
	/	—	\
		max TP	

x	$\rightarrow$	a	$\rightarrow$
$f'(x)$	$-$	0	$+$
	\	—	/
		min TP	

x	$\rightarrow$	a	$\rightarrow$
$f'(x)$	$-$	0	$-$
	\	—	\
		point of inflexion	

1 a The display shows the graph
   $y = 2x^3 + 3x^2 - 36x - 10$.
   (i) Find the coordinates of the two stationary points.
   (ii) Confirm, using differentiation, that one is a maximum and the other a minimum stationary point.

b This display shows the graph of $y = f(x)$ where
   $f(x) = 3x^4 + 4x^3 - 12x^2$
   (i) Find the coordinates of the three stationary points.
   (ii) Confirm, using differentiation, that one is a maximum and the other two are minimum stationary points.

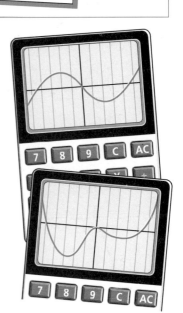

2 For each of the following curves find the coordinates of their stationary points and use differentiation to determine their nature:

a $y = 2x^3 - 9x^2 + 12x - 5$

b $y = \frac{1}{3}x^3 - x$

c $y = x^3 + 3x^2 - 9x - 20$

d $y = \frac{2}{3}x^3 - x^2 + 1$

e $y = 3x^3 - 3x^2$

f $y = \frac{1}{3}x^3 + x^2 - 1$

g $y = 2x^3 - \frac{3}{2}x^2 - 3x - 1$

h $y = \frac{1}{3}x^3 + 4x^2 + 16x$

Outcome 3 Assessment

1 Given that $y = \dfrac{x^4 + 2x}{x^2}$, find $\dfrac{dy}{dx}$.

2 If $f(x) = \dfrac{1}{x^2} - \dfrac{3}{\sqrt{x}}$, find $f'(x)$.

3 The diagram shows the sketch of the function
$y = x^2 - 3x - 10$ near the origin. A tangent is
drawn to the point $(3, -10)$.
Calculate the gradient of this tangent.

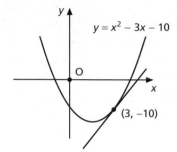

4

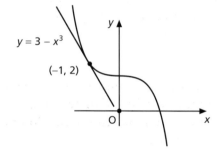

Calculate the gradient of the curve $y = 3 - x^3$ at the point where $x = -1$.

5 Calculate the coordinates of the stationary points of the curve with equation
$y = x^3 - 3x^2 - 9x + 4$.
Determine their nature.

6 Find the stationary points of the function $f(x) = 3x^5 - 5x^3 + 1$.
Determine their nature.

Preparation for Unit Assessment

OUTCOME 4a
Define and interpret a recurrence relation in the form
$u_{n+1} = mu_n + c$ (m, c constants) in a mathematical model

1 a The number, u_n, of insects alive in a tank after n days is given by
$u_n = 0.6u_{n-1} + 10$. If $u_0 = 400$ find how many are alive after:
(i) 1 day   (ii) 2 days   (iii) 3 days.

b u_n plants are diseased after n days. If $u_{n+1} = \frac{3}{4}u_n + 64$ and $u_0 = 1024$,
how many are diseased after:
(i) 1 day   (ii) 2 days   (iii) 4 days?

c There are u_n seedlings visible after n days. If $u_{n+1} = \frac{1}{2}u_n + 16$ with $u_0 = 256$,
how many are visible after:
(i) 2 days   (ii) 4 days   (iii) 5 days?

d During a course of injections the number of units, u_n, of a drug in a patient's
blood after n hours is given by the recurrence relation $u_n = 0.8u_{n-1} + 10$.
If $u_0 = 25$ how many units remain after:
(i) 1 hour   (ii) 2 hours   (iii) 3 hours?

2 a In a butterfly enclosure, one third of the butterflies die during the day and are
replaced before opening the next day by 20 new butterflies. If there are u_n
butterflies at opening on a particular day, write down a recurrence relation for
u_{n+1}, the number of butterflies at opening the next day.

b In a fish farm, one quarter of the fish in a tank are removed during each week.
Each weekend 1000 new young fish are added to the tank. At the start of one
particular week u_n fish are in the tank. Write a recurrence relation for u_{n+1}, the
number of fish in the tank at the start of the next week.

c Each month one fifth of the length of a coastal path is lost to sea erosion. The
local council reclaims 80 metres of path at the end of each month due to repair
work. If there are u_n metres of path at the start of a particular month, write a
recurrence relation for u_{n+1}, the number of metres of existing path at the start of
the next month.

d 10% of the ripe apples are picked each day in an orchard. A further 600 apples
become ripe overnight. If u_n apples are ripe at the start of a particular day, write a
recurrence relation for u_{n+1}, the number of ripe apples at the start of the next day.

3 For each of the following write a recurrence relation that describes the situation.
Explain clearly the meaning of the notation that you use.

a 80% of pollutants are removed each week from a loch by a purifying plant. At the
weekend a local factory discharges a further 3 tonnes of pollutant into the loch.

b During the course of each month 5% of the road length in a town becomes
'unsuitable' and requires resurfacing. At the end of each month 8 km of roads are
resurfaced and become 'suitable' again.

c A lending library finds that 8% of its CD stock is damaged each week so they add
25 new CDs to the stock each weekend.

Preparation for Unit Assessment

OUTCOME 4b
Find and interpret the limit of a sequence generated by a recurrence relation in a mathematical model (where the limit exists)

Reminder

A recurrence relation of the form $u_{n+1} = au_n + b$ has a limit when $-1 < a < 1$. a is often referred to as the multiplier.

The limit, when it exists, is
$$L = \frac{b}{(1-a)}$$

---

1 In each recurrence relation, there is a limit since the multiplier lies between -1 and 1. In each case find this limit:

a $u_{n+1} = \frac{1}{2}u_n + 12$ **b** $u_{n+1} = 0.4u_n + 12$ **c** $u_{n+1} = 0.2u_n + 1$

d $u_{n+1} = \frac{2}{3}u_n + 5$ **e** $u_{n+1} = 0.9u_n + 300$ **f** $u_{n+1} = \frac{3}{4}u_n + 7$

g $u_{n+1} = 0.8u_n + 18$ **h** $u_{n+1} = \frac{2}{5}u_n + 24$

2 a The number, u_n, of fish alive in a pond after n months is given by
$u_n = 0.8u_{n-1} + 12$.
Find the limit of the sequence generated by this recurrence relation.
Interpret this limit in the context of the question.

b u_n shrubs are blighted by greenfly after n days.
If $u_{n+1} = 0.4u_n + 102$, calculate the limit of the sequence generated by this recurrence relation. Interpret this limit in the context of the question.

3 a Each month one quarter of the garbage in a city dump is burned in the incinerators. This is then topped up by 600 tonnes of new rubbish each month.
  (i) If there are u_n tonnes of garbage at the start of a particular month, write down a recurrence relation for u_{n+1}, the number of tonnes of garbage in the dump at the start of the next month.
  (ii) Calculate the limit of the sequence generated by this recurrence relation. Interpret this limit in the context of the question.

b 40% of a mushroom crop are collected each day. A further 800 mushrooms become ready overnight.
  (i) If u_n mushrooms are ready at the start of a particular day, write a recurrence relation for u_{n+1}, the number of mushrooms ready at the start of the next day.
  (ii) Calculate the limit of the sequence generated by this recurrence relation. Interpret this limit in the context of the question.

Outcome 4 Assessment

1 During each week seepage beneath a concrete wall causes one fifth of the water in a pond to be lost.
500 litres of water are pumped back in each weekend.
At the start of a particular week u_n litres are in the pond.
   a Find a recurrence relation for u_{n+1}, the number of litres in the pond at the start of the following week.
   b Find the limit of the sequence generated by this recurrence relation and explain what it means in the given context.

2 A building firm is testing a foundation pile. During each hour the platform loses 15% of its height at the start of the hour.
At the end of the hour the height of the platform is raised by 18 cm.
   a At the start of a particular hour the platform height is u_n cm.
      Write a recurrence relation for u_{n+1}, the height in centimetres at the start of the next hour.
   b This recurrence relation has a limit. Find this limit and explain its meaning in the context of this problem.

Preparation for Course Assessment

OUTCOME 1
Use the properties of the straight line

1 On a geological map two fault lines are shown. Fault line 1 passes through points (6, 11) and (−2, −9). Fault line 2 passes through the origin and has gradient $\frac{1}{2}$.

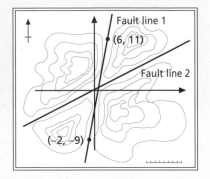

   a Write down the equation of Fault line 2.
   b Find the equation of Fault line 1.
   c Find the coordinates of the point where the two fault lines meet.
   d Calculate the distance of this meeting point from the point (−2, −9) if 1 unit on the map represents 2.5 km in real life.

2 The designs of two access ramps are shown. The equations of the lines of their top surfaces are
Ramp 1: $5y - 3x + 6 = 0$
Ramp 2: $7x - 10y - 14 = 0$.
To meet regulations the line of the top surface must make an angle

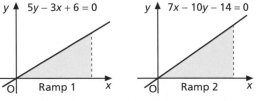

with the horizontal of no more than 34°. If the scales on the axes are equal in both diagrams decide if the two designs meet the regulations or not.

3 A vertical wedge is held in place by two steel supports BA and BN with A(−4, 8) and B(−6, 0). One edge of the wedge lies along the y-axis and the tip of the wedge rests at the origin. The support BN is perpendicular to edge AO of the wedge.
Find:

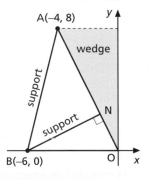

   a the equation of support BN
   b the coordinates of the point N where the support meets the edge of the wedge.

4

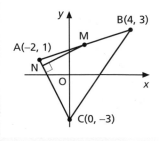

In triangle ABC, with A(−2, 1), B(4, 3) and C(0, −3), M is the midpoint of side AB. MN is drawn perpendicular to AC.
Find:
   a the coordinates of M
   b the equation of AC
   c the equation of MN
   d the coordinates of N.

5 A(−2, 9), B(−2, −1) and C(4, 1) are the vertices of triangle ABC.
  a Show that triangle ABC is isosceles.
  b Show also that if vertex B is moved 5 units parallel to the x-axis then triangle ABC remains isosceles.

6 The diagram shows a mathematical model of a road system. Points A(−3, −1) and B(3, 2) lie on a line representing Queen's Road. The line representing King's Street has equation $y + 3x = 18$.

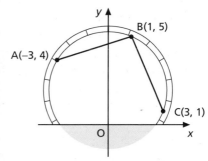

  a Find the equation of the line representing Queen's Road.
  b Calculate the coordinates of the point of intersection of the two roads.
  c **(i)** Determine the angle that each road makes with the positive direction of the x-axis.
      (You may assume that the scales on the two axes are the same.)
    (ii) Hence determine the angle through which a car must turn travelling from Queen's Road to drive *south* along King's Street. Give your answer to the nearest degree.

7 The diagram shows how an engineer plans to add two supports to shore up the crumbling roof of a Victorian sewer tunnel. The two supports are anchored at A(−3, 4) and C(3, 1) and meet at B(1, 5). It is essential that the angle between the two supports at point B is within 10° of a right angle. Determine whether this particular plan is acceptable.

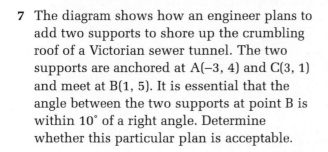

8 A triangle has vertices A(1, 3), B(−2, 1) and C(0, −4).
  a Find the equation of the median: **(i)** from B   **(ii)** from C.
  b Find the point of intersection of these two medians.
  c Show that this point of intersection lies on the third median.

9 The three sides of triangle ABC have equations as follows.
  AB: $y = x + 2$ BC: $y + 2x = 11$ AC: $2y + x = 1$
  A has coordinates (−1, 1).
  a Find the coordinates of **(i)** B   **(ii)** C.
  b A triangle whose vertices are P(x_1, y_1), Q(x_2, y_2) and R(x_3, y_3) has an area given by the formula:
    Area = $\frac{1}{2}(x_1y_2 + x_2y_3 + x_3y_1 − x_3y_2 − x_2y_1 − x_1y_3)$.
    (*Ignore any negative sign that may appear in the final answer.*)
    Find the area of triangle ABC.

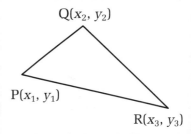

Preparation for Course Assessment

OUTCOME 2
Associate functions and graphs

1 **a** Show that the function $f(x) = 2x^2 - 6x + 5$ can be written in the form
   $f(x) = a(x + b)^2 + c$ where a, b and c are constants. State the values of a, b and c.
  b Hence, or otherwise, find the coordinates of the turning point of the graph
   $y = 2x^2 - 6x + 5$.

2 Sketch the graph $y = 3 \cos (x + 30)°$ for $0 \le x \le 360$ stating clearly the coordinates
   of the maximum and minimum turning points.

3 The functions f and g are defined by $f(x) = \dfrac{x-1}{x}$ $(x \ne 0)$ and $g(x) = \dfrac{1}{1-x}$ $(x \ne 1)$
  a Show that $f(g(x)) = x$
  b The function h is defined by $h(x) = \dfrac{1}{f(g(x))}$. State a suitable domain for h.

  c Find a simplified expression for $g(f(x))$.

4 The diagram shows the graphs of two logarithmic
   functions: $y = \log_a (x + b)$ and $y = \log_c (x - d)$.
   Find the values of the constants a, b, c and d.

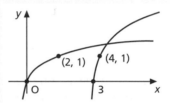

5

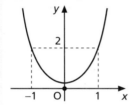

The diagram shows part
of the graph $y = f(x)$
  a Sketch: **(i)** $y = -f(x)$ **(ii)** $2 - f(x)$
  b Give a suitable domain for the function g
   defined by $g(x) = \dfrac{1}{2 - f(x)}$

6 **a** Sketch the graph $y = 2 \sin \left(x + \dfrac{\pi}{3}\right)$ for $0 \le x \le 2\pi$, clearly marking the points of
   intersection with the axes.
  b On the same diagram sketch $y = \cos x$ for $0 \le x \le 2\pi$.

  c Solutions to the equation $2 \sin \left(x + \dfrac{\pi}{3}\right) = \cos x$ are found where the two
   graphs intersect. How many solutions does this equation have for $0 \le x \le 2\pi$?

7 The diagram shows part of the graph
   $y = a \sin bx + c$.
   Determine the values of the constants a, b
   and c.

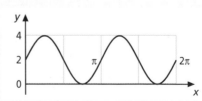

8 The function $f(x) = 7 - 6x - 3x^2$ can be written in the form $f(x) = a - b(x + c)^2$.
  a Determine the values of the constants a, b and c.
  b Hence, or otherwise, find the maximum value of the function f and the
   corresponding value of x.

9 a Give the exact value of $2 \sin^2 \dfrac{\pi}{4} - \tan \dfrac{\pi}{4}$.

b Show that $4 \cos^2 \dfrac{\pi}{6} - 2 \sin \dfrac{\pi}{6} - 1 = \sin \dfrac{\pi}{2}$.

10 Two functions f and g are defined, for suitable values of x, by $f(x) = \dfrac{1}{\sqrt{x}}$ and $g(x) = 2 + \dfrac{1}{x^2}$

a Find a simplified expression for $g(f(x))$.

b Show that $g(x) = \dfrac{2x^2 + 1}{x^2}$.

c Hence show that $f(g(x)) = \dfrac{x}{\sqrt{(2x^2 + 1)}}$.

d Find all the values of x for which $f(x)$ is not defined.

11 For each expression give:
(i) the maximum value with the corresponding value of x
(ii) the minimum value with the corresponding value of x.

a $1 + \cos x$ **b** $(1 + \sin x)^2 - 2$ **c** $\dfrac{1}{\cos x + 3}$

In each case consider only the range of values $0 \le x \le 2\pi$.

12 Martin is creating a design using a graph-plotting package on his PC. He bases his design on the exponential graph $y = 2^x$.

a Give equations for graphs 1, 2 and 3.

b Again based on the graph $y = 2^x$ he creates three graphs as shown with the y-axis intercepts equally spaced. Graph 4 passes through the origin. Give the equations for graphs 4, 5 and 6.

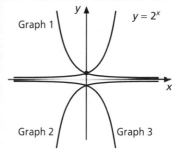

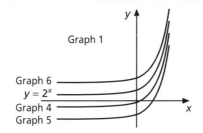 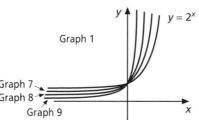

c He creates a new effect as shown with exponential graphs, one of which is $y = 2^x$. They all share the same y-axis intercept. Give possible equations for graphs 7, 8 and 9.

13 a Show that $f(\theta) = \sin^2 \theta + 8 \sin \theta + 18$ can be written in the form $(\sin \theta + a)^2 + b$ where a and b are constants

b Hence find the minimum and maximum values of f giving the corresponding values of θ for $0 \le \theta \le 2\pi$.

14 Two functions f and g are defined by $f(x) = 2 \sin x$ and $g(x) = x^2 - 2x + 3$.

a Show that $g(x)$ can be written in the form $(x + a)^2 + b$

b Hence find the *maximum* value of h where $h(x) = g(f(x))$ and the corresponding value of x where $0 \le x \le 2\pi$.

Preparation for Course Assessment

OUTCOME 3
Use basic differentiation

1 The diagram shows part of the graph
   $y = x^3 - 3x^2 + 3x - 1$.
   a Find the coordinates of A, the point where
      the graph crosses the y-axis.
   b Find the gradient of the tangent to the curve
      at the point A.
   c The tangent at the point B on the curve is
      parallel to the tangent at the point A.
      Find the coordinates of B.

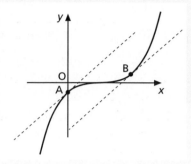

2 Calculate the exact value of $f'(9)$ where $f(x) = \dfrac{3 - \sqrt{x}}{x}$.

3

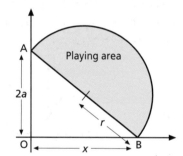

The diagram shows the plan for a
semi-circular playing area. Diameter
AB is a barrier which fences off a
triangular area between two walls, one
along the x-axis and the other along
the y-axis. All measurements on the
diagram are in metres. $AO = 2a$ metres
and $OB = x$ metres.

   a If the area of triangle AOB is 20 m^2 express a in terms of x.
   b If the radius of the semi-circular playing area is r metres show that $r^2 = a^2 + \frac{1}{4}x^2$
   c Hence show that the area of the semi-circular playing area is given by

   $$A(x) = \frac{200\pi}{x^2} + \frac{\pi}{8}x^2$$

   d Find the values of x and a that give the minimum area for the playing area.
      Give your answers to 3 significant figures.

4 a $f(x) = \dfrac{1 - \sqrt{x}}{x^2}$.   Find the exact value of $f'(4)$.

   b $g(x) = \dfrac{(2\sqrt{x} + 1)^2}{\sqrt{x}}$ Find the exact value of $g'(9)$.

   c $h(x) = \dfrac{(1 - 2\sqrt{x})(2 + 3\sqrt{x})}{x}$ Calculate $h'\left(\frac{1}{4}\right)$.

5

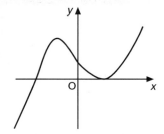

The path followed by a firework rocket is given by $y = -0.01x^2 + 1.5x$ where x metres is its horizontal distance and y metres its vertical height above its firing position.

a Use differentiation to determine the rocket's maximum vertical height above its firing position.

b The ground surface is modelled by the curve $y = 0.002x^2$. When the rocket is at its maximum vertical height above its firing position, calculate its height above the ground.

c Find a formula $h(x)$ for its height above the ground.

d Use differentiation to find the rocket's maximum height above the ground.

6 A log rolls down a hillside.
The distance, d metres, rolled after t seconds is given by $d(t) = 0.1t^3 + 0.5t$

a Calculate the velocity (rate of change of distance) of the log after 2 seconds.

b After how many seconds will the velocity of the log be 8 m/s?

7 The diagram shows an incomplete sketch of the graph of $y = (x - 2)^2(x + 3)$

a Write down the coordinates of the three points where the graph meets the axes.

b Use differentiation to find the coordinates of the turning points and to confirm their nature.

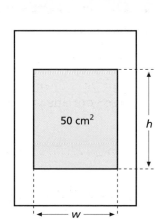

8 A rectangular advertisement in a magazine has a design as follows:

• a central rectangular area with a coverage of 50 cm^2

• a 4 cm margin at the top and bottom of the central area

• a 2 cm margin to the left and right of the central area.

a Find an expression for h in terms of w.

b Show that the total area, A cm^2, of the advertisement is given by:

$$A(w) = 8w + \frac{200}{w} + 82$$

c Find the dimensions of the advertisement that has a minimum total area.

Preparation for Course Assessment

OUTCOME 4
Design and interpret mathematical models of situations involving recurrence relations

1 Three sequences are defined by these three recurrence relations:

$u_{n+1} = 0.5u_n + 3$

$v_{n+1} = 1.5v_n + 1$

$w_{n+1} = 1.2w_n + 3.8$

a If $u_1 = 10$ and $v_1 = 2$ show that $u_3 = v_3$.

b Given that $w_2 = 5$, calculate w_1.

c Give a reason why only one of the sequences has a limit as n tends to infinity and find the exact value of this limit.

2 A sequence is generated by the recurrence relation $u_{n+1} = au_n + b$ (where a and b are constants).

If $u_1 = 2$, $u_2 = 3$ and $u_3 = 7$, find the values of a and b.

3 A sequence is generated by the recurrence relation: $u_{n+1} = au_n + 5$ (a is a constant).

a If $u_1 = 6$ find an expression in terms of a for u_3.

b If $u_3 = 11$ find the possible values of a.

c Explain why, with the given information, there is only one possible sequence for which a limit exists as n tends to infinity. Calculate the limit for this sequence.

4 Proposals for the purifying and removal of pollution from a Highland loch involve the testing of three different types of purifiers. They are initially tested in three different tanks, as shown in the table.

Type	Amount of pollutant removed in one 24-hour period	Tank
High	65	A
Medium	55	B
Low	40	C

The second table shows the amounts of pollutant added to each tank at the end of each 24-hour period during the test.

Tank	Amount of pollutant in litres
A	50
B	40
C	30

a For each tank set up a recurrence relation that models the situation.

You must explain clearly the meaning of any notation that you use.

b In the long run which tank contains the most pollutant and which the least?

5 An experiment was carried out to determine the effect on rats when a certain protein was injected into their blood. It was found that during the course of one day, 64% of the protein in the rat's blood at the start of the day had been destroyed.

Each new day the rats received an injection of 10 units of the protein into their blood. The initial level of the protein in their blood was 3 units.

a Set up a recurrence relation to model this situation. Explain clearly any notation you use. Remember to include the initial value information.

b Calculate the long-term effect of this course of injections on the rats' blood. Comment also on the greatest and the least number of units of protein present in the blood during the course of one complete day (again in the long term).

c If the minimum number of units must not eventually fall below 10 units in the blood, find the number of units necessary for each daily injection.

6 A particular car tyre should for safety reasons keep a pressure of no more than 40 psi. The tyre has a leak and loses 12% of its pressure during the course of one day's use. At the end of each day the owner pumps up the tyre's pressure by 4.9 psi.

a Set up a recurrence relation to describe this situation explaining clearly the notation that you use.

b If the tyre initially has a pressure of 38 psi, on which day will its pressure first be more than 39 psi (immediately after the end of the day's pumping up)?

c In the long run is increasing the pressure daily by 4.9 psi a safe course of action?

d Calculate the greatest daily increase in pressure that the owner can safely give the tyre.

7 A butterfly breeder notes the following death rates over the course of one week:

Temperature (°F)	% dead during 1 week
80	55
70	30
60	18

He sets up three enclosures, each containing 500 butterflies, and at the end of each week he adds a fresh batch of butterflies to each enclosure as follows:

	Temperature (°F)	Number in fresh batch added at end of week
Enclosure 1	60	150
Enclosure 2	80	450
Enclosure 3	70	300

a For each of the three enclosures construct a recurrence relation that models the situation, explaining carefully the notation that you use.

b In the long term compare the number of butterflies in each of the enclosures.

c The breeder wishes to alter the number in the end-of-week batch to ensure that in the long run each enclosure contains 500 butterflies. Explain how he does this, showing clearly your calculations.

d Having made these alterations he now decreases the temperature of Enclosure 2 to 70°F. What is the long-term effect on the number of butterflies in this enclosure due to this temperature drop?

Mathematics 2 (H) Contents

Preparation for Unit Assessment

OUTCOME 1a
Apply the Factor/Remainder Theorem to a polynomial function

1 Which of the following numbers are factors of 16?
2, 3, 4, 5, 6, 7, 8

> **Reminder**
> The Remainder Theorem
> $f(h)$ is the remainder when polynomial $f(x)$ is divided by $x - h$.

2 Show that:
a $(x - 2)$ is a factor of $x^2 + 3x - 10$
b $(x + 3)$ is a factor of $x^2 + 2x - 3$

3 Use the Remainder Theorem to determine the remainder on dividing:
a $2x^3 - 7x^2 - x + 4$ by $x - 3$
b $x^4 - 3x^2 + 4x + 1$ by $x - 1$
c $x^3 - 5x^2 + 2x - 4$ by $x + 2$
d $5x^3 + 2x^2 - 6$ by $x + 1$

4 Use the Factor Theorem to find which of the following are factors of $x^3 + 2x^2 - 5x - 6$:
a $x + 1$ b $x - 1$
c $x + 2$ d $x - 2$
e $x + 3$ f $x - 3$

> **Reminder**
> The Factor Theorem
> If $f(h) = 0$, then $x - h$ is a factor of polynomial $f(x)$.
> Conversely, if $x - h$ is a factor of the polynomial $f(x)$, then $f(h) = 0$.

5 Use the Factor Theorem to find the factors of:
a $x^3 + 6x^2 + 3x - 10$
b $2x^3 + 3x^2 - 8x - 12$
c $2x^3 + x^2 + 3x + 4$
d $3x^3 - x^2 - 27x + 9$

6 Use the Factor Theorem to show that 2 is a root of $3x^4 - 5x^3 - 4x^2 + 8x - 8 = 0$.

7 Determine the roots of these equations:
a $x^3 - 6x^2 + 11x - 6 = 0$
b $x^3 - 7x - 6 = 0$
c $2x^3 - 5x^2 - 14x + 8 = 0$
d $x^4 + 3x^3 - 3x^2 - 7x + 6 = 0$

8 Solve the equation: $3x^4 + 10x^3 - 9x^2 - 40x - 12 = 0$.

Preparation for Unit Assessment

OUTCOME 1b
Determine the nature of the roots of a quadratic equation using the discriminant

1 Solve the following equations, giving answers correct to 3 significant figures.

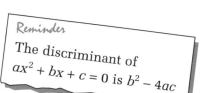

Reminder
The roots of $ax^2 + bx + c = 0$, $a \neq 0$ are

$$\frac{-b \pm \sqrt{(b^2 - 4ac)}}{2a}$$

   a $2x^2 + 3x - 7 = 0$ b $3x^2 - 5x + 1 = 0$

   c $2 - x - 5x^2 = 0$ d $3 + 2x - 4x^2 = 0$

2 Use the discriminant to determine whether or not the roots of these quadratic equations are real.

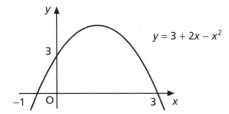

Reminder
The discriminant of $ax^2 + bx + c = 0$ is $b^2 - 4ac$

   a $x^2 + 3x - 4 = 0$ b $2x^2 + 7x - 1 = 0$

   c $x^2 - 2x + 3 = 0$ d $16x^2 - 8x + 1 = 0$

   e $5 + 2x - x^2 = 0$ f $3x^2 + 5x + 3 = 0$

   g $9x^2 - 12x + 4 = 0$ h $-25 + 10x - x^2 = 0$

3 Which of the quadratic equations in question **2** have equal roots and which have unequal roots?

4 a For what range of values of t does $2x^2 + 4x + t = 0$ have real roots?

   b For what value of t are the roots of $2x^2 + 4x + t = 0$ equal?

5 a For what range of values of p does $px^2 - 4x + 1 = 0$ have real roots?

   b For what value of p are the roots of $px^2 - 4x + 1 = 0$ equal?

6 Show that $y = 10x - 2$ is a tangent to the parabola $y = 3x^2 + 4x + 1$.

7 Use the discriminant to show that $y = 3 - x$ is not a tangent to the parabola $y = x^2 - 8x + 12$.

8 a From the graph, solve $x^2 - 8x + 7 < 0$

   b From the graph, solve $3 + 2x - x^2 < 0$

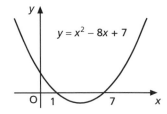

9 Determine the equation of a quadratic with roots −1 and 4.

10 Prove that $y = 5 + 4x - x^3$ has a root between 2 and 3, and find the root to 3 significant figures.

Unit 1 Assessment

1 Use the Remainder Theorem to find the remainder when:
  a $x^3 + 7x^2 - 4x - 6$ is divided by $x - 2$
  b $x^4 + 3x^3 - x + 2$ is divided by $x - 1$
  c $2x^3 + 5x^2 + 7$ is divided by $x + 3$

2 Use the Factor Theorem to find the factors of:
  a $x^3 + x^2 - 4x - 4$
  b $3x^3 + 7x^2 - 5x + 3$
  c $2x^3 - 5x^2 - 9x + 18$

3 Use the Factor Theorem to solve $2x^4 - 3x^3 - 15x^2 + 32x - 12 = 0$.

4 Use the discriminant to determine which of these quadratic equations have real roots:
  a $3x^2 - 5x + 2 = 0$
  b $2x^2 + 3x + 2 = 0$
  c $4x^2 + 3x - 2 = 0$
  d $5x^2 + x - 4 = 0$
  e $x^2 + 6x + 2 = 0$

5 Which of the equations in question **4** have equal roots and which have unequal roots?

Preparation for Unit Assessment

OUTCOME 2a
Integrate functions reducible to the sums of powers of x (definite and indefinite)

Reminder

$$\int f(x)\, dx = F(x) + c$$

where c is the constant of integration

$$\int ax^n\, dx = \frac{ax^{n+1}}{n+1} + c$$

where c is the constant of integration

1 Integrate with respect to x:

a x^2 **b** $6x^2$ **c** $\frac{1}{4}x$ **d** x^{-4}

e $3x^{-2}$ **f** $8x^{-3}$ **g** $\frac{1}{2}x^{-4}$ **h** $\frac{1}{x^5}$

i $\frac{3}{x^4}$ **j** $\frac{1}{6x^3}$ **k** $x^{\frac{3}{2}}$ **l** $4x^{-\frac{1}{2}}$

2 Integrate the following:

a $\int (4x + 3)\, dx$ **b** $\int (6x^2 - x)\, dx$ **c** $\int (4x^3 - 2 + 6x^{-3})\, dx$

d $\int (2x^{-2} + 4x^{-3})\, dx$ **e** $\int \left(x^2 - \frac{1}{x^3}\right) dx$ **f** $\int \left(x^{-\frac{1}{3}} + x^{\frac{1}{3}}\right) dx$

g $\int \left(4x^{\frac{3}{2}} - 3x^{\frac{1}{2}}\right) dx$ **h** $\int x(x^2 + 3)\, dx$ **i** $\int x(2x^2 - 3x^{-4})\, dx$

j $\int x^2(x^3 + x^{-1})\, dx$ **k** $\int \frac{(x^4 - x)}{x}\, dx$ **l** $\int \frac{(x - x^3 - x^5)}{x^3}\, dx$

3 Evaluate:

a $\int_0^1 (x^2 + 2)\, dx$ **b** $\int_0^2 (4x^3 - 6x)\, dx$

c $\int_2^3 (x - 1)\, dx$ **d** $\int_1^2 \left(4 - \frac{1}{x^2}\right) dx$

Reminder

$$\int_b^a f(x)\, dx = F(a) - F(b)$$

e $\int_{-2}^0 (x + 6x^2)\, dx$ **f** $\int_{-2}^2 \left(1 - 2x + \frac{x^3}{2}\right) dx$

g $\int_{-1}^1 (3x^{-2} + x^{-3})\, dx$ **h** $\int_{-1}^2 \left(x^3 + \frac{1}{x^3}\right) dx$ **i** $\int_{-3}^3 \left(\frac{4}{x^2} - \frac{6}{x^3}\right) dx$

4 Evaluate:

a $\int_0^2 \frac{(x^4 + x^3)}{x^2}\, dx$ **b** $\int_1^3 \frac{(2x^3 - 4x^2 + x)}{x}\, dx$

c $\int_{-1}^1 2x(x - 3x^{-3})\, dx$ **d** $\int_{-2}^1 \frac{(3x^2 + 4x)}{x^4}\, dx$

Preparation for Unit Assessment

OUTCOME 2b
Find the area between a curve and the x-axis using integration

1 Calculate the shaded areas.

a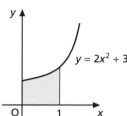
$y = 2x^2 + 3$

b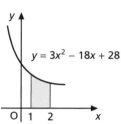
$y = 3x^2 - 18x + 28$

Reminder

The area bounded by the curve $y = f(x)$, the lines $x = a$ and $x = b$ and the x-axis is

- $A = \int_a^b f(x)\,dx$, if $f(x) \geq 0$ and $a \leq x \leq b$

- $A = -\int_a^b f(x)\,dx$, if $f(x) \leq 0$ and $a \leq x \leq b$

c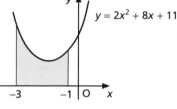
$y = 2x^2 + 8x + 11$

d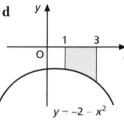
$y = -2 - x^2$

e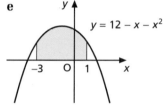
$y = 12 - x - x^2$

f
$y = x^2 - 3x - 10$

g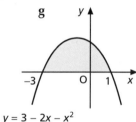
$y = 3 - 2x - x^2$

h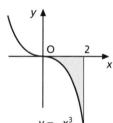
$y = -x^3$

i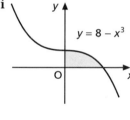
$y = 8 - x^3$

2 Calculate the shaded areas.

a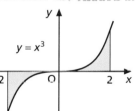
$y = x^3$

b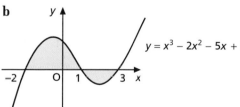
$y = x^3 - 2x^2 - 5x + 6$

c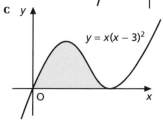
$y = x(x - 3)^2$

d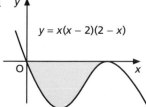
$y = x(x - 2)(2 - x)$

Preparation for Unit Assessment

OUTCOME 2c
Find the area between two curves using integration

1 Calculate the shaded areas.

a

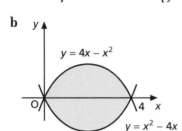

$y = \frac{1}{3}x^2$

6

$y = 8x - x^2$

> **Reminder**
>
> The area bounded by the curves $y = f(x)$, $y = g(x)$, and the lines $x = a$ and $x = b$ is
> $$A = \int_a^b f(x) - g(x)\,dx,$$
> if $f(x) \geq g(x)$ and $a \leq x \leq b$

b

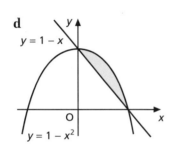

$y = 4x - x^2$

4

$y = x^2 - 4x$

c

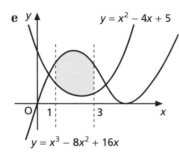

$y = 4x - x^2$

1   3

$y = x^2 - 4x$

d

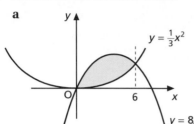

$y = 1 - x$

$y = 1 - x^2$

e

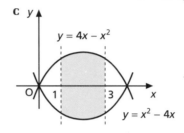

$y = x^2 - 4x + 5$

1   3

$y = x^3 - 8x^2 + 16x$

f

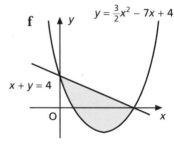

$y = \frac{3}{2}x^2 - 7x + 4$

$x + y = 4$

2 Find the area between the curves as indicated.

a

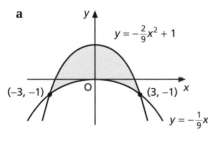

$y = -\frac{2}{9}x^2 + 1$

$(-3, -1)$ $(3, -1)$

$y = -\frac{1}{9}x^2$

b

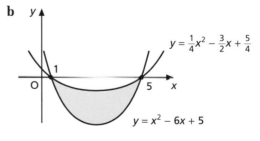

1

$y = \frac{1}{4}x^2 - \frac{3}{2}x + \frac{5}{4}$

5

$y = x^2 - 6x + 5$

3 Find the shaded areas A and B.

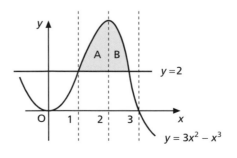

A   B

$y = 2$

1   2   3

$y = 3x^2 - x^3$

Unit 2 Assessment

1 Integrate these expressions with respect to x:

a $x(x^2 - x)$

b $\dfrac{1}{x^2} + \dfrac{1}{x^3}$

c $\dfrac{x^3 - x}{x}$

d $x^{\frac{1}{2}}\left(x - x^{\frac{1}{2}}\right)$

2 Evaluate:

a $\displaystyle\int_0^1 3x\left(1 - x^3\right)\,dx$

b $\displaystyle\int_1^3 \left(\dfrac{2}{x^3} - \dfrac{1}{3x^2}\right)\,dx$

c $\displaystyle\int_{-2}^2 \dfrac{(1 + x^2)}{x^2}\,dx$

3 Calculate the shaded area.

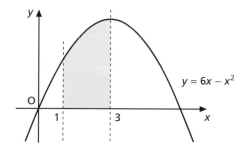

4 Find the total area enclosed by the curve
$y = x^3 - 4x$ and the x-axis.

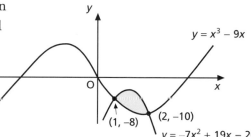

5 a Calculate the area between
the curves $y = x^3 - 9x$ and
$y = -7x^2 + 19x - 20$.

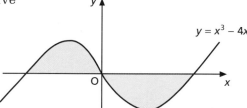

b Calculate the area between the curves
$y = x^{\frac{1}{2}}$ and $y = x^2$

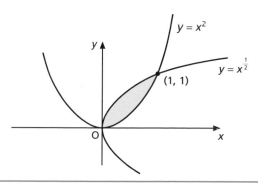

Preparation for Unit Assessment

OUTCOME 3a
Solve a trigonometric equation in a given interval

Reminder

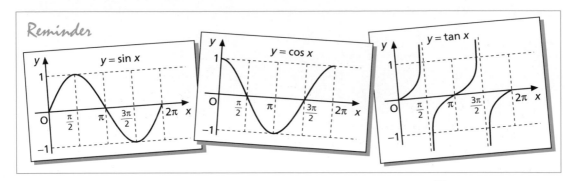

1 Solve each equation for x in the given interval:

  a $\sin x° = \frac{1}{2}$, $0 \le x \le 360$ **b** $\cos x° = 1$, $0 \le x \le 360$

  c $\tan x = \sqrt{3}$, $0 \le x \le 2\pi$ **d** $2 \sin x = -\sqrt{3}$, $0 \le x \le 2\pi$

Reminder

Sin $180 - x$	All x
Tan $180 + x$	Cos $360 - x$

2 Solve for x:

  a $\sin 2x = -1$ for $0 \le x \le 2\pi$

  b $2 \cos 2x = 1$ for $\pi < x < 2\pi$

  c $\sqrt{3} \tan 2x° = 1$ for $0 \le x \le 360$

  d $2 \cos 2x° + \sqrt{3} = 0$ for $0 \le x \le 360$

  e $\sqrt{2} \sin x = -1$ for $0 \le x \le 2\pi$ **f** $\tan 3x° = 1$ for $0 \le x \le 180$

3 Find the roots of these equations correct to 1 decimal place:

  a $\sin x° = 0.6$, $0 \le x \le 180$ **b** $\cos x = -0.9$, $0 \le x \le 2\pi$

  c $\tan x° = 1.5$, $180 \le x \le 360$ **d** $\sin 2x = 0.8$, $0 \le x \le 2\pi$

  e $3 \cos 2x - 1 = 0$, $0 \le x \le 2\pi$ **f** $2 \tan 2x° = -1$, $0 \le x \le 360$

4 Solve the equations for x:

  a $\sin (x + 20)° = 1$, $0 \le x \le 90$

  b $2 \cos (x + 10)° = 1$, $0 \le x \le 90$

  c $2 \tan (x - 30)° = 0$, $0 \le x \le 360$

  d $\sin \left(x + \frac{\pi}{6}\right) = 1$, $0 \le x \le \pi$

  e $\sqrt{2} \cos \left(x - \frac{\pi}{3}\right) = 1$, $0 \le x \le 2\pi$

  f $\tan \left(x - \frac{\pi}{4}\right) = 1$, $0 \le x \le 2\pi$

x	$0°$	$30°$	$45°$	$60°$	$90°$
$\sin x$	0	$\frac{1}{2}$	$\frac{1}{\sqrt{2}}$	$\frac{\sqrt{3}}{2}$	1
$\cos x$	1	$\frac{\sqrt{3}}{2}$	$\frac{1}{\sqrt{2}}$	$\frac{1}{2}$	0
$\tan x$	0	$\frac{1}{\sqrt{3}}$	1	$\sqrt{3}$	undefined

5 Solve correct to 1 decimal place:

  a $\cos (x - 30)° = 0.4$, $0 \le x \le 360$ **b** $\sin (x + 10)° = 0.7$, $0 \le x \le 360$

  c $\tan (x - 15)° = 2$, $0 \le x \le 360$ **d** $\sin \left(x - \frac{\pi}{5}\right) = 0.1$, $0 \le x \le \pi$

  e $\cos \left(x + \frac{\pi}{6}\right) = 0.3$, $0 \le x \le 2\pi$ **f** $\tan \left(2x - \frac{\pi}{2}\right) = 3$, $0 \le x \le \pi$

Preparation for Unit Assessment

OUTCOME 3b
Apply a trigonometric formula (addition formula) in the solution of a geometric problem

> **Reminder**
>
> **Addition formulae**
> $$\sin (A \pm B) = \sin A \cos B \pm \cos A \sin B$$
> $$\cos (A \pm B) = \cos A \cos B \mp \sin A \sin B$$
>
> **Double angle formulae**
> $$\sin 2A = 2 \sin A \cos A$$
> $$\cos 2A = \cos^2 A - \sin^2 A$$
> $$= 2 \cos^2 A - 1$$
> $$= 1 - 2 \sin^2 A$$

1 Use the addition formulae to expand the following:

   a $\sin (P - Q)$ **b** $\cos (C + D)$ **c** $\cos (3M - N)$ **d** $\sin (A + 2B)$

2 Expand using the double angle formulae:

   a $\cos 2P$ **b** $\sin 2X$ **c** $\cos 4M$ **d** $\sin 4E$

3

 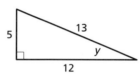

   Use the addition formulae to calculate the values of:

   a $\sin (x + y)°$ **b** $\cos (x + y)°$ **c** $\cos (x - y)°$ **d** $\sin (x - y)°$

4 Using the data in the triangles in question **3** show that:

   a $\sin 2x° = \dfrac{24}{25}$ **b** $\cos 2x° = \dfrac{7}{25}$ **c** $\sin 2y° = \dfrac{120}{169}$ **d** $\cos 2y° = \dfrac{119}{169}$

5 Using the triangle opposite, find the exact values of:

   a $\sin (a - b)$ **b** $\cos (a - b)$

   c $\sin 2a$ **d** $\cos 2b$

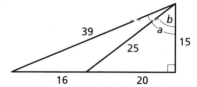

6

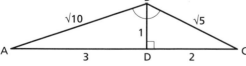

   Use an addition formula to show that:

   $$\sin \angle ABC = \dfrac{1}{\sqrt{2}}$$

7 Use addition formulae to show that:

   $\cos (180 - (x + y))° = - \cos (x + y)°$

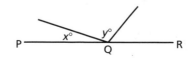

Preparation for Unit Assessment

OUTCOME 3c
Solve a trigonometric equation involving an addition formula in a given interval

1 Solve $\sin\left(x - \dfrac{\pi}{4}\right) = 0$ for $0 \le x \le 2\pi$

> **Reminder**
>
> $\sin A \cos B \pm \cos A \sin B = \sin (A \pm B)$
> $\cos A \cos B \mp \sin A \sin B = \cos (A \pm B)$

2 Solve $\cos (x + 60)° = 0$ for $0 \le x \le 360$

3 a Express $\cos x° \cos 40° - \sin x° \sin 40°$ in the form $\cos (A + B)$.
   b Hence, solve the equation $\cos x° \cos 40° - \sin x° \sin 40° = 0.4$.

4 In a similar fashion, solve these equations:
   a $\sin x° \cos 10° + \cos x° \sin 10° = 0.5$, $0 \le x \le 360$
   b $\cos x° \cos 35° - \sin x° \sin 35° = 0$, $0 \le x \le 360$
   c $\sin x \cos \dfrac{\pi}{5} - \cos x \sin \dfrac{\pi}{5} = \dfrac{1}{2}$, $0 \le x \le 2\pi$

5 Show that $\sin\left(x - \dfrac{\pi}{3}\right) + \cos\left(x + \dfrac{\pi}{6}\right)$ equals 0 for all x between 0 and 2π.

6 Solve:
   a $\sin (x + 30)° + \cos (x + 60)° = 0$, $0 \le x \le 360$
   b $\sin (x - 45)° - \cos (x + 45)° = 0$, $0 \le x \le 360$

7 Solve:
   a $\cos\left(x - \dfrac{\pi}{4}\right) - \sin\left(x - \dfrac{\pi}{4}\right) = \sqrt{2}$ for $0 \le x \le 2\pi$
   b $\sin\left(x + \dfrac{\pi}{3}\right) + \sin\left(x - \dfrac{\pi}{3}\right) = -\dfrac{\sqrt{3}}{2}$ for $\pi \le x \le 2\pi$

8 Use the double angle formulae to solve these equations:
   a $2 \sin x° \cos x° = 1$ for $0 \le x \le 360$
   b $\cos^2 x - \sin^2 x = \dfrac{1}{2}$ for $0 \le x \le 2\pi$
   c $\sin x° \cos x° = \dfrac{1}{4}$ for $0 \le x \le 180$

> **Reminder**
>
> $\sin 2A = 2 \sin A \cos A$
> $\cos 2A = \cos^2 A - \sin^2 A$
> $\qquad = 2 \cos^2 A - 1$
> $\qquad = 1 - 2 \sin^2 A$

Outcome 3 Assessment

1 Solve these equations for x in the given intervals. Where necessary give your answers correct to 1 decimal place.

   a $2 \sin 3x° = 1$, $0 \le x \le 90$

   b $3 \cos 2x + 2 = 0$, $0 \le x \le 2\pi$

   c $\tan 2x° - 2 = 0$, $0 \le x \le 360$

   d $2 \cos (x + 40)° = 1$, $0 \le x \le 360$

   e $3 \sin \left(x - \dfrac{\pi}{4} \right) = 1$, $0 \le x \le \pi$

2 By expanding $\cos (90 - x)°$ show it is equal to $\sin x°$.

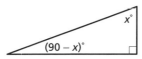

3 By expanding $\sin (180 - x)°$ show it is equal to $\sin x°$.

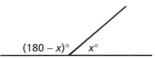

4 Determine the value of $\sin (a - b)$.

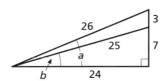

5 **a** Express $\cos x° \cos 30° + \sin x° \sin 30°$ in the form $\cos (A - B)$.

   b Hence find the exact values of x which satisfy the equation

   $\cos x° \cos 30° + \sin x° \sin 30° = \dfrac{\sqrt{3}}{2}$, $0 \le x \le 360$.

6 **a** Express $\sin x° \cos 25° + \cos x° \sin 25°$ in the form $\sin (A + B)$.

   b Hence find the exact values of x which satisfy the equation

   $\sin x° \cos 25° + \cos x° \sin 25° = \dfrac{1}{\sqrt{2}}$, $0 \le x \le 360$.

7 Solve these equations for x in the given intervals:

   a $\cos \left(x + \dfrac{\pi}{4} \right) - \sin \left(x + \dfrac{\pi}{4} \right) = \sqrt{2}$, $0 \le x \le 2\pi$

   b $\sin (x - 60)° + \cos (x - 30)° = -0.5$, $0 \le x \le 360$

Preparation for Unit Assessment

OUTCOME 4a

Given the centre (a, b) and radius r, find the equation of the circle in the form $(x - a)^2 + (y - b)^2 = r^2$

1 Write down the equation of the circle with centre at the origin and radius:

   a 1 unit

   b 4 units

   c 7 units

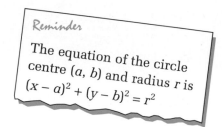

Reminder

The equation of the circle centre (a, b) and radius r is
$(x - a)^2 + (y - b)^2 = r^2$

2 What is the equation of the circle with diameter 20 units and centre at the origin?

3 Write down the equations of these circles:

   a centre (3, 0), radius 5 units   **b** centre (8, 0), radius 6 units

   c centre (−1, 0), radius 2 units   **d** centre (−4, 0), radius 1 unit

   e centre (0, 2), radius 3 units   **f** centre (0, −5), radius 8 units

4 Write down the centre and radius of each circle:

   a $x^2 + y^2 = 25$ **b** $(x - 6)^2 + y^2 = 16$ **c** $(x + 2)^2 + y^2 = 5$

   d $x^2 + (y - 7)^2 = 36$ **e** $(x - 9)^2 + (y + 1)^2 = 9$ **f** $(x + 4)^2 + (y - 5)^2 = 20$

5 Find the equation of each circle in the form $(x - a)^2 + (y - b)^2 = r^2$

   a centre (1, 2), radius 3   **b** centre (4, −3), radius 2

   c centre (−2, 6), radius √15   **d** centre (−5, −5), radius 6

   e centre (−3, 0), radius √8   **f** centre (−9, −1), radius 20

6 Determine the equation of the circle with centre (4, −7) and radius equal to half the radius of circle $(x - 1)^2 + (y + 1)^2 = 100$.

Preparation for Unit Assessment

OUTCOME 4b
Find the radius and centre of a circle given the equation in the form $x^2 + y^2 + 2gx + 2fy + c = 0$

1 Find the radius and centre of each circle:
  a $x^2 + y^2 - 16 = 0$
  b $x^2 + y^2 - 64 = 0$

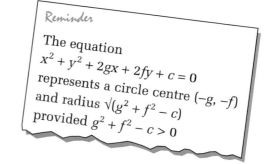

Reminder

The equation
$x^2 + y^2 + 2gx + 2fy + c = 0$
represents a circle centre $(-g, -f)$
and radius $\sqrt{(g^2 + f^2 - c)}$
provided $g^2 + f^2 - c > 0$

2 What is special about the 'circle'
$x^2 + y^2 = 0$?

3 Write down the coordinates of the centre of each of these circles:
  a $x^2 + y^2 + 6x = 0$
  b $x^2 + y^2 + 10x + 9 = 0$
  c $x^2 + y^2 - 10x - 1 = 0$
  d $x^2 + y^2 + 4y = 0$
  e $x^2 + y^2 + 8y + 15 = 0$
  f $x^2 + y^2 - 12y - 13 = 0$
  g $x^2 + y^2 + 5x + 4 = 0$
  h $x^2 + y^2 - 9y + 14 = 0$

4 Calculate the radius of each circle in question **3**.

5 Find the radius and centre of each circle:
  a $x^2 + y^2 - 6x - 8y = 0$
  b $x^2 + y^2 - 4x - 10y + 4 = 0$
  c $x^2 + y^2 + 12x - 12y + 8 = 0$
  d $x^2 + y^2 + 2x + 6y + 6 = 0$
  e $x^2 + y^2 - 10x + 8y + 20 = 0$
  f $x^2 + y^2 + 8x - 14y - 16 = 0$
  g $x^2 + y^2 + 4x - 10y - 7 = 0$
  h $x^2 + y^2 - 7x + 9y - 3.5 = 0$
  i $x^2 + y^2 + 4x - 5y - 10 = 0$
  j $x^2 + y^2 - 3x + 6y + 5 = 0$

OUTCOME 4c
Determine whether a given line is a tangent to a given circle

Reminder

The line $y = ax + b$
cuts the circle
$x^2 + y^2 + 2gx + 2fy + c = 0$
when
$x^2 + (ax + b)^2 + 2gx + 2f(ax + b) + c = 0$

A line is a tangent to a circle if there is only one point of contact.

A quadratic equation
$ax^2 + bx + c = 0$ has
equal roots if
$b^2 - 4ac$ is equal to 0.

1 State whether or not the lines are tangents to the circles:
   a $x^2 + y^2 = 1$; $x = 1$, $x = -1$, $y = 1$, $y = -1$
   b $x^2 + y^2 = 4$; $x = 4$, $x = -4$, $y = 4$, $y = -4$
   c $x^2 + y^2 = 9$; $x = 3$, $x = -3$, $y = 3$, $y = -3$

2 Show that the lines $y = 1$ and $y = -1$ are tangents to the circle $x^2 + y^2 - 6x + 8 = 0$.

3 a Show that the lines $x = 3$ and $x = -3$ are both tangents to the circle
      $x^2 + y^2 + 8y + 7 = 0$.
   b Show that the lines $y = -1$ and $y = -7$ are also tangents to the circle
      $x^2 + y^2 + 8y + 7 = 0$.

4 Show that the line $y = 3$ is not a tangent to the circle $x^2 + y^2 - 2x - 15 = 0$.

5 Determine if the line is a tangent to the circle:
   a $x^2 + y^2 = 8$, $y = 4 - x$
   b $x^2 + y^2 = 20$, $y = 2x - 10$
   c $x^2 + y^2 = 10$, $y = x + 4$
   d $x^2 + y^2 = 4$, $y = x - 4$
   e $x^2 + y^2 + 8x + 8 = 0$, $y = -x$
   f $x^2 + y^2 - 2x - 4y - 40 = 0$, $y = 2x + 5$
   g $x^2 + y^2 - 4x + 6y + 8 = 0$, $y = 6 - 2x$
   h $x^2 + y^2 - y + 4 = 0$, $y = 2x + 1$

Preparation for Unit Assessment

OUTCOME 4d
Determine the equation of the tangent to a given circle given the point of contact

> **Reminder**
>
> (a, b) is the centre of the circle with equation $(x - a)^2 + (y - b)^2 = r^2$
>
> $(-g, -f)$ is the centre of the circle with the equation
> $x^2 + y^2 + 2gx + 2fy + c = 0$

1 a Sketch the circle $x^2 + y^2 = 25$ on a coordinate diagram.
 b Write down the equations of four lines which are tangents to the circle.
 c For each of the four tangents write down the coordinates of the point of contact.

2 a Check that the point A$(-3, 4)$ lies on the circle $x^2 + y^2 = 25$.
 b Find the gradient of the radius OA.
 c Write down the gradient of the tangent at A.
 d Find the equation of the tangent to the circle at the point of contact $(-3, 4)$.
 e Repeat **a, b, c** and **d** for the point $(4, -3)$.

3 Find the equation of the tangent to the circle $x^2 + y^2 = 40$ at the point $(-6, 2)$.

4 a Write down the coordinates of the centre of the circle $(x - 2)^2 + (y + 3)^2 = 10$.
 b Check that the point P$(5, -2)$ lies on the circle and find the gradient of the tangent at P.
 c Find the equation of the tangent at $(5, -2)$.

5 Find the equation of the tangent to the circle $(x - 3)^2 + (y + 1)^2 = 13$ at the point $(6, 1)$.

6 a Write down the coordinates of the centre of the circle $x^2 + y^2 - 6x + 4y - 19 = 0$.
 b Find the equation of the tangent to the circle at the point of contact $(-1, 2)$.

7 For each circle, find the equation of the tangent at the given point of contact.
 a $x^2 + y^2 - 6y + 1 = 0$; point of contact $(2, 1)$
 b $x^2 + y^2 - 4x - 4 = 0$; point of contact $(0, 2)$
 c $x^2 + y^2 - 6x + 10y - 16 = 0$; point of contact $(2, -12)$
 d $x^2 + y^2 + 4x - 8y + 10 = 0$; point of contact $(1, 3)$
 e $x^2 + y^2 - 4x - 2y - 15 = 0$; point of contact $(4, -3)$
 f $x^2 + y^2 + 2x - 6y - 35 = 0$; point of contact $(2, -3)$
 g $x^2 + y^2 - 6x + 14y + 38 = 0$; point of contact $(1, -3)$
 h $x^2 + y^2 + 4x - 8y - 80 = 0$; point of contact $(4, -4)$

Outcome 4 Assessment

1 Write down the equation of each of these circles:
   a radius 6 units, centre the origin
   b radius 4 units, centre (0, 4)
   c radius 3 units, centre (5, −2)

2 Find the radius and coordinates of the centre of each of these circles:
   a $x^2 + y^2 + 10x + 16 = 0$
   b $x^2 + y^2 - 12x + 2y - 13 = 0$

3 Show that the line with equation $y = 2x + 8$ is a tangent to the circle with equation $x^2 + y^2 - 8x - 2y - 28 = 0$.

4 Determine whether the line $y = 5 - x$ is a tangent to the circle $x^2 + y^2 + 7x - 4y - 12 = 0$.

5 Find the equation of the tangent to the circle $x^2 + y^2 - 8x - 1 = 0$ at the point of contact (0, −1).

6 Find the equation of the tangent to the circle $x^2 + y^2 - 8x + 12y + 18 = 0$ at the point of contact (1, −1).

7 The point B(−2, −6) lies on the circle with centre (1, 3). Find the equation of the tangent ABC.

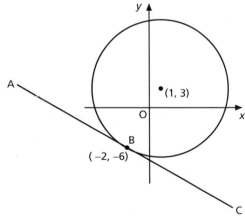

OUTCOME 1
Use the Factor/Remainder Theorem and apply quadratic theory

1 Use the Factor Theorem to determine the factors of each polynomial:
   a $f(x) = 4x^4 - 4x^3 - 19x^2 + 16x + 12$
   b $f(x) = 2x^3 + 7x^2 + 4x + 3$
   c $f(x) = 8x^3 - 4x^2 - 18x + 9$
   d $f(x) = x^4 + x$

2 a Show that $(x + 2)$ is a factor of $f(x) = x^3 + 2x^2 - 9x - 18$ and find the other factors.
   b Write down the coordinates of the points at which the graph of $y = f(x)$ meets the axes.

3 Find p if:
   a $(x - 2)$ is a factor of $2x^3 + x^2 + px + 6$
   b $(x + 1)$ is a factor of $2x^3 + px^2 - 2x - 1$

4 Use the Remainder Theorem to determine the remainder on dividing:
   a $f(x) = x^4 - 3x^2 + 4$ by $x - 2$
   b $f(x) = 3x^4 + x^3 + 6x + 1$ by $x + 3$
   c $f(x) = x^4 - 2x^3 + x - 3$ by $x - 1$
   d $f(x) = x^3 - 2x^2 + 4x - 1$ by $x - \frac{1}{2}$
   e $f(x) = 2x^3 - 3x + 2$ by $x + \frac{1}{2}$

5 The remainder is -20 when $f(x) = x^4 - x^3 + mx^2 + nx + 18$ is divided by $(x + 2)$. One factor of $f(x)$ is $(x - 2)$. Find the values of m and n.

6 Find the roots of these quadratic equations correct to 2 significant figures:
   a $3x^2 - 4x - 5 = 0$ b $1 - 5x - 2x^3 = 0$ c $x(2x + 7) = 1$

7 a Find algebraically the two values of x where the quadratics $y = x^2 + 5x - 1$ and $y = 2 - 3x - 2x^2$ intersect.
   b Find algebraically, correct to 2 significant figures, the two values of x where the quadratics $y = 2x^2 + 3x - 4$ and $y = 1 - 2x - 3x^2$ intersect.

8 Use the discriminant to show that the line $y = \frac{1}{2}x + 2$ is not a tangent of the parabola $y = x^2 - 2x + 5$.

9 a For what values of k does $4x^2 + kx + 1 = 0$ have equal roots?
   b Find the range of values of t for which $4x^2 + tx + 1 = 0$ has real roots.

10 $\dfrac{x^2 + 1}{(x + 2)^2} = m$, $m \in R$. Find the value of m for the given equation to have two equal roots.

11 Find the value of a for the equation $a(x - 1)^2 + ax - 3 = 0$ to have two equal roots $(a \neq 0)$.

12 Find the range of values of t for which $\dfrac{1 + 2x^2}{t(1 + 2x)^2} = 1$ has real roots $(t \neq 0)$.

13 Find the condition on m for $m(x - 2)^2 + m(x - 2) + m - 2 = 0$ to have real roots $(m \neq 0)$.

14 Show that for all real numbers k, the roots of the equation $2x^2 - 3kx + 3k - 2 = 0$ are always real numbers.

15 The roots of the equation $(x - 2)(x + k) = -16$ are equal. Find the values of k.

16 Show that the line $y = 9x - 10$ is a tangent to the parabola $y = 3x^2 - 3x + 2$.

17 Determine if the line $y = 3x + 2$ and the circle $x^2 + y^2 - 3x + 8y + 12 = 0$:
    a do not touch   b meet at a point   c have two points of intersection.

18 Repeat question 17 for the line $y + 4x = 1$ and the circle $x^2 + y^2 + 2x - 12y + 10 = 0$.

19 Show that $y + 2x = 2$ is a tangent to the circles $x^2 + y^2 + 10x - 4y + 9 = 0$ and $x^2 + y^2 - 2x - 10y + 21 = 0$.

20 The line with equation $y - 2x = k$ is a tangent to the circle $x^2 + y^2 + 4x - 2y - 40 = 0$.
    a Find the two possible values of k.
    b Find the equation of the diameter joining the points of contact.

21 Find the possible values of k for which $y = 2x + k$ is a tangent to the circle $x^2 + y^2 = 20$.

22 The line $y = mx + c$ is a tangent to the parabola $y = x^2 + x - 6$ at the point $(2, 0)$.
    a Find a relationship between c and m.
    b Find the equation of the tangent.

23 For what value of k will the graph of $y = -k + 6x - kx^2$ touch the x-axis?

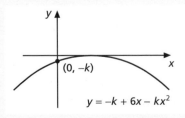

24 a

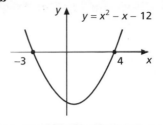

From the graph solve
$x^2 - 2x - 3 < 0$.

b

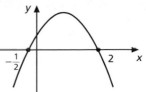

From the graph solve
$x^2 - x - 12 \geq 0$.

c

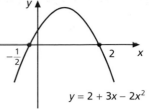

From the graph solve
$2 + 3x - 2x^2 < 0$.

25 Sketch the graph of $y = x^2 + 2x - 8$ and use it to solve the inequality
$x^2 + 2x - 8 < 0$.

26 Solve the inequality $3 + 5x - 2x^2 \leq 0$.

27 Solve the inequalities: **a** $2x^2 + 7x - 4 > 0$ **b** $2 + x - 6x^2 \leq 0$

28 Determine a possible equation for a quadratic with roots:

   a -1 and 4 **b** $-\dfrac{3}{2}$ and $\dfrac{1}{3}$ **c** $\dfrac{1}{4}$ and $-\dfrac{3}{4}$

29 Prove that the equation $2x^2 - 3x - 7 = 0$ has a root between 2 and 3. Find this root correct to 3 significant figures.

30 Prove that the equation $x^3 - 4x^2 + 6 = 0$ has a root between 1 and 2 and find the root correct to 3 significant figures.

31 Prove that the equation $2x^3 + 5x + 6 = 0$ has a root between -1 and 0 and find the root to 2 significant figures.

32 Prove that the equation $x^3 + 2x^2 - 5x - 8 = 0$ has a root between 2 and 3 and a root between -2 and -1. Find both roots correct to 3 significant figures.

33 The diagram shows a sketch of the polynomial
$y = \dfrac{1}{2}x^3 - 2x^2 - 2x + 8$ and the line $y = 2$.

   a State the number of roots which the
     equation $\dfrac{1}{2}x^3 - 2x^2 - 2x + 6 = 0$ has.

   b Calculate the negative root to 3
     significant figures.

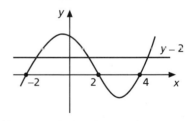

34 A manufacturer makes a cuboid box. Its volume can be determined from the
formula $V(x) = 6 - 11x + 6x^2 - x^3$ where x cm is a particular measurement used
in the making of the box.

   a Factorise $6 - 11x + 6x^2 - x^3$.

   b For what values of x is $V(x) = 0$?

   c By sketching, or otherwise, find the range of values it is possible for such a
     measurement, x, to take.

OUTCOME 2
Use basic integration

1 Integrate with respect to x:

a $x^3 + \dfrac{1}{x^3}$

b $3x^2 - \dfrac{2}{x^5}$

c $1 + \dfrac{1}{3x^4}$

d $\dfrac{1}{2x^2} - \dfrac{1}{2} + \dfrac{3}{4x^3}$

e $x^{\frac{1}{2}} - 2x^{\frac{1}{3}}$

f $4 - x^{\frac{3}{4}}$

g $\sqrt{x} - \sqrt[3]{x}$

h $\dfrac{1}{x^{\frac{1}{2}}} + \dfrac{2}{x^{\frac{1}{4}}} + \dfrac{3}{2x^{\frac{1}{3}}}$

2 Carry out these integrations:

a $\displaystyle\int (2x - 1)^2 dx$

b $\displaystyle\int x^2(x^3 - 2)dx$

c $\displaystyle\int 3x^{\frac{1}{2}}\left(x^{\frac{1}{2}} + 2x^{-\frac{1}{2}}\right)dx$

d $\displaystyle\int x^4\left(\dfrac{1}{x^2} - \dfrac{1}{x}\right)dx$

e $\displaystyle\int \sqrt{x}\left(x^2 - \dfrac{1}{x^2}\right)dx$

f $\displaystyle\int \dfrac{x - x^2}{x}dx$

g $\displaystyle\int \dfrac{1 + 2x - 3x^3}{x^3}dx$

h $\displaystyle\int \dfrac{\left(x^{\frac{1}{5}} + x^{\frac{3}{5}} + x\right)}{2x^{\frac{2}{5}}}dx$

3 Find the value of :

a $\displaystyle\int_0^1 (3x^2 + 2)dx$

b $\displaystyle\int_1^3 (2x^3 - 5x)dx$

c $\displaystyle\int_2^3 \left(\dfrac{1}{x^2} + \dfrac{2}{x^3}\right)dx$

d $\displaystyle\int_1^9 \sqrt{x}\,dx$

e $\displaystyle\int_{-1}^1 (3x - 2)^2 dx$

f $\displaystyle\int_{-2}^0 x(x^2 - 4)dx$

g $\displaystyle\int_1^4 \dfrac{1 - x^2}{\sqrt{x}}dx$

h $\displaystyle\int_1^2 \dfrac{x^2 - 3}{3x^2}dx$

4 Evaluate: $\displaystyle\int_{-1}^2 (1 - x^2)\,dx$ and draw a sketch to explain your answer.

5 Calculate the shaded areas:

a
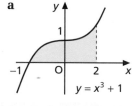

b
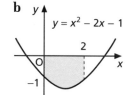

c
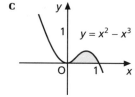

6 a Show that $\displaystyle\int_{-1}^1 (2x^3 - 2x)dx$ equals zero.

b Calculate the area enclosed by $y = 2x^3 - 2x$ and the x-axis.

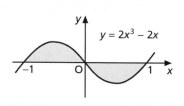

7 Calculate the shaded areas:

a
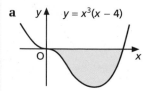

b
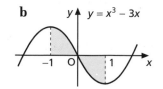

c
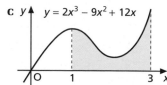

8 a Calculate the area trapped between the parabola

$y = 2 + \frac{1}{2}x - \frac{1}{4}x^2$ and the line $y = 2 - \frac{1}{2}x$.

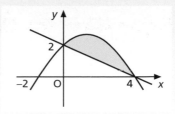

b

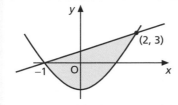

Calculate the area between the parabola
$y = x^2 - 1$ and the line $y = x + 1$.

9 a Make a sketch of the graphs of $y = x^3$ and $y = x$.

b Calculate the area enclosed by the two curves.

10

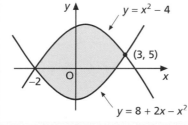

Calculate the shaded area.

11 Calculate the area enclosed by the curves
$y = x^2 - 1$ and $y = 1 - x^2$.

12 The leaf of a birch tree is symmetrical.
One half of the leaf can be represented on
a coordinate diagram as shown. Calculate
the area of the leaf.

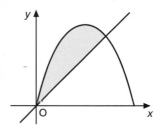

13

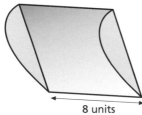

The cuttings collector of
a lawnmower is a prism
with a cross-section as
shown. It can be
represented on the
coordinate plane as

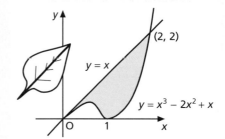

the area bounded by the parabola $y = 4x - x^2$ and
the line $y = x$.

a Calculate the shaded area in square units.

b Hence calculate the capacity of the collector if it is 8 units wide.

14 The outline of a new surfboard can be represented
on the coordinate plane as the area bounded by

the parabolae $y = \frac{1}{4}x^2$ and $y = 2x - \frac{1}{4}x^2$

a Calculate the area of the board in square units.

b If each unit is worth 0.4 m, calculate the
area of the board in square metres.

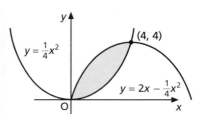

15 An architect is commissioned
to design a playground. The
area she must use is fixed.
A couple of her suggestions
have been modelled as
shown.

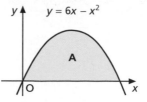

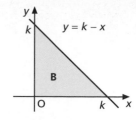

  a (i) Calculate area A.
     (ii) Using the fact that the
          areas A and B must be the same,
          calculate the value of k.
  b A third design, shown here, is based on
     the sine wave $y = a \sin x$. Calculate the
     value of a.

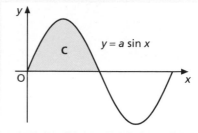

16

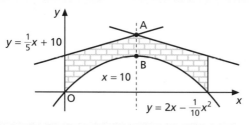

The diagram shows the side view
of a bridge represented on a
coordinate diagram. The bridge is
symmetrical about the line $x = 10$.

  a State the coordinates of (i) A (ii) B.
  b Calculate the area of the side of the bridge.

17 Calculate the total shaded area.

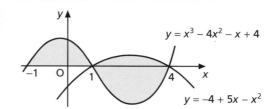

18

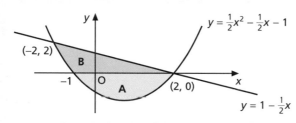

Calculate:
  a area A
  b area B.

19 a $\dfrac{dy}{dx} = 4 - x$ and $y = 1$ when $x = 2$. Find the value of y when $x = 4$.

    b $\dfrac{dy}{dx} = \dfrac{1}{\sqrt{x}}$ and $y = -4$ when $x = 4$. Find the value of y when $x = 16$.

    c $\dfrac{dy}{dx} = \dfrac{2}{x^3}$ and $y = 0$ when $x = \dfrac{1}{2}$. Find the value of y when $x = \dfrac{1}{3}$.

20 $\dfrac{dy}{dx} = \dfrac{-4}{x^2}$ and $y = 4$ when $x = 1$. Show that $\dfrac{dy}{dx} = \dfrac{-y}{x}$.

Preparation for Course Assessment

OUTCOME 3
Solve trigonometric equations and apply trigonometric formulae

1 Solve these equations for x, giving answers correct to 3 significant figures where necessary:

  a $2 \cos x° = 1$, $0 \le x \le 360$
        b $\sin 2x - 1 = 0$, $0 \le x \le 2\pi$

  c $\tan 2x° = 3$, $0 \le x \le 360$
        d $3 \cos 2x - 1 = 0$, $0 \le x \le 2\pi$

  e $2 \sin \frac{1}{2}x° = 1$, $0 \le x \le 360$
     f $3 \cos \frac{1}{2}x = 2$, $0 \le x \le 2\pi$

  g $\sin^2 3x° = 1$, $0 \le x \le 180$
      h $\tan^2 2x = 4$, $0 \le x \le \pi$

  i $4 \cos^2 2x° = 1$, $0 \le x \le 360$
     j $3 \tan^2 4x = 1$, $0 \le x \le \dfrac{\pi}{2}$

2 A mirror reflects a beam of light back to its source at A. A lies on the circumference of a circle centre M and radius 1. When the mirror is rotated through $x°$, the reflected light is rotated through $2x°$, as shown, to arrive back on the circumference at B.

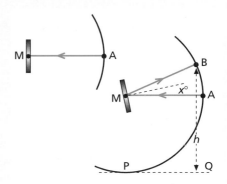

  a Show that the height, h, of B above the base line PQ is given by $h = \sin 2x + 1$.

  b Calculate the possible angles the mirror might turn through to make $h = 1.4$.

3 Solve for x, correct to 3 significant figures where necessary:

  a $2 \sin^2 x° + 5 \sin x° - 3 = 0$, $0 \le x \le 360$

  b $2 \cos^2 x - \cos x - 1 = 0$, $0 \le x \le 2\pi$

  c $3 \sin^2 x + 2 \sin x - 1 = 0$, $0 \le x \le 2\pi$

  d $2 \tan^2 x° - 3 \tan x° + 1 = 0$, $0 \le x \le 360$

  e $4 \cos^2 x° - 8 \cos x° + 3 = 0$, $0 \le x \le 2\pi$

  f $3 \tan^2 x + 5 \tan x = 2$, $0 \le x \le 2\pi$

4 **a** Writing 135 as $90 + 45$ and using an addition formula, verify that $\cos 135° = -\dfrac{1}{\sqrt{2}}$.

  b Expressing $\cos 105°$ as $\cos (60 + 45)°$, use the appropriate addition formula to show that the exact value of $\cos 105°$ is $\dfrac{1 - \sqrt{3}}{2\sqrt{2}}$.

5 **a** Simplify $\cos \left(x + \dfrac{\pi}{3}\right) + \cos \left(x - \dfrac{\pi}{3}\right)$.

  b Hence or otherwise solve the equation $\cos \left(x + \dfrac{\pi}{3}\right) + \cos \left(x - \dfrac{\pi}{3}\right) = 0.4$; $0 \le x \le 2\pi$.

  c Similarly, solve the equation $\sin \left(x - \dfrac{\pi}{4}\right) + \cos \left(x - \dfrac{\pi}{4}\right) = 0.4$; $0 \le x \le 2\pi$.

6 Show that: **a** $\sin 4M = 4 \sin M \cos M (1 - 2 \sin^2 M)$

               b $\cos 4M = 1 - 8 \sin^2 M + 8 \sin^4 M$

7 For acute angles M and N, $\cos M = \frac{4}{5}$ and $\cos N = \frac{5}{13}$. Find the exact values of:

   a $\cos (M - N)$ **b** $\sin (M - N)$ **c** $\tan (M - N)$

8 If $\tan A° = \frac{2}{\sqrt{3}}$ and A is acute, find the exact value of $\cos (A + 60)°$

9 A is the point with coordinates $(\sin (x + 45)°, \cos (x - 45)°)$ and B is the point with coordinates $(\cos (x + 45)°, \sin (x - 45)°)$.

   a Find in its simplest form an expression for the gradient of the line AB.
   b Calculate the length of the line AB.

10 Given that $\tan A = \frac{\sqrt{5}}{2}, 0 < A < \frac{\pi}{2}$, find the exact values of:

   a $\sin A$ **b** $\cos A$ **c** $\sin 2A$ **d** $\cos 2A$ **e** $\tan 2A$.

11 Find the exact value of $\cos \left(\frac{2\pi}{3} - \varnothing \right) + \sin \left(\frac{5\pi}{6} + \varnothing \right)$.

12 If $\sin P = \frac{5}{13}, 0 < P < \frac{\pi}{2}$, find the exact value of

   a $\sin 2P$ **b** $\cos 2P$ **c** $\cos \frac{1}{2}P$ **d** $\sin 4P$.

13 **a** By expanding $\sin (x + y)$ show that it is equal to $\frac{56}{65}$.

   b Show that $\sin \angle ABC = \frac{56}{65}$.

   c Similarly, find the value of $\cos \angle ABC$.

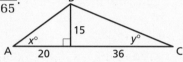

14 **a** Calculate the exact value of: **(i)** $\sin \angle RPS$ **(ii)** $\sin \angle QPS$.

   b Hence calculate the exact value of $\sin \angle QPR$.

   c Calculate the exact value of $\cos \angle QPR$.

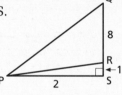

15

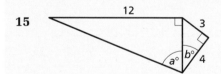

Calculate the exact value
of $\tan (a + b)°$.

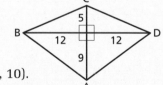

16 ABCD is a kite. Calculate the exact value of $\cos \angle ADC$.

17 Lines are drawn from the origin, O, to A(6, 8) and B(24, 10).
Work out the exact value of $\sin (\angle AOB)$.

18 In this scalene triangle, $\sin y = \frac{1}{2}$.
Show that $a = 2(\sqrt{3} \sin x + \cos x)$.

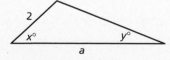

19 **a** $\angle PQS = \angle SQR$. By considering the *double angle* formulae
     calculate the *exact* value of:
     (i) $\sin \angle PQR$ **(ii)** $\cos \angle PQR$ **(iii)** $\tan \angle PQR$

   b Hence calculate the exact value of PR.

   c Without using a calculator why might you say
     that $\angle PQR \approx 45°$?

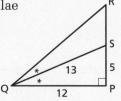

20 a By using an addition formula, find the exact value of sin ∠ABC.

b Hence find the exact value of ∠ABC, given that it is obtuse.

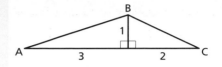

21 Solve the following equations using suitable double angle formulae:

a $\sin 2x° + \cos x° = 0$, $0 \le x < 360$ **b** $2 \sin 2x° - \sin x° = 0$, $0 \le x < 360$

c $3 \cos 2x° + \sin x° - 2 = 0$, $0 \le x < 360$ **d** $2 \cos 2x + \cos x - 1 = 0$, $0 \le x < 2\pi$

e $\sin x° + \sin \frac{1}{2}x° = 0$, $0 \le x < 360$ **f** $3 \cos x° + 7 \cos \frac{1}{2}x° = 0$, $0 \le x < 360$

22 a Show that $\cos 2x° - 4 \cos^2 x° = 2 \sin^2 x° - 3$.

b Hence solve the equation

$\cos 2x° - 4 \cos^2 x = 5 \sin x°$ for $0 \le x < 360$.

23 The diagram shows the curves $y = 2 \sin 2x°$ and $y = -\sin x$ for $0 \le x < 360$.
Find the x-coordinate of the point of intersection at A.

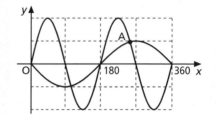

24 Relative to a certain set of axes, a satellite traces out a path in the night sky which can be represented by the equation $y = 2 + 2 \cos x°$ where y units is its height above the horizon and $x°$ is its bearing, $0 \le x \le 360$. A second satellite has a path described by $y = \cos 2x°$.

a By solving a suitable equation find the bearings at which these two satellites appear to be at the same height.

b Calculate the height at which this occurs.

25 A meter has a dial on which there are two hands. The tip of the larger hand moves round the dial according to the formula $y = 2 \cos 2x° + 2$ where y is the height of the tip above the bottom of the dial and $0 \le x \le 360$. The tip of the smaller hand moves round according to the formula $y = \sin x° + 1$.
Calculate when the tips are at the same height.

26 The diagram represents a roof structure with apex at C. Prove that $\sin ∠ACB = \frac{w}{h} \sin a \sin b$.

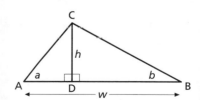

27 a Show that $\dfrac{1 - \cos A}{\sin A} = \tan \frac{1}{2}A$; $0 < A < \pi$.

b Hence solve the equation $\dfrac{1 - \cos A}{\sin A} = \frac{1}{2}$; $0 < A < \pi$.

Preparation for Course Assessment

OUTCOME 4
Use the equation of the circle

1 Write down the radius and coordinates of the centre of the circle with equation $(x - 3)^2 + (y + 1)^2 = 100$.

2 Write down the equations of these circles:
   a centre(0, 0), radius 5
   b centre(−2, 0), radius 4
   c centre(0, 2), radius 2
   d centre(3, −5), radius 1

3 Calculate the radius and the coordinates of the centre of each of these circles:
   a $x^2 + y^2 + 4x + 6y - 3 = 0$
   b $x^2 + y^2 - 2x + 10y + 10 = 0$
   c $x^2 + y^2 + 8x - 8y - 8 = 0$
   d $x^2 + y^2 - 3x + 4y = 0$

4 Which of these equations do not represent circles? Give a reason for your answer.
   a $x^2 + y^2 + 3x + 6y - 7 = 0$
   b $x^2 + y^2 - 2x + 5y + 8 = 0$
   c $x^2 + y^2 - 4x - 4y + 12 = 0$
   d $x^2 + y^2 + 6x - 2y + 9 = 0$

5 Find the points of intersection of:
   a the line $y = 6 - 3x$ and the circle $x^2 + y^2 - 8x + 2y - 8 = 0$
   b the line $y = 2x + 5$ and the circle $x^2 + y^2 - 4x - 8y + 10 = 0$
   c the line $2y + x = 5$ and the circle $x^2 + y^2 + 2x + 4y - 20 = 0$

6 Find the equation of the circle which has A(−3, 2) and B(5, −4) as the end points of a diameter.

7 The straight line $y = x - 2$ cuts the circle $x^2 + y^2 - 10x + 2y + 16 = 0$ at the points P and Q.
   a Find the coordinates of P and Q.
   b Find the equation of the circle which has PQ as diameter.

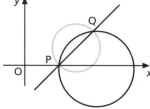

8 Show that the line $y = 2x - 5$ is a tangent to the circle $x^2 + y^2 + 12x - 6y - 35 = 0$ and find the coordinates of the point of contact.

9 The line $2y - x + 12 = 0$ is a tangent to the circle $x^2 + y^2 + 2x - 2y - 43 = 0$.
   a Prove this.
   b Find the coordinates of the point of contact.

10 Find the equation of the tangent to the circle $x^2 + y^2 + 3x + 5y + 8 = 0$ at the point (2, −1).

11 a Find the points of intersection of the circle $x^2 + y^2 + \frac{1}{2}x - \frac{1}{2}y - 21 = 0$ with the line $y = x - 2$.
   b Find the lines parallel to $y = x - 2$ which are tangents to the circle and find the coordinates of the points of contact.

12 Given the line $y = 3x + 2$ and the circle $x^2 + y^2 - 3x + 8y + 12 = 0$, determine if the line:
a intersects the circle at two points
b is a tangent to the circle
c does not meet the circle.

13 Determine the relationship between the line $y = 1 - 4x$ and the circle $x^2 + y^2 + 2x - 12y + 10 = 0$.

14 The shadow of the sun on the ground during an eclipse can be modelled by the circle $x^2 + y^2 + 4x + 6y + 8 = 0$. The line along which its centre runs has equation $y = 2x + 1$. Work out the equations of the two tangents which form the boundaries of the path of the shadow. (Hint: consider the lines $y = 2x + k$.)

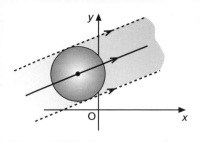

15 The line $y = x + k$ is a tangent to the circle $x^2 + y^2 + 2x - 12y + 19 = 0$.
a Find two possible values of k.
b Find the equation of the line joining the points of contact.

16 The line $y = 3 - 2x$ is a tangent to the circle $x^2 + y^2 + kx - 6y + 14 = 0$. Find the possible values of k.

17 PQ is a tangent to the circle with centre C and equation $(x - 5)^2 + (y + 2)^2 = 16$. P is the point $(0, 1)$. Find the area of triangle PQC, leaving your answer in surd form.

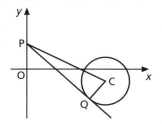

18 Show that the circles $x^2 + y^2 + 8x - 14y - 35 = 0$ and $x^2 + y^2 - 16x + 4y + 43 = 0$ touch each other.

19 Determine if the circles $x^2 + y^2 - 24x - 32y + 231 = 0$ and $x^2 + y^2 + 6x + 40y - 267 = 0$ touch each other.

20

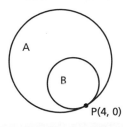

A: $x^2 + y^2 - 12y - 16 = 0$
B: $x^2 + y^2 - 4x - 6y = 0$

Circles A and B touch at the point $P(4, 0)$.
a Show that the centre of circle A lies on the circumference of circle B.
b Show that P lies on the line of centres of the two circles.
c Find the equation of the common tangent at P.
d Determine the area of each circle.

21 With suitable axes the circular weight of a pendulum can be represented by the equation $x^2 + y^2 + 22y + 112 = 0$, with the top of the arm at the origin.

   a Calculate the length of the arm.

   b The centre of the weight moves through the arc of a circle as it swings. What is the equation of this circle?

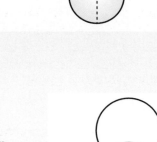

22 Two circles touch at the point (3, 4). The radius of circle C1 is twice that of circle C2. The equation of circle C2 is $x^2 + y^2 - 10x - 2y + 13 = 0$. Find the equation of circle C1.

23 The circle $x^2 + y^2 - 8x - 2y - 8 = 0$ is reflected in the x-axis. Find its new equation.

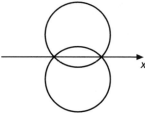

24 The circle with equation $x^2 + y^2 + 6x - 8y + 10 = 0$ is given a translation so that its new centre is at the point (−2, 3). Find the equation of the circle in its new position.

25

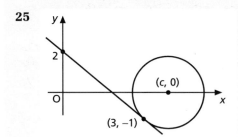

$y = 2 - x$ is a tangent to the circle at the point (3, −1). The centre of the circle lies on the x-axis.

   a Find the equation of the circle.

   b Write down the equation of the circle after a 90° clockwise rotation about O.

26 A circle passes through the points (0, 0) and (0, −8). The line $x = 6$ is a tangent to the circle. Find the equation of the circle.

27 One of the following represents a circle. Which one? Write down the coordinates of the centre of the circle.

   a $5x^2 + 5y^2 - 4x + 6y + 6 = 0$

   b $3x^2 + 3y^2 - 12x + 8y + 6 = 0$

Mathematics 3 (H) Contents

Preparation for Unit Assessment

OUTCOME 1a
Determine whether three points with given coordinates are collinear

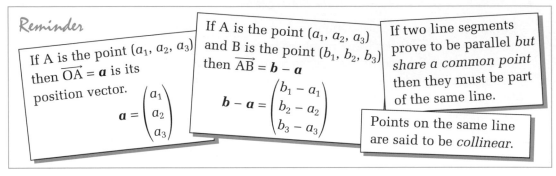

Reminder

If A is the point (a_1, a_2, a_3) then $\overrightarrow{OA} = \boldsymbol{a}$ is its position vector.

$$\boldsymbol{a} = \begin{pmatrix} a_1 \\ a_2 \\ a_3 \end{pmatrix}$$

If A is the point (a_1, a_2, a_3) and B is the point (b_1, b_2, b_3) then $\overrightarrow{AB} = \boldsymbol{b} - \boldsymbol{a}$

$$\boldsymbol{b} - \boldsymbol{a} = \begin{pmatrix} b_1 - a_1 \\ b_2 - a_2 \\ b_3 - a_3 \end{pmatrix}$$

If two line segments prove to be parallel *but* share a *common point* then they must be part of the same line.

Points on the same line are said to be *collinear*.

1 Write down the position vectors of each of the following points:

  a B(3, 1, 2)   **b** C(−2, 3, 1)   **c** K(−2, −5, 2)   **d** P(1, −2, −3)

2 Write down the vector requested, given the following points:

  a $\overrightarrow{BC}$; B(3, 1, 2) and C(3, 2, 4)   **b** $\overrightarrow{PQ}$; P(5, 0, 4) and Q(1, 3, 1)

  c $\overrightarrow{RT}$; R(−1, 2, 4) and T(−3, 4, −1)   **d** $\overrightarrow{MN}$; M(0, −2, 0) and N(−2, −5, −1)

3 In each case calculate $\overrightarrow{AB}$ and $\overrightarrow{CD}$ then say whether or not the lines AB and CD are parallel.

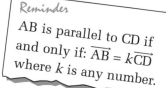

Reminder

AB is parallel to CD if and only if: $\overrightarrow{AB} = k\overrightarrow{CD}$ where k is any number.

  a A(2, 2, 2), B(3, 4, 4), C(0, 2, 1) and D(3, 8, 7)

  b A(1, 0, 4), B(3, −1, 8), C(7, −2, 2) and D(17, −7, 22)

  c A(−1, −2, 4), B(2, −2, 3), C(2, 0, 0) and D(−10, 0, 4)

  d A(3, −1, 5), B(5, 0, 2), C(6, 1, −1) and D(12, 4, −9)

  e A(0, −4, 6), B(5, 6, 1), C(−2, 4, 7) and D(1, 10, 4)

4 For each pair of directed line segments: **(i)** state why you know they are parallel **(ii)** name a point common to both segments if it can be identified **(iii)** declare what conclusion, if any, you can make about them.

  a $\overrightarrow{AB} = \begin{pmatrix} 2 \\ 4 \\ 1 \end{pmatrix}$, $\overrightarrow{BC} = \begin{pmatrix} 6 \\ 12 \\ 3 \end{pmatrix}$ **b** $\overrightarrow{PQ} = \begin{pmatrix} -2 \\ 4 \\ 1 \end{pmatrix}$, $\overrightarrow{PR} = \begin{pmatrix} -4 \\ 8 \\ 2 \end{pmatrix}$ **c** $\overrightarrow{SK} = \begin{pmatrix} 2 \\ 4 \\ -2 \end{pmatrix}$, $\overrightarrow{TK} = \begin{pmatrix} 3 \\ 6 \\ -3 \end{pmatrix}$

  d $\overrightarrow{SP} = \begin{pmatrix} 6 \\ 2 \\ -4 \end{pmatrix}$, $\overrightarrow{QR} = \begin{pmatrix} 15 \\ 5 \\ -10 \end{pmatrix}$ **e** $\overrightarrow{EF} = \begin{pmatrix} -4 \\ 4 \\ 8 \end{pmatrix}$, $\overrightarrow{FG} = \begin{pmatrix} 5 \\ -5 \\ -10 \end{pmatrix}$ **f** $\overrightarrow{GH} = \begin{pmatrix} 4 \\ 1 \\ 3 \end{pmatrix}$, $\overrightarrow{JK} = \begin{pmatrix} 2 \\ 0.5 \\ 1.5 \end{pmatrix}$

5 For each set of points: **(i)** write down, in component form, a directed line segment joining the first to the second point; **(ii)** write down a directed line segment joining the second to the third point; **(iii)** work out if the points in the set are collinear.

  a A(2, 1, 1), B(3, 2, 5), C(9, 4, 13)   **b** D(1, 0, −1), E(2, −1, 0), F(5, −4, 3)

  c G(3, 6, 5), H(4, 8, 8), I(5, 10, 10)   **d** J(2, 0, 0), K(8, 9, −3), L(16, 21, −7)

  e M(0, 4, −1), N(2, 12, −7), P(5, 24, −16)   **f** Q(5, −3, −4), R(6, −2, −3), S(3, −4, −6)

Preparation for Unit Assessment

OUTCOME 1b

Determine the coordinates of the point which divides the join of two given points internally in a given ratio

---

Example

A is the point $(1, 2, 4)$

B is the point $(13, 10, -12)$

Find the point P (p_1, p_2, p_3) which divides this line in the ratio $1 : 3$.

$$\overrightarrow{AP} : \overrightarrow{PB} = 1 : 3$$

$$\Rightarrow \frac{\overrightarrow{AP}}{\overrightarrow{PB}} = \frac{1}{3}$$

$$\Rightarrow 3\overrightarrow{AP} = \overrightarrow{PB}$$

$$3\overrightarrow{AP} = \overrightarrow{PB}$$
$$3(\boldsymbol{p} - \boldsymbol{a}) = \boldsymbol{b} - \boldsymbol{p}$$
$$3\boldsymbol{p} - 3\boldsymbol{a} = \boldsymbol{b} - \boldsymbol{p}$$
$$4\boldsymbol{p} = \boldsymbol{b} + 3\boldsymbol{a}$$

$$4\begin{pmatrix} p_1 \\ p_2 \\ p_3 \end{pmatrix} = \begin{pmatrix} 13 \\ 10 \\ -12 \end{pmatrix} + 3\begin{pmatrix} 1 \\ 2 \\ 4 \end{pmatrix}$$

$$= \begin{pmatrix} 13 + 3 \\ 10 + 6 \\ -12 + 12 \end{pmatrix} = \begin{pmatrix} 16 \\ 16 \\ 0 \end{pmatrix}$$

$$\begin{pmatrix} p_1 \\ p_2 \\ p_3 \end{pmatrix} = \frac{1}{4}\begin{pmatrix} 16 \\ 16 \\ 0 \end{pmatrix} = \begin{pmatrix} 4 \\ 4 \\ 0 \end{pmatrix}$$

So P is the point $(4, 4, 0)$.

---

1 P divides AB internally in the ratio $1 : 3$ means $\overrightarrow{AP} : \overrightarrow{PB} = 1 : 3$ or $\dfrac{\overrightarrow{AP}}{\overrightarrow{PB}} = \dfrac{1}{3}$ and so $3\overrightarrow{AP} = \overrightarrow{PB}$. Make similar statements about the following:

  a P divides AB internally in the ratio $1 : 5$.
  b S divides PQ internally in the ratio $1 : 4$.
  c T divides CD internally in the ratio $2 : 3$.
  d R divides GF internally in the ratio $3 : 4$.

2 $3\overrightarrow{AP} = \overrightarrow{PB}$ implies that the position vectors are related by the equation $4\boldsymbol{p} = \boldsymbol{b} + 3\boldsymbol{a}$. Work out similar equations for the following:

  a $2\overrightarrow{AP} = \overrightarrow{PB}$ **b** $4\overrightarrow{AP} = \overrightarrow{PB}$ **c** $2\overrightarrow{AP} = 3\overrightarrow{PB}$
  d $3\overrightarrow{AP} = 2\overrightarrow{PB}$ **e** $3\overrightarrow{AP} = 4\overrightarrow{PB}$ **f** $\overrightarrow{AP} = 4\overrightarrow{PB}$

3 Solve the following equations: **a** $5\begin{pmatrix} p_1 \\ p_2 \\ p_3 \end{pmatrix} = \begin{pmatrix} 8 \\ 4 \\ 5 \end{pmatrix} + 2\begin{pmatrix} 1 \\ 3 \\ 0 \end{pmatrix}$

  b $6\begin{pmatrix} p_1 \\ p_2 \\ p_3 \end{pmatrix} = \begin{pmatrix} 4 \\ 4 \\ 10 \end{pmatrix} + 4\begin{pmatrix} 5 \\ 2 \\ -1 \end{pmatrix}$ **c** $4\begin{pmatrix} p_1 \\ p_2 \\ p_3 \end{pmatrix} = 2\begin{pmatrix} 3 \\ 1 \\ 2 \end{pmatrix} + 3\begin{pmatrix} 2 \\ 6 \\ 8 \end{pmatrix}$ **d** $8\begin{pmatrix} p_1 \\ p_2 \\ p_3 \end{pmatrix} = 3\begin{pmatrix} 4 \\ 1 \\ 7 \end{pmatrix} + 5\begin{pmatrix} 4 \\ 9 \\ 7 \end{pmatrix}$

4 Find p when:

    a $a = \begin{pmatrix} -1 \\ -1 \\ 2 \end{pmatrix}$ $b = \begin{pmatrix} 4 \\ 9 \\ 7 \end{pmatrix}$ and $5p = b + 4a$

    b $a = \begin{pmatrix} 2 \\ 1 \\ 5 \end{pmatrix}$ $b = \begin{pmatrix} 7 \\ -4 \\ 15 \end{pmatrix}$ and $5p = 2b + 3a$

    c $a = \begin{pmatrix} -3 \\ 2 \\ 1 \end{pmatrix}$ $b = \begin{pmatrix} -17 \\ 9 \\ 29 \end{pmatrix}$ and $7p = 2b + 5a$

5   **a**   A is the point $(-5, -2, 1)$. B is the point $(-2, 4, 4)$.

        Find the point P (p_1, p_2, p_3) which divides this line in the ratio $1:2$.

   b   A is the point $(-3, 0, -5)$. B is the point $(5, -8, 7)$.

        Find the point P (p_1, p_2, p_3) which divides this line in the ratio $1:3$.

   c   A is the point $(12, -6, -7)$. B is the point $(2, -1, 8)$.

        Find the point P which divides this line in the ratio $2:3$.

   d   A is the point $(-20, -10, 6)$. B is the point $(8, 4, -1)$.

        Find the point P which divides AB in the ratio $5:2$.

   e   A is the point $(10, 10, -10)$. B is the point $(-5, 10, 15)$.

        Find the point P which divides AB in the ratio $4:1$.

Preparation for Unit Assessment

OUTCOME 1c
Use the scalar product

Work to 1 decimal place where appropriate.

1 Calculate the scalar product for each pair of vectors:

a $\begin{pmatrix} 1 \\ 2 \\ 1 \end{pmatrix}, \begin{pmatrix} 3 \\ 2 \\ 5 \end{pmatrix}$
   b $\begin{pmatrix} 2 \\ 1 \\ 4 \end{pmatrix}, \begin{pmatrix} 2 \\ 2 \\ 0 \end{pmatrix}$
   c $\begin{pmatrix} 2 \\ -2 \\ 3 \end{pmatrix}, \begin{pmatrix} 3 \\ -2 \\ -4 \end{pmatrix}$
   d $\begin{pmatrix} -1 \\ 0 \\ 6 \end{pmatrix}, \begin{pmatrix} -5 \\ 3 \\ -2 \end{pmatrix}$

2 Calculate the magnitude of the following vectors:

a $\begin{pmatrix} 3 \\ 4 \\ 12 \end{pmatrix}$
   b $\begin{pmatrix} 9 \\ 12 \\ 8 \end{pmatrix}$
   c $\begin{pmatrix} 15 \\ 80 \\ 36 \end{pmatrix}$
   d $\begin{pmatrix} -8 \\ 144 \\ 15 \end{pmatrix}$

3 Calculate the scalar product for each diagram.

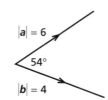

a $|\mathbf{a}| = 6$, $54°$, $|\mathbf{b}| = 4$

b $|\mathbf{a}| = 3$, $148°$, $|\mathbf{b}| = 5$

4 Which of the following pairs of vectors are perpendicular?

a $\begin{pmatrix} 3 \\ 4 \\ -2 \end{pmatrix}, \begin{pmatrix} 2 \\ -4 \\ -5 \end{pmatrix}$
   b $\begin{pmatrix} 1 \\ -2 \\ 11 \end{pmatrix}, \begin{pmatrix} -5 \\ 3 \\ 1 \end{pmatrix}$

c $\begin{pmatrix} 3 \\ -4 \\ 6 \end{pmatrix}, \begin{pmatrix} 4 \\ 6 \\ 2 \end{pmatrix}$
   d $\begin{pmatrix} 5 \\ 3 \\ -2 \end{pmatrix}, \begin{pmatrix} 1 \\ -3 \\ -3 \end{pmatrix}$

5 Find the angle between the following pairs of vectors.

a $\begin{pmatrix} 1 \\ 2 \\ 1 \end{pmatrix}, \begin{pmatrix} 3 \\ 1 \\ 5 \end{pmatrix}$ b $\begin{pmatrix} 2 \\ -1 \\ 3 \end{pmatrix}, \begin{pmatrix} -1 \\ 1 \\ -1 \end{pmatrix}$

Reminder

$\cos \theta = \dfrac{a.b}{|a|\,|b|}$

$0 \le \theta \le 180$

c $\begin{pmatrix} -1 \\ 2 \\ 4 \end{pmatrix}, \begin{pmatrix} 2 \\ -2 \\ 3 \end{pmatrix}$ d $\begin{pmatrix} -1 \\ -1 \\ 2 \end{pmatrix}, \begin{pmatrix} 4 \\ 5 \\ 5 \end{pmatrix}$

6 Find the *acute* angle between each of these pairs of vectors.

a $\begin{pmatrix} -1 \\ -2 \\ -3 \end{pmatrix}, \begin{pmatrix} 1 \\ 2 \\ 5 \end{pmatrix}$ b $\begin{pmatrix} 3 \\ 1 \\ 9 \end{pmatrix}, \begin{pmatrix} -2 \\ 2 \\ 5 \end{pmatrix}$ c $\begin{pmatrix} 1 \\ -3 \\ 5 \end{pmatrix}, \begin{pmatrix} 1 \\ 7 \\ 3 \end{pmatrix}$ d $\begin{pmatrix} 1 \\ 5 \\ -2 \end{pmatrix}, \begin{pmatrix} 3 \\ -1 \\ -2 \end{pmatrix}$

7 Given three points A(1, 2, 6), B(2, −3, 1), C(1, 4, 2):

a Calculate $\overrightarrow{AB}$ and $\overrightarrow{AC}$

b Hence find the size of ∠BAC

c Calculate $\overrightarrow{BA}$ and $\overrightarrow{BC}$ and hence calculate the size of ∠ABC.

8 Calculate each of the angles indicated.

a ∠ABC given the points A(1, 2, 3), B(2, 2, 2) and C(1, −1, 5)

b ∠PQR given the points P(−1, 3, 1), Q(7, 1, 2) and R(5, 0, 4)

c ∠HAL given the points A(1, 0, 2), H(−5, −2, −1) and L(3, 7, 1)

Outcome 1 Assessment

1 Prove that A(1, 5, −7), B(2, 3, −4) and C(5, −3, 5) are collinear.

2 Which set of points all lie on the same straight line?
   a A(−5, −4, 5), B(1, 2, 2) and C(3, 4, 2)
   b D(−5, 4, 6), E(−1, 2, 4) and F(5, −1, 1)
   c G(1, 2, 3), H(−2, 1, 9) and K(−4, 2, 13)

3 A is the point (−4, 6, −9) and B is the point (6, 1, 6). Find the point P that divides AB internally in the ratio 1 : 4.

4 S and R are the points (7, −5, −6) and (0, 2, 8) respectively. Find the point T that divides SR internally in the ratio 3 : 4.

5 Show the vectors $\begin{pmatrix} 3 \\ -5 \\ 2 \end{pmatrix}$ and $\begin{pmatrix} -4 \\ -2 \\ 1 \end{pmatrix}$ are perpendicular to each other.

6 A, B, C and D are the points A(1, 2, 1), B(5, 8, −7), C(3, 4, −3) and D(6, 6, 0). Use the scalar product $\overrightarrow{AB}.\overrightarrow{CD}$ to prove that AB and CD are perpendicular.

7 Find the acute angle between the vectors $\begin{pmatrix} 2 \\ 1 \\ 3 \end{pmatrix}$ and $\begin{pmatrix} -1 \\ 2 \\ -3 \end{pmatrix}$.

8 A, B and C are the points A(3, 1, 1), B(2, 7, 4), C(−2, 1, −3). Calculate the size of the angle BCA.

Preparation for Unit Assessment

OUTCOME 2a
Differentiate k sin x, k cos x

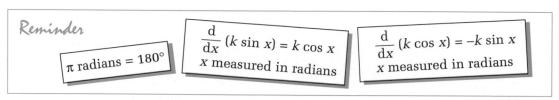

Reminder

π radians = 180°

$$\frac{d}{dx}(k \sin x) = k \cos x$$
x measured in radians

$$\frac{d}{dx}(k \cos x) = -k \sin x$$
x measured in radians

1 Express the following in radians using π.
  a 90° **b** 60° **c** 45° **d** 30° **e** 150°

2 Express the following in degrees.
  a $\dfrac{\pi}{5}$ **b** $\dfrac{2\pi}{5}$ **c** $\dfrac{\pi}{6}$ **d** $\dfrac{5\pi}{6}$ **e** $\dfrac{2\pi}{3}$

3 Differentiate the following:
  a $3 \sin x$ **b** $5 \sin x$ **c** $-2 \sin x$ **d** $-6 \sin x$ **e** $\dfrac{2}{3} \sin x$

4 Differentiate:
  a $4 \cos x$ **b** $3 \cos x$ **c** $-3 \cos x$ **d** $-2 \cos x$ **e** $\dfrac{3}{4} \cos x$

5 Find the derivative of:
  a $2 \cos x$ **b** $4 \sin x$ **c** $-3 \sin x$ **d** $-5 \cos x$

6 Find $\dfrac{dy}{dx}$ for each: **a** $y = \cos x + 3 \sin x$ **b** $y = 2 \sin x - 3 \cos x$
  c $y = 3 \cos x - \sin x$ **d** $y = \sin x - \cos x$

Reminder

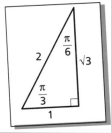

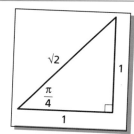

7 Without the aid of a calculator find the value of:
  a $f'(x)$ when $f(x) = \sin x$ and $x =$ **(i)** $\dfrac{\pi}{3}$ **(ii)** $\dfrac{\pi}{6}$ **(iii)** $\dfrac{\pi}{4}$
  b $f'(x)$ when $f(x) = \cos x$ and $x =$ **(i)** $\dfrac{\pi}{3}$ **(ii)** $\dfrac{\pi}{6}$ **(iii)** $\dfrac{\pi}{4}$
  c $f'(x)$ when $f(x) = 3 \cos x$ and $x =$ **(i)** $\dfrac{\pi}{3}$ **(ii)** $\dfrac{\pi}{6}$ **(iii)** $\dfrac{\pi}{2}$
  d $f'(x)$ when $f(x) = 2 \sin x$ and $x =$ **(i)** $\dfrac{\pi}{3}$ **(ii)** $\dfrac{\pi}{2}$ **(iii)** $\dfrac{\pi}{6}$

8 **a** $f(x) = 2 \sin x + 3 \cos x$. Find the value of: **(i)** $f'\left(\dfrac{\pi}{3}\right)$ **(ii)** $f'\left(\dfrac{\pi}{6}\right)$ **(iii)** $f'(0)$

  b $f(x) = 3 \sin x - 5 \cos x$. Find the value of: **(i)** $f'\left(\dfrac{\pi}{4}\right)$ **(ii)** $f'\left(\dfrac{\pi}{6}\right)$ **(iii)** $f'(0)$

Preparation for Unit Assessment

OUTCOME 2b
Differentiate using the function of a function rule

> **Examples**
>
> $$y = 4(3x + 1)^5 \qquad\qquad y = (3x + 1)^5 \qquad\qquad y = 4\sin(3x + 1)$$
> $$y = f(g(x)) \qquad\qquad y = f(g(x)) \qquad\qquad y = f(g(x))$$
> where $f(x) = 4x^5$ where $g(x) = 3x + 1$ where $f(x) = 4\sin x$
> and $\quad g(x) = 3x + 1$ $\qquad \dfrac{dy}{dx} = g'(x) \times f'(g(x))$ and $\quad g(x) = 3x + 1$
> $$= 3 \times 5(3x + 1)^4$$
> $$= 15(3x + 1)^4$$
> $$y = \sin^2 x$$
> $$y = (\sin x)^2$$
> $$f(x) = x^2$$
> and $\quad g(x) = \sin x$

1 Each of the following is a composite function of the form $y = f(g(x))$.
Identify $f(x)$ and $g(x)$ in each case.

  a $(x + 2)^3$ **b** $(2x - 3)^4$ **c** $(3x + 5)^{-1}$ **d** $3(x - 1)^2$ **e** $4(3 - 2x)^5$

  f $\dfrac{5}{(3x + 5)}$ **g** $\sqrt{(2x - 1)}$ **h** $(3 - 2x)^{\frac{1}{2}}$ **i** $(3x^2 + 2x + 5)^3$

2 Differentiate each of the following:

  a $(2x + 1)^4$ **b** $(5x - 4)^3$ **c** $(3 - 5x)^6$ **d** $(4 - 2x)^5$ **e** $(x + 3)^{-2}$

  f $(7x - 2)^{-1}$ **g** $(2 - x)^{-3}$ **h** $(5 - 3x)^{-1}$ **i** $\sqrt{3x - 1}$ **j** $\sqrt{2x - 1}$

  k $\sqrt{3 - 2x}$ **l** $\sqrt{4 - x}$ **m** $2(x + 4)^2$ **n** $3(6x - 1)^4$ **o** $2(1 - x)^{-3}$

  p $4(1 - 4x)^{-1}$ **q** $\dfrac{3}{x + 4}$ **r** $\dfrac{4}{2x + 1}$ **s** $\dfrac{2}{1 - 3x}$ **t** $\dfrac{1}{3x - 4}$

  u $(x^2 + 2x + 1)^4$ **v** $2(3x^2 - 4)^3$ **w** $(3 - x - x^3)^4$

  x $(4 - 2x^4)^5$ **y** $(2x^2 - 3x + 1)^{-1}$ **z** $\sqrt{(2x^3 - 1)^3}$

3 Each of the following is a composite function of the form $y = f(g(x))$.
Identify $f(x)$ and $g(x)$ in each case.

  a $\sin(2x + 1)$ **b** $\cos(3x - 1)$ **c** $\cos(2x + 7)$ **d** $\sin(4 - x)$ **e** $\sin(3 - x^2)$

  f $\cos(3x - 1)$ **g** $\sin\sqrt{x}$ **h** $\cos^3 x$ **i** $\sin^4 x$ **j** $\sin\left(\dfrac{1}{x}\right)$

4 Differentiate each of the following:

  a $\sin(3x + 1)$ **b** $\cos(2x - 3)$ **c** $\cos(1 - 3x)$ **d** $\sin(2 - 5x)$

  e $\sin 2x$ **f** $\cos 4x$ **g** $\cos 5x$ **h** $\sin(-3x)$

  i $\sin^3 x$ **j** $\cos^4 x$ **k** $\sin\sqrt{x}$ **l** $\cos(4 - x^3)$

  m $\sin(x^2 + 1)$ **n** $\cos(3x^4 - 1)$ **o** $\cos(1 - x^{-3})$ **p** $\sin(2 - 3x^{-1})$

  q $\sin\left(\dfrac{1}{x}\right)$ **r** $\cos\left(\dfrac{2}{x}\right)$ **s** $\cos\left(\dfrac{1}{x} + x\right)$ **t** $\cos(2x^2 + x + 1)$

  u $\sin(2x^2 - 1)$ **v** $\sin(3 - 2x - x^2)$ **w** $\cos(1 - x^4)$ **x** $\sin(x^2 - 5x - 1)$

  y $\sin(3x^5 - 2)$

Preparation for Unit Assessment

OUTCOME 2c
Integrate functions of the form $f(x) = (x + \theta)^n$, n rational except for -1, $f(x) = p \cos x$ and $f(x) = p \sin x$

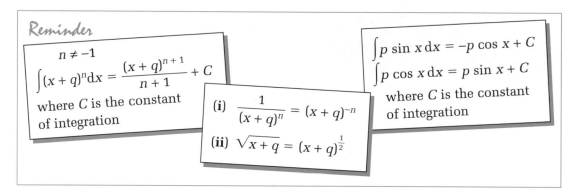

Reminder

$n \neq -1$

$$\int (x + q)^n dx = \frac{(x + q)^{n+1}}{n+1} + C$$

where C is the constant of integration

(i) $\dfrac{1}{(x + q)^n} = (x + q)^{-n}$

(ii) $\sqrt{x + q} = (x + q)^{\frac{1}{2}}$

$$\int p \sin x \, dx = -p \cos x + C$$

$$\int p \cos x \, dx = p \sin x + C$$

where C is the constant of integration

1 Integrate the following:

a $(x + 1)^4$ **b** $(x + 3)^5$ **c** $(x - 4)^2$ **d** $(x - 5)^3$ **e** $(x + 7)^{-2}$

f $(x - 1)^{-3}$ **g** $(x - 5)^{-3}$ **h** $(x + 2)^{-6}$ **i** $(x + 3)^{\frac{1}{2}}$ **j** $(x + 4)^{\frac{2}{3}}$

k $(x - 3)^{\frac{1}{3}}$ **l** $(x - 6)^{\frac{4}{3}}$ **m** $(x + 2)^{\frac{1}{3}}$ **n** $(x - 5)^{\frac{3}{5}}$ **o** $(x + 1)^{\frac{1}{4}}$

p $(x + 3)^{\frac{5}{4}}$ **q** $(x - 2)^{-\frac{3}{2}}$ **r** $(x + 8)^{-\frac{2}{3}}$ **s** $(x - 1)^{-\frac{1}{2}}$ **t** $(x - 4)^{-\frac{5}{3}}$

2 Find:

a $\displaystyle\int (x + 2)^4 \, dx$ **b** $\displaystyle\int (x + 3)^5 \, dx$ **c** $\displaystyle\int (x - 9)^3 \, dx$ **d** $\displaystyle\int (x - 5)^2 \, dx$

e $\displaystyle\int (x + 1)^{-3} \, dx$ **f** $\displaystyle\int (x + 5)^{-4} \, dx$ **g** $\displaystyle\int (x - 7)^{-5} \, dx$ **h** $\displaystyle\int (x - 8)^{-3} \, dx$

i $\displaystyle\int (x + 1)^{\frac{1}{2}} \, dx$ **j** $\displaystyle\int (x + 4)^{\frac{1}{5}} \, dx$ **k** $\displaystyle\int (x - 2)^{\frac{3}{4}} \, dx$ **l** $\displaystyle\int (x - 1)^{\frac{5}{2}} \, dx$

m $\displaystyle\int (x + 4)^{-\frac{1}{3}} \, dx$ **n** $\displaystyle\int (x + 3)^{-\frac{2}{3}} \, dx$ **o** $\displaystyle\int (x - 5)^{-\frac{4}{3}} \, dx$ **p** $\displaystyle\int (x + 6)^{-\frac{4}{7}} \, dx$

3 Find:

a $\displaystyle\int \frac{dx}{(x + 1)^4}$ **b** $\displaystyle\int \frac{dx}{(x + 3)^2}$ **c** $\displaystyle\int \frac{dx}{(x - 2)^3}$

d $\displaystyle\int \sqrt{x + 2} \, dx$ **e** $\displaystyle\int \sqrt{x - 3} \, dx$ **f** $\displaystyle\int \sqrt{x + 5} \, dx$

4 Integrate the following:

a $3 \sin x$ **b** $2 \cos x$ **c** $5 \cos x$ **d** $-2 \sin x$ **e** $-\cos x$

f $\frac{1}{2} \cos x$ **g** $\frac{3}{4} \sin x$ **h** $\frac{4}{5} \sin x$ **i** $-\frac{1}{2} \cos x$ **j** $-\frac{1}{2} \sin x$

5 Find:

a $\displaystyle\int 3 \cos x \, dx$ **b** $\displaystyle\int 2 \sin x \, dx$ **c** $\displaystyle\int -7 \cos x \, dx$ **d** $\displaystyle\int - \sin x \, dx$

e $\displaystyle\int \frac{1}{3} \sin x \, dx$ **f** $\displaystyle\int \frac{2}{5} \cos x \, dx$ **g** $\displaystyle\int -\frac{1}{4} \cos x \, dx$ **h** $\displaystyle\int -\frac{1}{6} \sin x \, dx$

Outcome 2 Assessment

1 Differentiate:
  a $3 \cos x$ **b** $2 \sin x$ **c** $-\cos x$ **d** $-3 \sin x$

2 Find the derivative of:
  a $5 \cos x$ **b** $7 \sin x$ **c** $-2 \sin x$ **d** $-3 \cos x$

3 Find $\dfrac{dy}{dx}$ for each:
  a $y = \sin x + 2 \cos x$ **b** $y = 2 \cos x - 3 \sin x$

4 Differentiate each of the following:
  a $(x + 2)^3$ **b** $(x - 1)^{-3}$ **c** $(1 + x)^4$ **d** $(4 + x)^{-1}$
  e $\sqrt{x + 3}$ **f** $\sqrt{3 - x}$ **g** $(2 - x)^{\frac{1}{2}}$ **h** $(4 + x)^{-\frac{1}{2}}$

5 Find the derivative of:
  a $\sin (x + 1)$ **b** $\cos (x - 2)$ **c** $\sin^2 x$ **d** $\cos^3 x$

6 Integrate the following:
  a $(x + 2)^3$ **b** $(x + 1)^{-4}$ **c** $(x - 3)^{\frac{2}{3}}$ **d** $(x - 2)^{-\frac{3}{5}}$

7 Find:
  a $\int (x + 1)^3 \, dx$ **b** $\int (x + 3)^{-2} \, dx$ **c** $\int (x - 2)^{\frac{1}{2}} \, dx$ **d** $\int (x + 4)^{-\frac{1}{3}} \, dx$

8 Find:
  a $\int 2 \cos x \, dx$ **b** $\int 3 \sin x \, dx$ **c** $\int -5 \cos x \, dx$ **d** $\int -4 \sin x \, dx$

Preparation for Unit Assessment

OUTCOME 3a
Simplify a numerical expression using the laws of logarithms

Simplify:

1 **a** $\log_a 3 + \log_a 4$
    c $\log_a 4 + \log_a 5$
    e $\log_a 2 + \log_a 7$
    g $\log_a 5 + \log_a 4 + \log_a 3$

  b $\log_a 5 + \log_a 2$
  d $\log_a 1 + \log_a 6$
  f $\log_a 3 + \log_a 3$
  h $\log_a 5 + \log_a 1 + \log_a 3$

> **Reminder**
>
> $\log_a x + \log_a y = \log_a xy$

2 **a** $\log_a 8 - \log_a 4$
    c $\log_a 12 - \log_a 3$
    e $\log_a 30 - \log_a 6$
    g $\log_a 24 - \log_a 4 - \log_a 3$
    h $\log_a 36 - \log_a 6 - \log_a 2$

  b $\log_a 6 - \log_a 1$
  d $\log_a 1 - \log_a 2$
  f $\log_a 5 - \log_a 5$

> **Reminder**
>
> $\log_a x - \log_a y = \log_a \dfrac{x}{y}$

3 **a** $\log_a 5 + \log_a 4$
    c $\log_a 90 - \log_a 10$
    e $\log_a 6 - \log_a 4$
    g $\log_a 8 + \log_a 6 - \log_a 12$

  b $\log_a 9 - \log_a 3$
  d $\log_a 15 + \log_a 2$
  f $\log_a 9 - \log_a 2$
  h $\log_a 40 - \log_a 4 + \log_a 5$

4 **a** $\log_a 5^2$
    c $\log_a 8^{-3}$
    e $\log_a 4^5 + \log_a 4^8$
    g $\log_a 8^3 - \log_a 8^2 + \log_a 8^4$
    h $\log_a 9^2 + \log_a 9^3 - \log_a 9^7$

  b $\log_a 3^4$
  d $\log_a 6^2 + \log_a 6^3$
  f $\log_a 2^7 - \log_a 2^2$

> **Reminder**
>
> $\log_a x^n = n\log_a x$

5 **a** $\log_3 3^2$
    c $\log_2 8$
    e $5\log_9 3 - \log_9 27$
    g $2\log_6 3 + 2\log_6 8 - 4\log_6 2$
    h $\log_6 36 + \log_3 27 - \log_4 4$

  b $\log_4 16$
  d $\log_5 25 + \log_5 125$
  f $2\log_{10} 2 + 2\log_{10} 5$

> **Reminder**
>
> $\log_a 1 = 0$
> $\log_a a = 1$

Preparation for Unit Assessment

OUTCOME 3b
Solve simple logarithmic and exponential equations

Example 1

$$6^x = 24$$
$$\Rightarrow \ \log 6^x = \log 24$$
$$\Rightarrow x \log 6 = \log 24$$
$$\Rightarrow \qquad x = \frac{\log 24}{\log 6}$$

By calculator,
using base 10
or base e:
$$x = 1.77 \text{ (to 2 d.p.)}$$

Example 2

$$\log_{10} x = 2.7$$
$$\Rightarrow \qquad x = 10^{2.7}$$
Using a calculator this
is approximately
$$x = 501.19 \text{ (to 2 d.p.)}$$

1 Find an expression for x, involving logarithms to the base 10:
   a $5^x = 20$ b $3^x = 21$ c $7^x = 300$ d $2^x = 30$

2 Find an expression for x, involving logarithms to the base e, then simplify where
   possible:
   a $6^x = 7776$ b $2^x = 1024$ c $4^x = 4096$ d $25^x = 5$

3 (i) Find an *exact* expression for x, involving logarithms to the base e
   (ii) then use your calculator to find an approximate answer correct to 2 decimal places:
   a $5^x = 20$ b $3^x = 12$ c $9^x = 429$ d $20^x = 2$

4 (i) Find an *exact* expression for x, involving logarithms to the base 10
   (ii) then use your calculator to find an approximate answer correct to 2 decimal places:
   a $4^x = 100$ b $2^x = 90$ c $500^x = 20$ d $26^x = 12$

5 Express x as a power of 10 in each case:
   a $\log_{10} x = 1.8$ b $\log_{10} x = 0.35$ c $\log_{10} x = -1.3$

6 Express x as a power of e in each case:
   a $\log_e x = 24$ b $\log_e x = 2.7$ c $\log_e x = 0.6$

7 Use your calculator to evaluate x, correct to 2 decimal places:
   a $x = 10^{2.1}$ b $x = 10^{0.23}$ c $x = e^{3.2}$ d $x = e^{4.5}$

8 (i) Express the *exact* value of x as a power of 10
   (ii) then use your calculator to find an approximate value for x in each case, correct
        to 2 decimal places:
   a $\log_{10} x = 2.5$ b $\log_{10} x = 0.12$ c $\log_{10} x = 1.4$ d $\log_{10} x = 0.25$
   e $\log_{10} x = -1.2$ f $\log_{10} x = 0.05$ g $\log_{10} x = -1.5$ h $\log_{10} x = -2.3$

9 (i) Express the *exact* value of x as a power of e
   (ii) then use your calculator to find an approximate value for x in each case, correct
        to 2 decimal places:
   a $\log_e x = 1.9$ b $\log_e x = 0.23$ c $\log_e x = -1.26$ d $\log_e x = -0.9$

Outcome 3 Assessment

1 Simplify:
- **a** $\log_a 5 + \log_a 7$
- **b** $\log_a 84 - \log_a 7$
- **c** $\log_a 9 + \log_a 5 - \log_a 3$
- **d** $\log_a 5^2 + \log_a 5^6$
- **e** $2 \log_6 3 + \log_6 24$
- **f** $2 \log_5 10 - 2 \log_5 2$

2 If $x = \dfrac{\log_{10} 12}{\log_{10} 2}$ calculate x correct to 2 decimal places.

3 If $x = \dfrac{\log_e 9}{\log_e 12}$ find an approximation for x correct to 2 decimal places.

4 Write down an exact expression for x, given that $\log_{10} x = 0.28$.

5 Write down an exact expression for x, given that $\log_e x = 3.14$.

6 When $\log_{10} x = 3.14$, calculate x correct to 2 decimal places.

7 When $\log_e x = 0.152$, calculate x correct to 2 decimal places.

8 Calculate x to 2 decimal places when $x = 10^{0.301}$.

9 Calculate the approximate value of x (to 2 decimal places) when $x = e^{1.041}$.

Preparation for Unit Assessment

OUTCOME 4a
Express a cos θ + b sin θ in the form r cos (θ ± α) or r sin (θ ± α)

1 Expand:
   a $r \cos (\theta + \alpha)$ **b** $r \cos (\theta - \alpha)$
   c $r \sin (\theta + \alpha)$ **d** $r \sin (\theta - \alpha)$

> **Reminder**
>
> $\cos (A + B) = \cos A \cos B - \sin A \sin B$
> $\cos (A - B) = \cos A \cos B + \sin A \sin B$

2 **a** Expand $5 \cos (\theta + \alpha)$.
   b Write down the coefficient of
      (i) $\cos \theta$ **(ii)** $\sin \theta$.
   c Repeat parts **a** and **b** for:
      (i) $3 \sin (\theta + \alpha)$ **(ii)** $4 \cos (\theta - \alpha)$.

> **Reminder**
>
> $\sin (A + B) = \sin A \cos B + \cos A \sin B$
> $\sin (A - B) = \sin A \cos B - \cos A \sin B$

3 **a** When expanded, $2 \sin (\theta + \alpha) = a \cos \theta + b \sin \theta$.
     Write down, in terms of θ, an expression for **(i)** a **(ii)** b.
   b When expanded, $2 \cos (\theta + \alpha) = p \cos \theta + q \sin \theta$.
     Write down, in terms of θ, an expression for **(i)** p **(ii)** q.

Examples

$2 \sin \theta° = 4;\ 2 \cos \theta° = -7$

$\Rightarrow \dfrac{2 \sin \theta°}{2 \cos \theta°} \Rightarrow \tan \theta° = -\dfrac{4}{7}$

$\tan^{-1}\left(-\dfrac{4}{7}\right) = -29.7$ (calculator)

sin positive cos negative	sin positive
cos negative	

$\theta = 180 + (-29.7)$
$ = 150.3°$

$R \sin \theta = 3;\ R \cos \theta = 4$
$\Rightarrow R^2 \sin^2 \theta + R^2 \cos^2 \theta = 9 + 16$
$\Rightarrow R^2 (\sin^2 \theta + \cos^2 \theta) = 25$
$\Rightarrow R^2 = 25$
$\Rightarrow R = 5$

---

4 Solve the following pairs of equations for $0 \le \theta < 360$.
   a $3 \sin \theta° = 4;\ 3 \cos \theta° = 2$ **b** $5 \sin \theta° = 3;\ 5 \cos \theta° = -4$
   c $\sin \theta° = -4;\ \cos \theta° = -3$ **d** $2 \sin \theta° = -3;\ 2 \cos \theta° = 4$
   e $R \sin \theta° = -2;\ R \cos \theta° = -3$ **f** $k \sin \theta° = 6;\ k \cos \theta° = -2$

5 Solve the following pairs of equations for R:
   a $R \sin \theta = 3;\ R \cos \theta = 4$ **b** $R \sin \theta = 5;\ R \cos \theta = -12$
   c $R \sin \theta = -1.5;\ R \cos \theta = 2$ **d** $R \sin \theta = -15;\ R \cos \theta = 8$

6 **a** Express $8 \cos \theta° + 15 \sin \theta°$ in the form $R \cos (\theta - \alpha)°$.
   b Express $20 \cos \theta° + 21 \sin \theta°$ in the form $R \sin (\theta + \alpha)°$.
   c Express $24 \cos \theta° + 7 \sin \theta°$ in the form $R \cos (\theta + \alpha)°$.
   d Express $9 \cos \theta° + 40 \sin \theta°$ in the form $R \sin (\theta - \alpha)°$.
   e Express $2 \cos \theta° - 3 \sin \theta°$ in the form $R \sin (\theta + \alpha)°$.
   f Express $7 \cos \theta° - \sin \theta°$ in the form $R \cos (\theta + \alpha)°$.
   g Express $-4 \cos \theta° - 3 \sin \theta°$ in the form $R \sin (\theta + \alpha)°$.

1 Express $6 \cos \theta° + 8 \sin \theta°$ in the form $R \cos (\theta - \alpha)°$.

2 Express $12 \cos \theta° + 5 \sin \theta°$ in the form $R \sin (\theta + \alpha)°$.

3 Express $10 \cos \theta° + 24 \sin \theta°$ in the form $R \cos (\theta + \alpha)°$.

4 Express $35 \cos \theta° + 12 \sin \theta°$ in the form $R \sin (\theta - \alpha)°$.

5 Express $4 \cos \theta° - 9 \sin \theta°$ in the form $R \sin (\theta + \alpha)°$.

6 Express $5 \cos \theta° - 2 \sin \theta°$ in the form $R \cos (\theta + \alpha)°$.

7 Express $-32 \cos \theta° - 60 \sin \theta°$ in the form $R \sin (\theta + \alpha)°$.

8 Express $-11 \cos \theta° - 60 \sin \theta°$ in the form $R \cos (\theta + \alpha)°$.

Preparation for Course Assessment

OUTCOME 1
Use vectors in three dimensions

1 $\overrightarrow{PS}$, $\overrightarrow{PR}$ and $\overrightarrow{PQ}$ represent the vectors *a*, *b* and *c* respectively.
  a Express $\overrightarrow{SR}$ in terms of *a* and *b*.
  b Express $\overrightarrow{RQ}$ in terms of *b* and *c*.
  c Express $\overrightarrow{SQ}$ in terms of *a* and *c*.
  d T is the midpoint of $\overrightarrow{SQ}$. Express $\overrightarrow{TR}$ in terms of *a*, *b* and *c*.

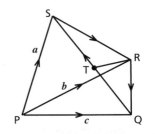

2 During a manoeuvre, a helicopter moves from position P(−15, −10, 11) to position Q(45, 14, 18).
  a Express this displacement as a vector in component form.
  b Calculate its magnitude.
  c Calculate, correct to 1 decimal place, the distance that P and Q are from an observer at the origin.
  d A second helicopter moves from R(−40, −20, −10) to T(80, 28, 4). Prove that it is moving in a parallel path to the first helicopter.

3

One planet eclipses another when the observer and the planets are collinear. The observer is at the point A(1, −2, 1). One planet is at B(11, −7, −9). The other is at C(71, −37, −69). Prove that the observer is viewing an eclipse.

4

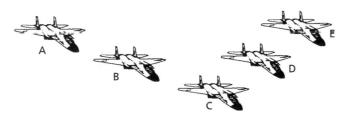

Flying in formation, jets at A, B and C should be in a straight line. Jets at C, D and E should also be in line. The coordinates of the jets are:
A(1, 2, 6), B(2, 0, 9), C(3, −2, 12), D(5, 1, 11) and E(7, 4, 12).
  a Prove that A, B and C are in line.
  b (i) Prove that C, D and E are not.
     (ii) Suggest a simple change to E's position to remedy the situation.

5 On a model of the UK, Edinburgh is represented by a point with coordinates (1, 2, 1) and London by (21, −8, 16). A radio station at Edinburgh links to one in London via a booster station sited at a point which divides the line EL internally in the ratio 2:3. What are the coordinates of this point on the map?

6

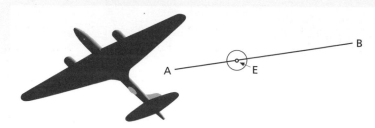

If the wing of the plane can be modelled by the line with endpoints A(−4, −2, 3) and B(20, 10, 11) then the engine's centre can be modelled by the point E where E divides AB internally in the ratio 1:3.

a Calculate the coordinates of E.

b Calculate the length of (**i**) AB and (**ii**) AE and hence verify the division.

7 The Flying Circus sky-writing expert forms a star. The coordinates of A are (1, 2, 2) and of B are (4, 11, 17). C divides AB *externally* in the ratio 5:2.

a Calculate the coordinates of C.

b D divides AC *externally* in the ratio 8:3. Calculate the coordinates of D.

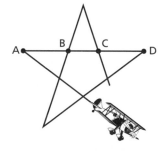

8

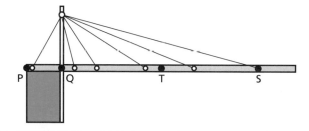

In the cantilever bridge, P is the point (4, 2, 2) and Q is the point (7, 3, 2). S is the point where the longest cable is secured to the platform of the bridge. S divides PQ externally in the ratio 8:7.

a Calculate the coordinates of S.

b T is the midpoint of QS. In what ratio does it divide PQ?

9 $\boldsymbol{a} = \begin{pmatrix} 1 \\ 2 \\ -3 \end{pmatrix}$ $\boldsymbol{b} = \begin{pmatrix} 2 \\ -1 \\ -2 \end{pmatrix}$

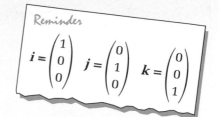

Reminder

$\boldsymbol{i} = \begin{pmatrix} 1 \\ 0 \\ 0 \end{pmatrix}$ $\boldsymbol{j} = \begin{pmatrix} 0 \\ 1 \\ 0 \end{pmatrix}$ $\boldsymbol{k} = \begin{pmatrix} 0 \\ 0 \\ 1 \end{pmatrix}$

a Express the following in terms of $\boldsymbol{i}$, $\boldsymbol{j}$ and $\boldsymbol{k}$.
   (i) $\boldsymbol{a}$ **(ii)** $\boldsymbol{b}$ **(iii)** $\boldsymbol{a} + \boldsymbol{b}$
   (iv) $3\boldsymbol{a} + \boldsymbol{b}$ **(v)** $4\boldsymbol{a} - 3\boldsymbol{b}$
b Calculate the magnitude of each correct to 1 decimal place.

10 a The vector $\boldsymbol{d} = 6\boldsymbol{i} + x\boldsymbol{j} + 24\boldsymbol{k}$ has a magnitude of 26. Calculate the value of x.
 b The vector $\boldsymbol{e} = n\boldsymbol{i} + m\boldsymbol{j} + 18\boldsymbol{k}$ is parallel to $\boldsymbol{d}$. Calculate the values of n and m.
 c The vector $\boldsymbol{g} = a\boldsymbol{i} + 3\boldsymbol{j} - 2\boldsymbol{k}$ is perpendicular to $\boldsymbol{d}$.
   Calculate the value of a.

11 As the racing car takes the bend on the
hill it undergoes the following forces:
   $\boldsymbol{p} = 9\boldsymbol{i} + 7\boldsymbol{j}; \boldsymbol{q} = 12\boldsymbol{i} + 9\boldsymbol{j} + 6\boldsymbol{k}; \boldsymbol{r} = 6\boldsymbol{k}$

a Express the resultant force in terms
   of $\boldsymbol{i}$, $\boldsymbol{j}$ and $\boldsymbol{k}$.
b Calculate the magnitude of the force.

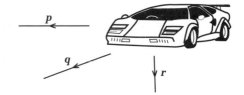

12

The downhill racer is being affected by
two forces:

$$\boldsymbol{u} = \begin{pmatrix} 3 \\ 12 \\ 20 \end{pmatrix} \text{ and } \boldsymbol{v} = \begin{pmatrix} 6 \\ 12 \\ 12 \end{pmatrix}$$

a Calculate the resultant force.
b Calculate the magnitude of the resultant.
c Calculate the acute angle between the
   two forces.

13

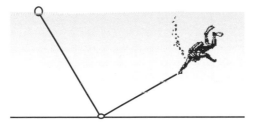

A diver at (1, 2, −5) is trying to anchor a buoy. He has pulled the rope through a
link at (−2, 4, −9). The buoy is at (−5, 3, 1).
Calculate the size of the angle made by the rope passing through the link at the
anchor point.

Preparation for Course Assessment

OUTCOME 2
Use further differentiation and integration

1 Find the equation of the tangent to the curve $y = 3 \sin x + 4 \cos x$ at $x = \dfrac{\pi}{4}$.

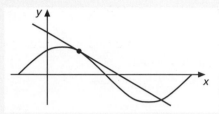

2 The fraction of the moon visible at any time in the year can be calculated from the formula $y = \dfrac{1}{2} + \dfrac{1}{2} \cos \dfrac{\pi}{14} x$ where x is the number of days since the start of the year.

  a Find $\dfrac{dy}{dx}$.

  b Find the rate of change of the fraction, y, on day 7.

  c Is the moon waxing or waning on day 20? (Is the derivative greater than or less than zero?)

3 The height of a carriage on a ferris wheel can be calculated using the formula $y = 5 \sin x + 12 \cos x$ where x is the angle through which the wheel has turned since the start of the ride.

  a Differentiate to find the maximum height of the carriage.

  b What is the smallest angle through which the wheel has to turn to reach this maximum?

  c Describe, in the first turn of the wheel, when the carriage is (**i**) rising (**ii**) falling.

4 **a** For $y = x^2$ (**i**) find $\dfrac{dy}{dx}$ (**ii**) express x in terms of y

    (**iii**) find $\dfrac{dx}{dy}$ (**iv**) use $y = x^2$ to express $\dfrac{dx}{dy}$ in terms of x

    (**v**) comment on the relation between $\dfrac{dy}{dx}$ and $\dfrac{dx}{dy}$.

  b Repeat this process for the following:

    (**i**) $y = x^4$ (**ii**) $y = x^3 + 2$ (**iii**) $y = (2x + 1)^{\frac{1}{2}}$

  c A function is defined in the interval $-\dfrac{\pi}{2} \le x \le \dfrac{\pi}{2}$

    $y = \sin^{-1} x \Rightarrow x = \sin y$.

    Use your findings from **a** and **b** above to express $\dfrac{dy}{dx}$ in terms of x.

5 A rectangle of card, length 12 cm and height h cm, is folded to make a cuboid tube of volume 1000 cm^3.

  a Show that $h = 1000(6x - x^2)^{-1}$.

  b Find the value of x which makes this height a minimum.

  c What is this minimum height?

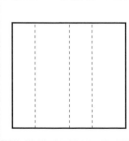
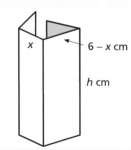

6 A box whose cross-section is a 5×12 rectangle is to be pushed through a window as shown. The angle that the 12 unit side makes with the horizontal is θ radians. The height of the window is h units where $h = h_1 + h_2$ as shown.

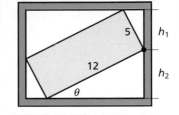

  a Using simple trigonometry, express h in terms of θ.

  b Find the value of θ which makes this height a maximum.

  c Find the dimensions of the window which correspond to this value of θ.

7

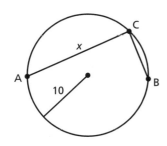

A circular field of radius 10 metres has a diameter AB. A rope is pulled from A to a point, C, on the circumference and then to B.

  a $AC = x$ metres. Express CB in terms of x.

  b Express the total length of rope, L metres, in terms of x.

  c **(i)** Find the value of x which minimises this length of rope.

  (ii) Work out the minimum length of rope.

8 Liquid is leaking from a conical hopper at the rate of 10 cubic units per second $\left(\dfrac{dV}{dt} = 10\right)$. The cone has a radius of 12 units and a height of 20. The liquid in the hopper forms a cone of radius r and height h.

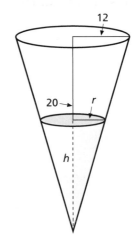

  a Use similar triangles to help you express h in terms of r.

  b Find V, the volume of liquid, in terms of r.

  c Find $\dfrac{dV}{dr}$.

  d $\dfrac{dr}{dV} = 1/\dfrac{dV}{dr}$. Express $\dfrac{dr}{dV}$ in terms of r.

  e Use the chain rule $\dfrac{dr}{dt} = \dfrac{dr}{dV} \times \dfrac{dV}{dt}$ to find the rate at which the radius, r, is changing per second when $r = 4$ units.

9 Find:

  a $\displaystyle\int (4x - 3)^3 \, dx$
  b $\displaystyle\int (2x - 1)^{-\frac{1}{3}} \, dx$
  c $\displaystyle\int \sqrt{3x - 4} \, dx$

10 Evaluate:

  a $\displaystyle\int_1^2 (x - 1)^2 \, dx$
  b $\displaystyle\int_0^1 (5x - 2)^{-2} \, dx$
  c $\displaystyle\int_1^2 \dfrac{dx}{x^2 - 6x + 9}$
  d $\displaystyle\int_0^5 dx$

11 On a speed/time graph the area under the curve represents the distance travelled. This graph shows a car, initially travelling at 1 km/minute, slowing down according to the formula $v = \dfrac{1}{(2t + 1)^2}$ where v is the speed in km/minute and t is the time in minutes.

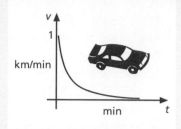

a Evaluate $\displaystyle\int_0^1 \dfrac{1}{(2t + 1)^2}\, dt$ to calculate how far the car travelled in the first minute.

b How far does it travel in the second minute?

12 The cross-section of a stream at a bend can be modelled by $y = \dfrac{x^4 + 9}{10x^2}$

To study *flow*, it is important to find the area of this cross-section.

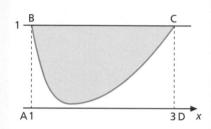

a Find the area *under* the curve from $x = 1$ to $x = 3$.

b Find the area of the rectangle ABCD.

c Calculate the area of the cross-section.

13

The tail piece of a plane is modelled by the area trapped between the curves $y = (x^2 - 5x + 4)^2$ and $y = 5(1 - x)(x - 4)$.

a Find the points where these two curves intersect.

b Find the shaded area trapped between the curves.

14 Find:

a $\displaystyle\int \sin (2x + 4)\, dx$
b $\displaystyle\int \cos (3x + 5)\, dx$
c $\displaystyle\int \sin (5 - 3x)\, dx$

d $\displaystyle\int 3 \cos (2x - 1)\, dx$
e $\displaystyle\int (\sin (2x + 4) - \cos (3x - 1))\, dx$
f $\displaystyle\int 5 \sin (2 - 5x)\, dx$

15 Evaluate:

a $\displaystyle\int_0^{\frac{\pi}{2}} \sin 2x\, dx$
b $\displaystyle\int_0^{\frac{\pi}{3}} \cos 3x\, dx$
c $\displaystyle\int_{\frac{\pi}{4}}^{\frac{\pi}{3}} -\sin 2x\, dx$
d $\displaystyle\int_{\frac{\pi}{3}}^{\frac{\pi}{2}} \cos 4x\, dx$

e $\displaystyle\int_0^{\frac{\pi}{2}} \sin \left(2x + \dfrac{\pi}{2}\right) dx$
f $\displaystyle\int_{\frac{\pi}{3}}^{\frac{\pi}{2}} \cos (3x + \pi)\, dx$
g $\displaystyle\int_0^{\pi} \sin (\pi - 2x)\, dx$

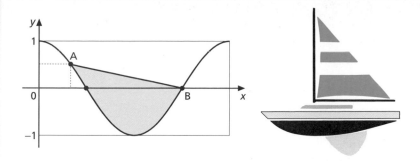

16

The keel of a yacht can be modelled by the area trapped between the line
$6x + 14\pi y - 9\pi = 0$ and the curve $y = \cos x$.

a Verify that the points A and B are $\left(\dfrac{\pi}{3}, \dfrac{1}{2}\right)$ and $\left(\dfrac{3\pi}{2}, 0\right)$ respectively.

b Calculate the shaded area by integrating between suitable limits.

17 A logo for the Forth Bridge Tourist Board is
based on the two curves $y = \sin 2x$ and
$y = 1 - \sin 2x$.
a Find the four points of intersection P, Q, R
and S.
b The shaded areas are to be red and the rest of
the rectangle is yellow.
  (i) Work out the shaded area.
  (ii) Calculate the proportion of the logo
     which is yellow.

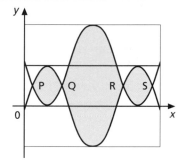

Preparation for Course Assessment

OUTCOME 3
Use properties of logarithmic and exponential functions

1 A block of ice melts losing weight according to the formula $W_t = W_0 (0.88)^t$
   where W_t is the weight after t minutes and W_0 is the starting weight.
   a The original weight of the block is 1 kg. What is its weight after 3 minutes?
   b How much weight was lost in the fourth minute?
      (Hint: consider *after 3 and after 4*.)
   c When will the block be half its original weight?

2 The surface area of a cabbage increases according to the formula $S_t = S_0 (1.8)^t$
   where S^t is the area after t days and S_0 is the initial area.
   a The original surface area is 100 cm^2. What is its area after 5 days?
   b How much area is gained in the third day?
   c When will the cabbage be twice its original area?

3 The temperature of a cup of tea falls from 100 °C to 20 °C in 10 minutes.
   It cools according to the formula $T_t = T_0 a^t$ where T_t is the temperature
   after t minutes and T_0 is the starting temperature.
   a Substitute the given values into the formula to find the value of a^{10}.
   b Find the value of $\log_{10} a$ correct to 3 decimal places.
   c Hence calculate the value of a to 3 decimal places.
   d What was the cup of tea's temperature after 5 minutes?

4 The value of a house increases from £10 000 to £15 000 in 2 years.
   Its value appreciates according to the formula $V_t = V_0 p^t$ where
   V_t is the value after t years and V_0 is the initial value.
   a Calculate the value of p to 3 decimal places.
   b What will the house be worth after 4 years?
   c When will it be worth £20 000?

5 A car loses half its value in 10 years. This value depreciates according to the
   formula $C_t = C_0 b^t$ where C_t is the value after t years and C_0 is the initial value.
   a Write down an expression for C_t in terms of C_0 when $t = 10$.
   b Hence calculate the value of b.

6 A certain type of grass spreads very fast. The area it covers is a function of the
   number of weeks it has been growing. This can be modelled by $A(t) = 50e^{0.17t}$
   where $A(t)$ is the area covered after t weeks.
   a Estimate the area covered after (i) 4 weeks (ii) 6 weeks.
   b What is the increase in area in the fifth week?

7 The breeding rate of a type of laboratory mouse can be modelled by
$M(t) = 400e^{0.26t}$ where $M(t)$ is the number of mice after t weeks.
a Estimate the number of mice after (**i**) 1 week   (**ii**) 3 weeks.
b How long will it be before the mouse population exceeds 2000?

8 A volatile liquid evaporates when left open to the air. The evaporation can be
modelled by $L(t) = 10e^{-0.92t}$ where t is the time, measured in hours, and L is the
volume left in litres.
a How much liquid is there initially?
b How much evaporates in the first 3 hours?
c How much evaporates in the next 3 hours?

9 An oil spillage occurs in the bay. Environmentalists model the cleaning action of
the tides by $P(t) = 8000e^{-1.09t}$ where t is the time, measured in days, and P is the
volume of pollution in gallons.
a What is the size of the initial spillage?
b What is the amount of pollution left after one day?
c What is the daily percentage drop in the pollution?

10 An epidemic spreads through the population according to the model
$D(t) = 500e^{1.01t}$ where t is the time, measured in days since the outbreak became
apparent, and D is the number of patients.
a How many had the disease when the outbreak became apparent?
b Use logarithms to the base e to find how long it will be before 10 000 have
succumbed to the disease.

11 The depreciation of equipment at a factory is modelled for tax purposes by
$V(t) = ae^{bt}$ where t is the time, measured in years since the equipment was
bought, V is its value at time t, and a and b are constants.
a If the equipment is initially worth £50 000 and worth £40 000 after a year
what are the values of a and b?
b When will it only be worth £10 000?

12 Two variables are connected by the formula $K(P) = ae^{bP}$.
When $K = 10$, $P = 1$; when $K = 20$, $P = 3$,
a Form two exponential equations involving a and b.
b By division find the value of b.
c By substitution find the value of a.
d Write out the formula connecting P to K and find K when $P = 5$.

13 What is the value of $\log_8 9$?
a Let $x = \log_8 9$ and rewrite the equation in exponential form.
b Take the logarithm to the base e of both sides of the equation.
c Use the laws of logarithms to help you solve the equation for x correct to
3 decimal places.
d If the logarithm to the base 10 had been used, what difference would it have
made?

14 Using logarithms to the base 10, calculate the value of $\log_e 5$.

15 $4000 = 4 \times 10^3$.
  a Use the laws of logarithms to help explain why $\log_{10} 4000 = 3 + \log_{10} 4$.
  b Estimate the value of $\log_{10} 4\,537\,000\,000\,000$.

16 Workers at a recycling plant reckon that only a quarter of the aluminium cans survive a cycle. The connection between t, the time measured in cycles, and n, the number of cans, is described by $t = 15 - 3 \log_{10} n$.
  a After how many cycles will the number of cans fall below 1000?
  b How many cans were there at the start ($t = 0$)?

17 Astronomers describe either the brightness of a star (E) or the magnitude of a star (m). The relation between brightness and magnitude is given by $\log_{10} E = -0.4(m + 14.2)$. (The unit of brightness is the *lux*.)
  a The magnitude generally ranges in value from 1 to 6, with 1 being the brightest. Calculate an equivalent range in brightnesses, giving your answer in standard form.
  b A star has a brightness of 3×10^{-8} lux. What is its magnitude (to 1 decimal place)?

18 A certain deciduous tree sheds its leaves over a month. The percentage of leaves left t days after the start of the shedding is given by $L(t) = 100 - 29 \ln(t + 1)$.
  a **(i)** Verify that $L(0) = 100$.
    (ii) How do you interpret this fact?
  b What percentage of leaves are left on day 25?
  c On which day will the tree have lost half its leaves?

19 A crowd empties out of the stadium after the big match. The size of the crowd, C, still in the grounds t minutes after the final whistle is modelled by the function $C(t) = a - b \ln(t + 1)$ where a and b are constants.
  a At the final whistle $C(0) = 10\,000$. (There are 10 000 people at the match.) Calculate the value of a.
  b The exits are designed so that after 10 minutes the last person has just left. Calculate the value of b to the nearest whole number.
  c How many people are still in the grounds 1 minute after the final whistle?
  d After how many minutes will there be only 1000 people left in the grounds?

20 There are 1000 birds in a local aviary. A certain infection passing through the birds is modelled by the formula $\ln \left(\dfrac{B}{1000 - B} \right) = kt + c$ where B is the number of infected birds, t is the time in days since the start of the infection and k and c are constants.
  a When $t = 0$, one bird is infected. After 10 days 500 birds are infected. Calculate the values of K and c.
  b On which day will **(i)** 400 birds **(ii)** 600 birds be infected?
  c How many birds will be infected after 8 days?

21 a Two variables are connected by a relationship of the form $y = ab^x$ where a and b are constants. Use the laws of logarithms to help you show that a linear relationship exists between $\log_{10} y$ and x.

b Two variables are connected by a relationship of the form $y = ax^b$ where a and b are constants. Show that a linear relationship exists between $\log_{10} y$ and $\log_{10} x$

c In a similar fashion explore relationships when **(i)** $y = ae^{bx}$ **(ii)** $y = a \times 10^{bx}$

22 As a frogman dives to a depth x, the intensity of light from his torch, y, drops due to particles in the water. It is thought that the two variables are related by a formula of the form $y = ae^{bx}$. Readings are taken and a table formed.

x	0	1	2	3	4	5
y	10	9.05	8.19	7.41	6.70	6.07

a Copy and complete this table.

x	0	1	2	3	4	5
$\ln y$						

b When plotted on a graph the points $(x, \ln y)$ lie on a straight line.
   (i) Two points on this line are $(0, p)$ and $(5, q)$. What are the values of p and q?
   (ii) What is the equation of the line?
c Use this linear relation between x and $\ln y$ to find the values of a and b.

23 On a cold day the engine block of a car cools down. $T(t)$ is its temperature in degrees Celsius t minutes after the engine is turned off. The function is of the form $T(t) = ab^t$.

a Show that $\log_{10} T$ has a linear relationship with t.

b Use the graph to help you calculate a and b.

c Use your model to calculate the temperature when $t = 7$.

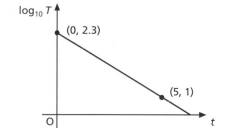

24 The distance to the horizon, D km, is related to the observer's height, h metres, above sea level by a formula of the form $D = ah^b$.
a Show that $\log D$ has a linear relationship with $\log h$.
b

h	0	10	20	30	40	50
D	0	12.0	17.0	20.8	24.0	26.9

A table of values is given. Use this table to help you calculate a and b.
c Use your model to calculate the distance to the horizon as seen from a plane flying at a height of 1000 metres.

Preparation for Course Assessment

OUTCOME 4
Apply further trigonometric relationships

1 Solve the equation $5 \cos \theta° + 12 \sin \theta° = 8$ for $0 \leq \theta < 360$.

2 a Express $7 \cos x° + 3 \sin x°$ in the form $R \cos (x + a)°$.
   b Hence solve the equation $7 \cos x° + 3 \sin x° = 5$ for $0 \leq x < 360$.

3 Solve the equation $4 \cos \theta - 11 \sin \theta = 6$ for $0 \leq \theta < 2\pi$.

4 a Express $12 \cos x - 5 \sin x$ in the form $R \sin (x + a)$.
   b Hence solve the equation $12 \cos x - 5 \sin x = 10$ for $0 \leq x < 2\pi$.

5 a Express $84 \cos x + 13 \sin x$ in the form $R \sin (x + a)$.
   b Hence find the maximum value of $84 \cos x + 13 \sin x + 15$.
   c For what values of x, $0 \leq x < 2\pi$, does the expression reach this maximum?

6 a Express $33 \cos x + 56 \sin x$ in the form $R \sin (x + a)$.

   b Hence find the minimum value of $\dfrac{1}{33 \cos x + 56 \sin x}$.

   c For what value of x, $0 \leq x < \dfrac{\pi}{2}$, does the expression reach this minimum?

7 Find the minimum value of $\dfrac{1}{3 \cos x° + 2 \sin x°}$ and the lowest positive value of x for which this minimum occurs.

8 A 10 m fence, PQ, is placed in the corner of a field to partition off a triangular area. $\angle PRQ = \theta°$.
   a Find an expression for the perimeter of the triangle in terms of θ.
   b Write this expression in the form $R \cos (\theta - a)° + b$.
   c (i) Calculate the value of θ which maximises the perimeter.
   (ii) What is the maximum perimeter?

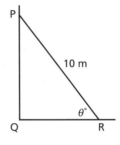

9 A designer is considering a baby chair for a car. The back, AB, is 5 units long; the seat, BC, is 2 units long and the angle that AB makes with the horizontal is $x°$. $\angle ABC = 90°$. K and L are vertically below A and C respectively.

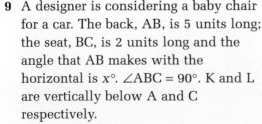
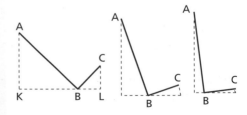

   a Find an expression for KL in terms of x.
   b Write this expression in the form $R \sin (x + a)°$.
   c Calculate the maximum value of KL and the angle at which it occurs.

10 Using convenient units of measurement, the height of a
particle on the wheel is modelled by $y = 3 \sin x° + 3$
and the height of the tip of the rider's shoe is modelled by
$y = \cos x° + 2$ where $x°$ is the angle turned through by the
wheel since the start of observations.

  a Form an equation in x to model the moment when the
   particle and the shoe tip are at the same height.
  b Solve the equation to find the values of x in the first turn of the wheel when
   this happens.
  c Find the corresponding heights.

11 An observer at A watches two moons orbiting
their planet. The moon Phobos appears to
zig-zag back and forth according to the formula
$y = 5 \sin x°$ where y is the distance to the right
of the planet, measured in convenient units.
The motion of Demos can similarly be modelled

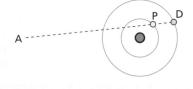

by $y = 8 \cos x°$. When these y values are the same, then both moons seem to be
at the same spot in the sky, as shown in the sketch.

  a The alignment occurs when $5 \sin x° - 8 \cos x° = 0$. Express $5 \sin x° - 8 \cos x°$
   in the form $R \cos (x + a)°$.
  b Solve $5 \sin x° - 8 \cos x° = 0$ for $0 \le x < 360$ to find x and y at the times of
   alignment.
  c $5 \sin x° - 8 \cos x°$ is an expression for the apparent separation of the two moons.
   (i) What is the maximum separation?
   (ii) What is the value of x when this maximum occurs? ($0 \le x < 360$)

12 At a certain place on earth the number of hours of sunshine per day can be
modelled by the formula $h = 0.9 \sin x° - 4.9 \cos x° + 6$ where x is the number of
days since January 1st.

  a Express $0.9 \sin x° - 4.9 \cos x°$ in the form $R \sin (x + a)$.
  b Find on which days of the year there are 8 hours of sunshine according to
   the model.
  c What is **(i)** the maximum **(ii)** the minimum number of hours per day?

13 The movement of a piston in a car engine is modelled by $y = 5 \sin 3x° + 12 \cos$
$3x° + 14$ where y is height of the crank above the piston head measured in
suitable units and x is the angle turned by the shaft.

  a Express $5 \sin 3x° + 12 \cos 3x°$ in the form $R \cos (3x - a)$.
  b Calculate for what values of x this height is 10 units. ($0 \le x < 360$)
  c What is **(i)** the maximum **(ii)** the minimum height?

14 The depth of water in a tidal loch is modelled by $y = 8 \sin \dfrac{\pi}{12}x - 5 \cos \dfrac{\pi}{12}x + 12$
(reckoning in radians).

  a Express $8 \sin \dfrac{\pi}{12}x - 5 \cos \dfrac{\pi}{12}x$ in the form $R \sin \left(\dfrac{\pi}{12}x - a \right)$.
  b Calculate for what values of x this depth is 6 units. ($0 \le x < 24$)
  c What is **(i)** the maximum **(ii)** the minimum depth?

Statistics (H) Contents

Preparation for Unit Assessment

OUTCOME 1a
Interpret the results of an EDA

1 A group of students recorded their pulse rates
   while sitting quietly. Their results are shown
   in the boxplot. How do the pulse rates for
   these male and female students compare?

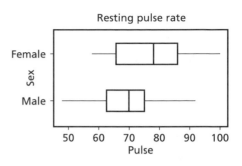

Resting pulse rate

2 When a chemical arrives at a factory it has to
   be analysed for its manganese content.
   The chemical arrives in seven batches and a
   small sample is taken from each. Each sample
   is split into two parts. One part is analysed by
   the factory's own equipment, the other part by
   the calibrating equipment of another
   laboratory. How does the performance of the
   factory's equipment compare to that of the
   specialist laboratory?

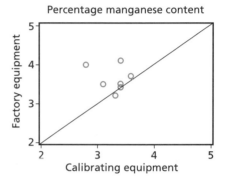

Percentage manganese content

3 The blood cholesterol levels of a group of
   heart attack patients were recorded 2 days
   after the attack. The levels of a group of
   healthy individuals were also recorded as
   a control. The results are summarised in
   this boxplot:

   a How do the cholesterol levels of these
       two groups compare?

   The heart attack sufferers also had their
   cholesterol level measured 4 days after the
   attack. These results are compared with
   their earlier cholesterol levels in the
   diagram opposite.

   b Describe how the cholesterol level
       changes over this period of time for
       these patients.

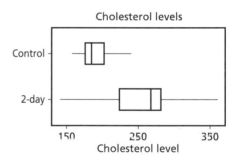

Cholesterol levels

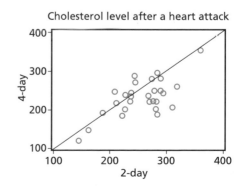

Cholesterol level after a heart attack

4 A group of students recorded their pulse rates before and after a short period of brisk exercise. The change in rate was calculated for each student. The diagram shows these changes for both female and male students.

   a Compare the change in pulse rate for these female and male students.

   b Do you think these findings can be generalised? Give a reason for your answer.

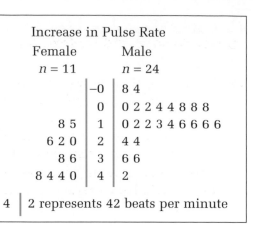

Increase in Pulse Rate

Female n = 11		Male n = 24
	−0	8 4
	0	0 2 2 4 4 8 8 8
8 5	1	0 2 2 3 4 6 6 6 6
6 2 0	2	4 4
8 6	3	6 6
8 4 4 0	4	2

4 | 2 represents 42 beats per minute

5 This stem-and-leaf diagram shows the number of words per sentence in a selected passage from Charles Dickens's novel *Bleak House*. A passage of 40 sentences was selected from *Vet in a Spin* by James Herriot. The number of words per sentence in this sample had a median of 10 and an inter-quartile range of 8.

   a Compare the length of sentences in these two passages.

   b Do you feel you could use this information to make a general statement about the length of sentences in works by Dickens and Herriot? Give a reason for your answer.

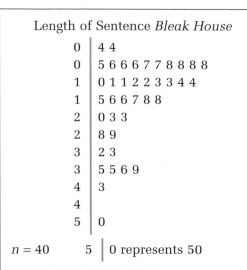

Length of Sentence *Bleak House*

0	4 4
0	5 6 6 6 7 7 8 8 8 8
1	0 1 1 2 2 3 3 4 4
1	5 6 6 7 8 8
2	0 3 3
2	8 9
3	2 3
3	5 5 6 9
4	3
4	
5	0

n = 40   5 | 0 represents 50

6 The lifetimes of random samples of three brands of a certain type of battery are summarised in this multiple boxplot.

   a Compare the performance of these three brands.

   b Which brand would you choose if you require batteries which last for at least 95 hours? Give a reason for your answer.

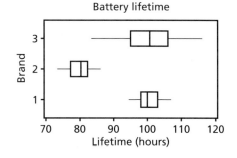

Battery lifetime

7 Twenty-four patients suffering from a painful disease were assigned to one of two groups at random. One group received a drug to relieve the pain. The other group was given a placebo (inactive substitute). The dotplots show the change in the level of pain reported by the patients, where

Change = Initial Pain − Final Pain

"and pain is measured on a scale of 0 to 10."

Comment critically on these data. Is there any evidence that the drug is effective for reducing pain?

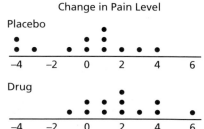

Change in Pain Level

Outcome 1 Assessment

1 Two groups of maths teachers were asked to indicate, on a scale of 0 to 100, the strength of their agreement with each of the following statements:

    Statement 1   *Statistics is more useful than trigonometry.*
    Statement 2   *I find statistics difficult.*
    Statement 3   *Including statistics in school maths courses is a good idea.*

Larger scores indicate greater agreement. The responses for each of the groups are displayed in these boxplots. Describe and compare the views of these two groups of teachers.

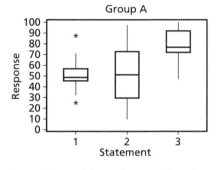
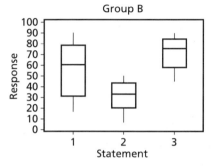

2 The values of four financial indicators were noted for a number of new companies in 1988. The indicators were the following ratios:

(**i**) Cash Flow to Total Debt   (**ii**) Net Income to Total Assets
(**iii**) Current Assets to Current Liabilities   (**iv**) Current Assets to Net Sales

Two years later it was noted whether the company was solvent or bankrupt. These boxplots compare the values of each indicator for the two types of company. Describe how the values of each of these indicators may or may not be used to predict future success in business.

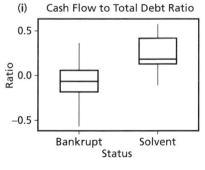
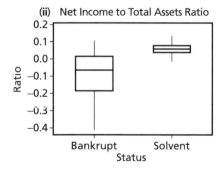

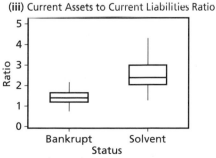
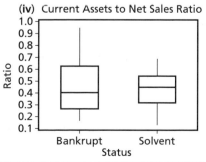

Preparation for Unit Assessment

OUTCOME 2a
Calculate the probability of an event which involves the laws of probability

---

Reminder

- The **sample space** S lists all the possible outcomes of a random experiment.
- An **event** E consists of one or more outcomes from S.
- The probability of an event is given by
$$P(E) = \frac{\text{number of outcomes in } E}{\text{number of outcomes in } S}$$
provided each outcome is equally likely.
- The **complement** of E, written $\overline{E}$, is the event containing all outcomes in S not in E.
$$P(\overline{E}) = 1 - P(E)$$

- **Mutually exclusive events** have no outcomes in common.
- **Addition Law**: If A and B are mutually exclusive events then
$$P(A \text{ or } B) = P(A) + P(B)$$
- **Independent events** result when the occurrence of one event does not affect the occurrence of the other.
- **Multiplication Law**: If A and B are independent events then
$$P(A \text{ and } B) = P(A) \times P(B)$$

---

1 A random experiment consists of tossing three fair coins.
   a List the sample space S.
   b The event E is 'there are more heads than tails'. List the outcomes in the event E.
   c Write down the probabilities $P(E)$ and $P(\overline{E})$. Interpret the meaning of $\overline{E}$.

2 The number of passengers on one sailing of a particular ferry was noted along with how they had boarded the ship:

coach	car	lorry	motorbike	cycle	foot
38	46	4	3	2	7

Assuming that the numbers in this sample are representative of the traffic on this crossing, estimate the probability that a randomly chosen passenger is travelling by:
   a coach   b motorbike or cycle.

3 A particular game involves rolling five dice. What is the probability:
   a of rolling 5 sixes
   b that all five dice show the same number of spots?

4 A computer is programmed to produce random digits 0, 1, 2, ... , 9.
If the computer program produces two such digits, what is the probability they are:
a both equal to 3 **b** both the same **c** not the same?

5 A bag contains 5 red and 7 green balls. What is the probability of withdrawing:
a 2 red balls when sampling **(i)** with **(ii)** without replacement
b a red and a green ball when sampling **(i)** with **(ii)** without replacement?

6 In a large batch of components, 5% are known to be defective. Calculate the probability that:
a a component chosen at random is not defective
b a random sample of three components contains only one that is defective.

7 From long experience it is known that 65% of customers at a restaurant pay by credit card.
a Calculate the probability that the next three customers all pay by credit card.
b What assumption have you made when performing this calculation?

8 The probabilities that three friends pass their driving test first time are 0.4, 0.6 and 0.9. Assuming independence, calculate the probability at least one of them passes first time.

Preparation for Unit Assessment

OUTCOME 2b
Construct the probability distribution of a given random variable

Reminder

A **random variable** is a function whose value depends on the outcome of a random experiment. If the number of values that a random variable can take is countable, then the random variable is said to be **discrete**.

The probability distribution of a discrete random variable is a table or formula giving the probabilities p_i associated with each value of the random variable where
$0 \leq p_i \leq 1$ and $\Sigma p_i = 1$

1 A random experiment involves tossing three fair coins.
   a List the sample space.
   b A random variable X is defined as the number of heads showing.
       List the values of X.
   c Calculate the probability $P(X = 1)$.
   d Construct the probability distribution for X.

2 A random experiment involves rolling a blue and a red die.
   a List the sample space in a table.
   b A random variable T is defined as the total score on the two dice.
       List the values of T.
   c Calculate the probability $P(T = 7)$.
   d Construct the probability distribution for T.

3 In a large study, the time for 20 000 first class letters to reach their destination was recorded:

No. of days	1	2	3 or more
No. of letters	18 564	826	610

Assuming this sample is representative of the population of all first class letters, estimate the probability distribution of the random variable D, the number of days taken for delivery of first class letters.

4 A coin is biased so that 'heads' is twice as likely as 'tails'. The random variable Y represents the number of heads which appear on two independent tosses of the coin. Construct the probability distribution for Y.

5 Which of the following could be the probability distribution of a discrete random variable?

a $f(x) = \dfrac{x + 2}{25}$, for $x = 1, 2, 3, 4, 5$

b $f(x) = \dfrac{x - 2}{5}$ for $x = 1, 2, 3, 4, 5$

c $f(x) = \dfrac{x^2}{30}$, for $x = 0, 1, 2, 3, 4$

d $f(x) = \dfrac{1}{6}$ for $x = 0, 1, 2, 3, 4, 5, 6$

6 For each of the following, determine the value of k which results in a possible probability distribution for a discrete random variable:

a $f(x) = kx$, for $x = 1, 2, 3, 4, 5$

b $f(x) = k\left(\dfrac{1}{2}\right)^x$, for $x = 1, 2, 3$

c

x	1	2	3	4
$P(X = x)$	0.2	k	0.3	k

d $f(x) = k(3 - x)$, for $x = 0, 1, 2$

7 It is believed that 40% of the population are of blood type O. Assume that the blood type of one person is independent of that of any other person. Two people are selected at random and Y is the random variable representing the number in the sample with blood type O. Construct the probability distribution for Y.

8 In a particular class of 30 pupils, five are suffering from hay fever. A random sample of three pupils is selected from the class without replacement. The random variable H represents the number of pupils in the sample who have hay fever. Construct the probability distribution of H. What assumption have you made?

Preparation for Unit Assessment

OUTCOME 2c
Calculate the mean and variance of a random variable

> **Reminder**
>
> To calculate the mean, E(D) of the discrete random variable D, evaluate the sum
> $$E(D) = \Sigma p_i d_i$$
> where p_i is the probability associated with the value d_i of D.
>
> To calculate the variance, Var(D), of the discrete random variable D, evaluate
> $$Var(D) = E(D^2) - [E(D)]^2$$
> where $E(D^2) = \Sigma p_i d_i^2$

1 A random variable X has a probability distribution:

x	0	1	2	3
P(X = x)	0.1	0.2	0.3	0.4

Calculate the mean, E(X). Calculate $E(X^2)$ and hence the variance, Var(X).

2 A random variable Y has a probability distribution:

y	−2	−1	0	1	2
P(Y = y)	0.2	0.1	0.1	0.2	0.4

Calculate the mean and variance of Y.

3 The discrete random variable S has a uniform distribution given by:

$$P(S = s) = \begin{cases} \dfrac{1}{n} & \text{for } s = 1, 2, 3, \ldots, n \\ 0 & \text{otherwise} \end{cases}$$

   a Construct a table showing the probability distribution of S when n = 6.
   b Calculate the mean and variance of S when n = 6.

4 The number of emergency call-outs of a tow truck each day is thought to be modelled by the random variable N with probability distribution:

n	0	1	2	3	4	5 or more
P(N − n)	0.05	0.1	0.4	0.35	0.1	0

Calculate the mean and variance of N.

5 A bag contains three black balls and three white balls. The random variable Z represents the number of balls that have to be withdrawn from the bag without replacement until the first white ball appears.
   a Construct the probability distribution for Z.
   b Calculate the mean and variance of Z.

6 Two badminton players are selected at random (without replacement) from a club team consisting of three men and five women. The random variable W represents the number of women selected.
   a Construct the probability distribution for W.
   b Calculate the mean and variance of W.

Preparation for Unit Assessment

OUTCOME 2d
Simulate the behaviour of a random variable

1 The following random numbers were produced by a calculator:
   0.444   0.196   0.358   0.599   0.824   0.902   0.610   0.265
   Use these random numbers to simulate:
   a tossing a coin eight times   **b** rolling a die eight times.

2 One of the rows in a table of random digits reads as follows:
   27564   81744   51909   36192   45263   33212   71808   24753   72644   74441
   The random variable X represents the number of breakdowns per week of a certain machine and is thought to have the probability distribution:

x	0	1	2	3	4 or more
$P(X = x)$	0.4	0.3	0.2	0.1	0

   Conduct ten simulations of the number of breakdowns per week for this machine.

3 The number of calls received each month by a residential phone number from telesales organisations is thought to be a random variable S with probability distribution:

s	0	1	2	3	4	5 or more
$P(S = s)$	0.1	0.1	0.4	0.3	0.1	0

   Use your calculator to generate random numbers and perform six simulations of the number of phone calls received in a month.

4 Use the random numbers   0.949   0.457   0.129   0.490   0.510
   to simulate five values of each of the following random variables:

   a $P(W = w) = \begin{cases} 0.1w & \text{for } w = 1, 2, 3, 4 \\ 0 & \text{otherwise} \end{cases}$

   b $P(R = r) = \begin{cases} \frac{1}{6}(3 - r) & \text{for } r = 0, 1, 2 \\ 0 & \text{otherwise} \end{cases}$

   c $P(T = t) = \begin{cases} \frac{2}{3}\left(\frac{1}{2}\right)^t & \text{for } t = 0, 1 \\ 0 & \text{otherwise} \end{cases}$

   d $P(X = x) = \begin{cases} 0.125x^2 & \text{for } r = -2, 2 \\ 0 & \text{otherwise} \end{cases}$

5 The following digits were taken from a row in a random number table:
   35653   53638   00564   57230   07395   10813   99194   81592   96834   21374
   Each game in a lottery consists of randomly drawing (without replacement) six balls plus a bonus ball from a set of balls numbered 1 to 49. Use the above random digits to simulate three games of this lottery.

Outcome 2 Assessment

1 This table shows the make-up of a multinational peace-keeping force by nationality and years of military service. Suppose one soldier is selected at random. What is the probability that the soldier:

	Military Service (years)			
	<1	1 to 3	>3	Total
British	367	2536	1063	3966
French	583	1262	625	2470
American	218	2084	1239	3541
Total	1168	5882	2927	9977

  a is British or French

  b is not French

  c is American and has more than 3 years service?

2 A laboratory tests blood samples for the presence of a virus. Their analysis is accurate 90% of the time. One day a doctor sends four blood samples to the lab for analysis. What is the probability that all four will be accurately diagnosed? What assumption have you made?

3 Three cards are picked, *with replacement,* from a deck of 52 playing cards. What is the probability that the first is a King, the second a diamond and the third a Jack?

4 A bag contains four blue and three red discs. Two discs are drawn at random from the bag *without replacement*. What is the probability that the two discs are different colours?

5 A test consists of five true-or-false questions and a student decides to answer each question by tossing a coin. The random variable X is the number of questions correctly answered.

  a Construct the probability distribution for X.

  b Calculate the mean and variance of X.

6 An anthropologist claims that in a particular society, the number of children per family is a random variable N with probability distribution as shown. Calculate the mean number of children per family and the variance.

n	0	1	2	3	4	>4
$P(N = n)$	0.05	0.15	0.35	0.25	0.2	0

7 A discrete random variable has the probability distribution

$$P(X = x) = \begin{cases} k(x - 2) & \text{for } x = 3, 5, 7 \\ 0 & \text{otherwise} \end{cases}$$

  a Find the value of k.

  b Calculate the mean and variance of X.

8 At the Peak Performance Gym, the number of press-ups achieved by members of the ladies gymnastics team during training sessions is thought to be a discrete random variable Y with probability distribution

$$P(Y = y) = \begin{cases} k & \text{for } y = 41, 42, \ldots, 49, 50 \\ 0 & \text{otherwise} \end{cases}$$

Determine the value of k and calculate the mean and variance of Y.

9 The following random numbers were produced by a calculator

0.322   0.161   0.922   0.153   0.664

Use these random numbers to simulate the number of children in each of five randomly chosen families from the society described in question **6**.

10 The number of vehicles inspected each day at an MOT station is thought to be a random variable X with probability distribution

$$P(X = x) = \begin{cases} 0.1(5 - x) & \text{for } x = 1, 2, 3, 4 \\ 0 & \text{otherwise} \end{cases}$$

Conduct ten simulations of X using this row from a table of random numbers:

23740   22505   07489   85986   74420   21744   97711   36648   35620   97949

Preparation for Unit Assessment

OUTCOME 3a
Calculate probability from the density function of a continuous random variable

> **Reminder**
>
> To show that $f(x)$ *could be* a probability density function for a continuous random variable X over the interval $a \le X \le b$, show that
>
> $$f(x) \ge 0 \text{ for } a \le X \le b, \text{ and } \int_a^b f(x)dx = 1$$
>
> To calculate the probability $P(x_1 \le X \le x_2)$ that the continuous random variable X takes values between x_1 and x_2, evaluate the definite integral $\int_{x_1}^{x_2} f(x)dx$ where $f(x)$ is the pdf of X.

1 Show that $f(x) = \begin{cases} 3x^2 & 0 \le x \le 1 \\ 0 & \text{otherwise} \end{cases}$ could be the pdf of a random variable X.

Calculate: **a** $P(0 \le X \le 0.5)$ **b** $P(0.5 \le X \le 1)$

2 Sketch the function $f(x) = \begin{cases} \frac{1}{2} & -1 \le x \le 1 \\ 0 & \text{otherwise} \end{cases}$ and show that $f(x)$ could be the pdf of

a continuous random variable X. By calculating areas evaluate $P\left(-\frac{1}{4} \le X \le \frac{1}{2}\right)$.

3 Sketch the probability density function $f(x) = \begin{cases} 1 - \frac{1}{2}x & P(0 \le X \le 2) \\ 0 & \text{otherwise} \end{cases}$

By calculating areas, evaluate $P(0 \le X \le 1)$.
Show how the same value of $P(0 \le X \le 1)$ can be achieved using calculus.

4 The standard symmetric triangular distribution has pdf $f(x) = \begin{cases} 4x & 0 \le x \le \frac{1}{2} \\ 4(1-x) & \frac{1}{2} \le x \le 1 \\ 0 & \text{otherwise} \end{cases}$

Using calculus, calculate, $P\left(\frac{1}{4} \le X \le \frac{1}{2}\right)$, $P\left(\frac{1}{2} \le X \le \frac{5}{8}\right)$ and hence write down $P\left(\frac{1}{4} \le X \le \frac{5}{8}\right)$.

S·T·A·T·I·S·T·I·C·S·(H)· Preparation for Unit Assessment

5 Find the value of k so that each of the following functions could be the pdf of a continuous random variable:

a $f(x) = \begin{cases} \dfrac{k}{x^2} & 1 \le x \le 5 \\ 0 & \text{otherwise} \end{cases}$

b $f(x) = \begin{cases} \frac{1}{2}k(6-x) & 0 \le x \le 6 \\ 0 & \text{otherwise} \end{cases}$

c $f(x) = \begin{cases} k\sqrt{x} & 0 \le x \le 4 \\ 0 & \text{otherwise} \end{cases}$

d $f(u) = \begin{cases} ku^2(1-u) & 0 \le u \le 1 \\ 0 & \text{otherwise} \end{cases}$

e Calculate $P(2 \le X \le 3)$ for each of the probability density functions **a**, **b** and **c**. Calculate $P(0 \le U \le 0.5)$ for the function in part **d**.

6 The lifetime, in thousands of hours, of an electronic component is represented by a random variable T, with probability density:

$$f(t) = \begin{cases} \dfrac{k}{t^3} & 1 \le t \le 2 \\ 0 & \text{otherwise} \end{cases}$$

a Calculate the value of k.

b Calculate the probability that such a component lasts between 1200 and 1400 hours.

Preparation for Unit Assessment

OUTCOME 3b

Obtain the mean and variance of a continuous random variable

Reminder

To calculate the mean μ or $E(X)$ of a continuous random variable X with probability density function $f(x)$, $a \leq X \leq b$, evaluate the definite integral

$$E(X) = \int_a^b xf(x)\, dx$$

To calculate the variance σ^2 or $Var(X)$ of a continuous random variable X with probability density function $f(x)$, $a \leq X \leq b$, evaluate $Var(X) = E(X^2) - [E(X)]^2$

where $E(X^2) = \int_a^b x^2 f(x)\, dx$

---

1 A random variable has the probability density function: $f(x) = \begin{cases} 2x & 0 \leq x \leq 1 \\ 0 & \text{otherwise} \end{cases}$
Calculate $E(X)$, $E(X^2)$ and $Var(X)$.

2 Calculate the mean and variance of the random variables with the following density functions:

a $f(x) = \begin{cases} 3x^2 & 0 \leq x \leq 1 \\ 0 & \text{otherwise} \end{cases}$

b $f(x) = \begin{cases} \frac{1}{2} & -1 \leq x \leq 1 \\ 0 & \text{otherwise} \end{cases}$

c $f(x) = \begin{cases} 1 - \frac{1}{2}x & 0 \leq x \leq 2 \\ 0 & \text{otherwise} \end{cases}$

d $f(x) = \begin{cases} \frac{3}{2}x(2 - x) & 0 \leq x \leq 1 \\ 0 & \text{otherwise} \end{cases}$

3 A sawmill is cutting fence posts 1.5 m long. The length of left-over off-cuts is a random variable L with density function $f(l)$:
Calculate the mean and variance of L.

$f(l) = \begin{cases} \frac{2}{3} & 0 \leq l \leq 1.5 \\ 0 & \text{otherwise} \end{cases}$

4 The length of calls to a telephone enquiry service, T, vary between 2 and 5 minutes with probability density $f(t)$:
Calculate the mean and variance for T.

$f(t) = \begin{cases} \frac{2}{9}(5 - t) & 2 \leq t \leq 5 \\ 0 & \text{otherwise} \end{cases}$

5 Jennifer's bus to work leaves at 8.00 am each week day. On most occasions she arrives at the bus stop X minutes early, where X is a random variable with probability density $f(x)$:

$f(x) = \begin{cases} \frac{1}{36}(5 + 4x - x^2) & -1 \leq x \leq 5 \\ 0 & \text{otherwise} \end{cases}$

a Calculate the mean and variance of X.
b Calculate the probability that she misses her bus.

6 The proportion of impurities in an ore is a random variable R with probability density $f(r)$:

   a Calculate the mean and variance of R.

   b Calculate the probability that the ore has more than 80% impurities.

$$f(r) = \begin{cases} 6r(1-r) & 0 \leq r \leq 1 \\ 0 & \text{otherwise} \end{cases}$$

7 The random variable T is the time, in seconds, between consecutive vehicles passing a particular point on a motorway.

The pdf proposed for T is $f(t)$: Calculate the mean and variance of T.

The Highway Code recommends that the time between vehicles should be at least 2 seconds. Calculate the probability that a vehicle is following too close to the one in front of it.

$$f(t) = \begin{cases} \dfrac{21-t}{200} & 1 \leq t \leq 21 \\ 0 & \text{otherwise} \end{cases}$$

1 Show that $f(x) = \begin{cases} 0.08(x-5) & 5 \le x \le 10 \\ 0 & \text{otherwise} \end{cases}$

could be the probability density function of a random variable X and calculate $P(X > 7.5)$.

2 Find the value of k so that $f(x) = \begin{cases} k(x^2 - 8x + 12) & 2 \le x \le 6 \\ 0 & \text{otherwise} \end{cases}$

could be the probability density function of a random variable X and calculate $P(3 < X < 5)$.

3 The time taken (in seconds) for a computer system to complete a certain task is a

random variable T with probability density function $f(t) = \begin{cases} \dfrac{k}{t^2} & 1 \le t \le 5 \\ 0 & \text{otherwise} \end{cases}$

Find the value of k and calculate the probability that the task takes more than 3 seconds.

4 The proportion of pupils at a certain school who come by car each day is thought to be a random variable X with probability density function:

$$f(x) = \begin{cases} 12(x - 2x^2 + x^3) & 0 \le x \le 1 \\ 0 & \text{otherwise} \end{cases}$$

a Calculate the probability that on a particular day more than half the pupils come to school by car.

b Calculate the mean and variance of X.

5 A manufacturer of colour televisions believes that the lifetime in years of the picture tube is a random variable with the probability density function:

$$f(x) = \begin{cases} 0.0032(25 - t) & 0 \le t \le 25 \\ 0 & \text{otherwise} \end{cases}$$

a Calculate the probability that the tube fails within the 12 month warranty period.

b Calculate the mean and variance for the lifetime of these picture tubes.

6 The amount of time in days that a cargo ship spends in a certain port is a random

variable with the probability density function: $f(x) = \begin{cases} \dfrac{k}{\sqrt{x}} & 1 \le x \le 3 \\ 0 & \text{otherwise} \end{cases}$

a Determine the value of k.

b Calculate the probability that a ship spends at least 2 days in this port.

7 a Calculate the mean and variance of the random

variable with probability density function: $f(x) = \begin{cases} 0.0192x^2(5 - x) & 0 \le x \le 5 \\ 0 & \text{otherwise} \end{cases}$

b What is the probability that the random variable takes a value between 2 and 3?

Preparation for Unit Assessment

OUTCOME 4a
Determine the equation of linear regression and use it for prediction

> **Reminder**
>
> The sums of squares and products are:
>
> $$S_{xx} = \Sigma(x_i - \bar{x})^2 = \Sigma x_i^2 - \frac{1}{n}(\Sigma x_i)^2$$
>
> $$S_{yy} = \Sigma(y_i - \bar{y})^2 = \Sigma y_i^2 - \frac{1}{n}(\Sigma y_i)^2$$
>
> $$S_{xy} = \Sigma(x_i - \bar{x})(y_i - \bar{y}) = \Sigma x_i y_i - \frac{1}{n}\Sigma x_i \Sigma y_i$$
>
> If a scatter plot shows a linear relationship then the equation of the regression line is
>
> $$y = a + bx$$
>
> where $a = \bar{y} - b\bar{x}$
>
> and $b = \dfrac{S_{xy}}{S_{xx}}$

1 In a science experiment, the length of the spring (y cm) is measured when different weights (x g) are suspended from it. A scatter plot shows that a linear model is appropriate.

Weight (x g)	100	150	200	300	350	400
Length (y cm)	20	23	25	29	33	36

For these data,
$\Sigma x = 1500$,
$\Sigma x^2 = 445\,000$,
$\Sigma y = 166$.

  a Calculate Σxy.
  b Determine the equation of the least squares regression line of length on weight and use it to predict the spring's length when a weight of 250 g is attached.

2 The scatter plot shows the height (y cm) and the length of the index finger (x mm) on the dominant hand of ten male sixth-year pupils.
For these data:
$\Sigma x = 928$, $\Sigma x^2 = 86\,464$, $\Sigma y = 1765$, $\Sigma xy = 164\,359$.
  a Determine the least squares regression equation of height on index finger length.
  b Use the equation to predict the height of a male pupil whose index finger is 90 mm long.

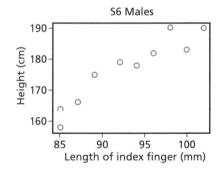

3 A research chemist records the reaction time (T seconds) when different amounts of a catalyst (M grams) are used. Here are her data:

M Amount of catalyst	0.2	0.4	0.6	1.0	1.2	1.4
T Reaction time	64.8	62.2	58.9	54.3	51.6	47.5

For these data, $\Sigma m = 4.80$, $\Sigma m^2 = 4.96$, $\Sigma t = 339.30$, $\Sigma mt = 255.90$.
A scatter plot confirms that a linear model is appropriate. Determine the regression equation and use it to predict the reaction time when 0.8 gram of catalyst is used.

4 As part of a dental hygiene study, the amount of plaque on the teeth of a random sample of ten patients was measured. The amount of plaque removed after each patient's teeth had been brushed in a controlled way was also determined. The study produced these data:

X Initial plaque	15	20	36	36	42	45	56	66	44	52
Y Plaque removed	3	7	12	16	18	18	25	30	19	28

A scatter plot suggests a linear model is appropriate and $\Sigma x^2 = 19\ 138$, $\Sigma xy = 8431$.

a Determine the equation of the least squares regression line of Y on X.

b Use the equation to predict the amount of plaque removed when the initial plaque is 50.

Preparation for Unit Assessment

OUTCOME 4b
Calculate the correlation coefficient and interpret the result

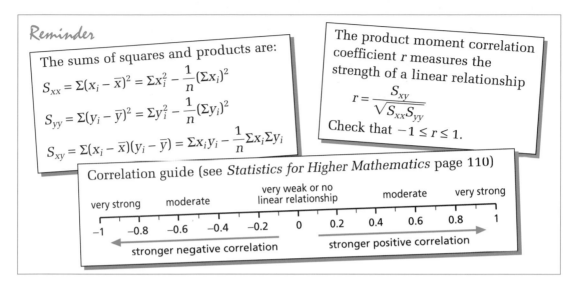

Reminder

The sums of squares and products are:

$$S_{xx} = \Sigma(x_i - \bar{x})^2 = \Sigma x_i^2 - \frac{1}{n}(\Sigma x_i)^2$$

$$S_{yy} = \Sigma(y_i - \bar{y})^2 = \Sigma y_i^2 - \frac{1}{n}(\Sigma y_i)^2$$

$$S_{xy} = \Sigma(x_i - \bar{x})(y_i - \bar{y}) = \Sigma x_i y_i - \frac{1}{n}\Sigma x_i \Sigma y_i$$

The product moment correlation coefficient r measures the strength of a linear relationship

$$r = \frac{S_{xy}}{\sqrt{S_{xx}S_{yy}}}$$

Check that $-1 \leq r \leq 1$.

Correlation guide (see *Statistics for Higher Mathematics* page 110)

1. Calculate the summary statistics Σx_i, Σy_i, Σx_i^2, Σy_i^2, $\Sigma x_i y_i$, $\bar{x}$, $\bar{y}$ for each of the following bivariate data sets:

   a
x	1	3	6	7	9
y	1.2	4.5	13.0	14.7	16.3

   b
x	1	2	3	7	9
y	5	12	25	33	16

   c
x	5	10	15	20	25	30
y	41	32	28	19	12	6

2. Calculate the sums of squares and products S_{xx}, S_{yy}, S_{xy} for each data set in question **1**. Draw scatter plots for these bivariate data sets and, if appropriate, calculate r.

3. The effectiveness of a weedkiller at various concentrations is recorded in the following data:

Concentration (g/litre)	1	2	3	4	5
No. of surviving weeds	12	9	7	6	3

   Calculate and interpret the product moment correlation coefficient.

4. The scatter plot shows the Standard Grade point average (X) and the Higher Grade Mathematics Band (Y) for 15 pupils in a certain school. Small values of X and Y represent good performance.

   $\Sigma x = 27.1$ $\Sigma x^2 = 53.27$

   $\Sigma y = 130.0$ $\Sigma y^2 = 1264.0$

   $\Sigma xy = 251.2$

   Calculate the correlation coefficient and describe the relationship between X and Y.

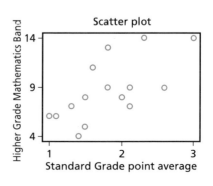

Unit 4 Assessment

1 A sample of eight leaves were collected from a laurel hedge, and the width and length of each leaf measured to the nearest millimetre.

Width (x mm)	32	40	44	42	46	51	57	57
Length (y mm)	70	93	90	102	98	114	126	120

  a Draw a scatter diagram for these data and comment on its appearance.
  b Calculate: Σx, Σy, Σxy, Σx^2, Σy^2.   **c** Calculate: S_{xx}, S_{xy}, S_{yy}.
  d Determine the product moment correlation coefficient and comment.
  e Determine the equation of the regression line and use it to estimate the length of a laurel leaf that is 35 mm wide.

2 Ten commercial lawn mowers of a particular model were studied to determine the relationship between the number of hours of operation between oil changes (x) and the number of years of satisfactory service they gave (y). The following data were produced:

Time between oil changes (x hours)	16	20	18	22	23	24	14	26	27	30
Years of service (y years)	12	10	11	10	8	7	14	5	5	4

A scatter diagram suggests a linear model and the following summaries are calculated: $\Sigma x = 220$ $\Sigma y = 86$ $\Sigma x^2 = 5070$ $\Sigma y^2 = 840$
  a Calculate Σxy.
  b Find the equation of the regression line and use it to estimate the number of years of service for a lawn mower that has its oil changed after every 25 hours of operation.
  c Calculate the correlation coefficient and comment.

3 The height, to the nearest centimetre, and the weight in kilograms of ten male students was measured and gave the following data:

Height (x cm)	183	168	178	178	165	188	168	175	178	173
Weight (y kg)	79.5	60.5	84.1	74.1	57.3	90.0	69.5	74.1	72.3	69.5

$\Sigma xy = 128\ 783$ $\Sigma y = 730.9$ $\Sigma x^2 = 308\ 112$ $\Sigma y^2 = 54\ 306$
  a Calculate Σx.
  b Calculate the sample correlation coefficient and comment.
  c Determine the equation of the least squares regression line and use it to estimate the average weight of students who are 180 cm tall.

4 Before sitting the final exam, students are given a practice test. The following data show the marks out of 80 for a group of students in the test and in the final exam:

Test (x)	10	15	18	26	28	35	38	42	46	49	55	56	66	73	76
Final (y)	6	15	8	20	10	35	40	40	40	30	40	46	50	60	70

$\Sigma x = 633$ $\Sigma y = 510$ $\Sigma xy = 26\ 740$ $\Sigma y^2 = 22\ 466$
  a Calculate Σx^2.   **b** Determine the equation of the regression line.
  c Estimate the average mark on the final exam for pupils who score 60 on the test.
  d Calculate the product moment correlation coefficient and comment.

Preparation for Course Assessment

OUTCOME 1
Interpret an Exploratory Data Analysis (EDA) on a data set

Reminder	Suspected outliers are	where
	values < lower fence	lower fence = $Q_1 - 1\frac{1}{2} \times (Q_3 - Q_1)$
	values > upper fence	upper fence = $Q_1 + 1\frac{1}{2} \times (Q_3 - Q_1)$

1 This stem-and-leaf diagram shows the heights of 15 women, measured to the nearest centimetre.
   a Find the median and quartiles of these data.
   b Calculate the lower and upper fences.
   c Identify any possible outliers.
   d Draw a modified boxplot for these data.

Heights

15	1
15	7
16	1 2 3 3 4 4 4
16	5 6 6 9
17	1
17	6

$n = 15$ 17 | 6 represents 176 cm

2

Paris	£84	Oslo	£123
Amsterdam	£93	Rome	£124
Frankfurt	£94	Madrid	£131
Barcelona	£111	Venice	£132
Munich	£111	Zurich	£142
Stockholm	£111	Vienna	£156
Milan	£111	Prague	£165

A travel agent listed these prices for return air fares to various European cities.
   a Identify any possible outliers.
   b Draw a modified boxplot for these data.

3 The following data show the closing prices (in pence) of eight Electricity stocks listed on the London Stock Exchange on a particular day:

548   288   418   419   606   585   535   643

   a Find the median and semi-interquartile range for these prices.
   b Calculate Σx and Σx^2 and hence find the sample mean and standard deviation.
   c The prices of stock in the Brewing, Information Technology and Chemical industries on the same day are summarised below:

	Breweries	Information Technology	Chemicals
n	35	51	26
$\bar{x}$	403.1	453.9	324.1
s	261.0	525.3	346.4
min	18	3	15
Q_1	159	132	86
median	363	278	171
Q_3	587	584	465
max	912	2735	1315

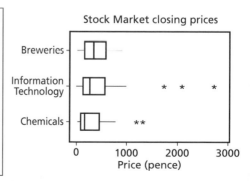

Stock Market closing prices

Calculate the semi-interquartile range for these three industries.
Compare your answers with the corresponding standard deviation and comment.

d By giving careful consideration to all the information available, compare the prices of stocks in the Electricity, Brewing, Information Technology and Chemical industries.

4 A study was conducted to compare two methods of determining the level of mercury in fish. The mercury level in each of 27 lake trout was determined by both methods. The diagram shows the results of the study. How do the two methods of determining mercury levels in fish compare?

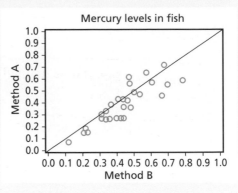

5

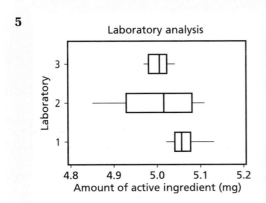

A certain medication in tablet form is supposed to contain 5 mg per tablet of the active ingredient. Tablets are ground up, thoroughly mixed and divided into samples each equivalent to the weight of one tablet. A number of samples are sent to each of three laboratories to be analysed for the amount of active ingredient in each sample. The findings of each lab are summarised in the boxplot. Compare the performance of the three labs.

6 This line graph shows the quarterly sales figures for a shop over a period of six years. Describe the patterns you see in these sales figures.

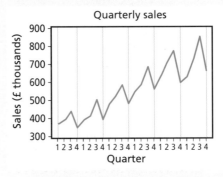

7

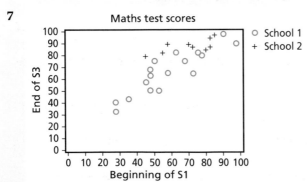

This scatter plot shows the maths test scores at the beginning of S1 and at the end of S3 for some pupils at each of two schools. Assuming these pupils sat equivalent tests under similar conditions, describe and compare the performance of these two groups of pupils.

Preparation for Course Assessment

OUTCOME 2
Work with discrete probability distributions

Reminder

$n!$, read as n factorial, is defined by
$$n! = n \times (n-1) \times (n-2) \times \ldots \times 1$$
$n!$ is the number of ordered arrangements of n distinct objects.

The number of arrangements of n objects of which k are identical is $\dfrac{n!}{k!}$

The number of ordered arrangements, or permutations, of r objects chosen from n distinct objects is $^nP_r = \dfrac{n!}{(n-r)!}$

The number of selections (in any order) or combinations of r objects chosen from n objects is
$$^nC_r = \dfrac{n!}{(n-r)!\,r!} = \binom{n}{r}$$

1 Evaluate: **a** $4!$ **b** $^9P_4$ **c** $\dfrac{^9P_4}{4!}$ **d** $^9C_4$

2 How many arrangements or permutations are there of:
  a 5 distinct objects
  b 6 objects of which 4 are identical
  c 2 objects chosen from 5 objects
  d 5 objects chosen from 8 objects?

3 How many selections or combinations are there of:
  a 2 objects chosen from 5 objects
  b 5 objects chosen from 8 objects
  c 3 objects chosen from 7 objects
  d 6 objects chosen from 12 objects?

4 Leigh separates out all the Hearts from a standard pack of cards.
  a How many 5-card hands can be dealt from these 13 Hearts?
  b Assuming the Hearts were thoroughly shuffled, what is the probability that Leigh deals a hand containing the Ace, King, Queen, Jack and 10 of Hearts (in any order)?
  c All the Hearts are returned to the pack and the whole pack is shuffled thoroughly. How many 5-card hands can be dealt from the whole pack of 52 cards?
  d What is the probability that Leigh deals a hand containing an Ace, King, Queen, Jack and a 10, all of the same suit (in any order)?

5 **a** How many five-digit numbers can be made using the following sets of digits?
    (i) 1, 2, 3, 4, 5   **(ii)** 3, 4, 8, 8, 8   **(iii)** 5, 5, 5, 7, 7   **(iv)** 0, 3, 5, 7, 9
  b For each of the sets of digits, calculate the probability that if the numbers are produced randomly, the result is divisible by 5.

6 Each game in a lottery consists of randomly drawing (without replacement) six balls from a set of balls numbered 1 to 49.
  a What is the probability that someone could guess which six numbers would be drawn?
  b What is the probability that someone selects none of the numbers drawn?

S·T·A·T·I·S·T·I·C·S·(H) Preparation for Course Assessment

107

7 The concentration of a pollutant, in parts per million, was measured at four locations on each of two beaches. Here are the data:

Beach A   35.3   34.6   36.8   34.2
Beach B   34.5   36.9   37.2   38.3

  a Assign ranks to these data, giving the value 34.2 rank 1, the value 34.5 rank 2, and so on, and show that the total rank sum for Beach A is 13.
  b List all the possible combinations of four ranks which result in a rank sum of 13 or less.
  c In how many ways can 4 ranks be chosen (in any order) from 8?
  d What is the probability that a rank sum of 13 or less happens by chance?

8 The probability of passing a certain maths test on the first attempt is 0.7. After a few days, those who failed the first sitting are permitted a second opportunity to pass an equivalent test and their probability of passing on the second attempt is 0.4. Students must have passed such a test before they can enter an external examination.

  a What is the probability that a randomly chosen student will sit the final examination?
  b If there are 100 students taking this maths course, how many of them would you expect to pass the test **(i)** altogether   **(ii)** on the second attempt?
  c What is the probability that a student chosen at random from those permitted to enter the final examination passed the test on the second attempt?

9 A card which allows cash to be withdrawn from a bank account at a cash dispenser requires the use of a **p**ersonal **i**dentification **n**umber (PIN). The PIN is four digits long, can be any value from 0000 to 9999 inclusive, and must be entered correctly before cash can be withdrawn.

  a What is the probability that someone could randomly guess the correct PIN?
  b If after three attempts the correct PIN has not been entered, the cash dispenser keeps the card. If a thief makes three different guesses, what is the probability that the machine keeps the card?
  c Andrea has forgotten the last two digits of her PIN. She remembers that the first two digits are 43 and that the other two are different from each other and from the first two. She makes three different guesses. What is the probability that her card is confiscated?

10 A pack of 52 cards is thoroughly shuffled and 2 cards are dealt. Find the probability that: **a** both cards are red   **b** both cards are of the same suit
              c exactly one card is a King   **d** at least one card is a Diamond.

11 Medical researchers have devised a test to detect whether or not a person has a particular virus. It is estimated that 2 people in every thousand of the population have this virus. However, the test is not perfect. It indicates that a person has the virus, i.e. tests positive, for 90% of those who do in fact have it and also for 5% of those who do not have the virus. What is the probability that a person chosen at random from the population:

  a has the virus and tests positive   **b** does not have the virus and tests positive?
  c Suppose the population consisted of 10 000 persons and they were all administered the test.
      (i) How many of these would you expect to test positive and actually have the virus?

(ii) How many in total would you expect to test positive?

d If the test indicated that someone had the virus, what is the probability that they do in fact actually have the virus?

12 A fair coin is tossed five times. The random variable X is the number of heads which result.

a Construct the probability distribution of X.

b Calculate the mean and variance of X.

13 A bag contains three red balls and five white balls. Three balls are withdrawn from the bag without replacement. The random variable R is the number of red balls withdrawn. Calculate the mean and variance of R.

14 A discrete random variable Z has the probability distribution:

$$P(Z = z) = \begin{cases} kz^2 & \text{for } z = 1, 3, 5 \\ 0 & \text{otherwise} \end{cases}$$

Calculate: **a** k **b** $E(Z)$ **c** $E(2Z - 3)$

15 A random variable X has the probability distribution:

x	−1	0	1	2
$P(X = x)$	k	$2k$	$3k$	$4k$

Find: **a** k **b** $P(-1 \leq X < 2)$ **c** $E(X)$ **d** $\text{Var}(X)$

16 Find expressions for the variance of the discrete random variables with these distributions:

a

y	0	k	$2k$
$P(Y = y)$	0.2	0.3	0.5

b

y	0	1
$P(Y = y)$	p	$(1 - p)$

17 **a** Find the value of k so that $P(X = x) = \begin{cases} k\binom{4}{x} & \text{for } x = 0, 1, 2, 3, 4 \\ 0 & \text{otherwise} \end{cases}$

could serve as the probability distribution of a discrete random variable X.

b Calculate the mean and variance of X.

18 Construct a table showing the probability distribution of the discrete random variable X where:

a $P(X = x) = \begin{cases} \dfrac{\binom{2}{x}\binom{4}{3 - x}}{\binom{6}{3}} & \text{for } x = 0, 1, 2 \\ 0 & \text{otherwise} \end{cases}$

b $P(X = x) = \begin{cases} \binom{3}{x}\left(\dfrac{1}{4}\right)^x\left(\dfrac{3}{4}\right)^{3 - x} & \text{for } x = 0, 1, 2, 3 \\ 0 & \text{otherwise} \end{cases}$

Calculate the mean and variance of X in each case.

19 Construct a table showing the cumulative probability distribution for the random variable X where:

$$P(X = x) = \begin{cases} \dfrac{x}{10} & \text{for } x = 1, 2, 3, 4 \\ 0 & \text{otherwise} \end{cases}$$

Reminder

A cumulative probability distribution gives the probability that a random variable takes any value *up to* a certain value.

Illustrate the cumulative probability distribution with a cumulative bar diagram.

20 The cumulative probability distribution for the discrete random variable X is:

$$P(X \le x) = \begin{cases} 0 & \text{for } x < 1 \\ \dfrac{x^2 + 4x}{32} & \text{for } x = 1, 2, 3, 4 \\ 1 & \text{for } x > 4 \end{cases}$$

Show that the probability distribution of X is given by:

$$P(X = x) = \begin{cases} \dfrac{2x + 3}{32} & \text{for } x = 1, 2, 3, 4 \\ 0 & \text{otherwise} \end{cases}$$

21 Find the cumulative probability distribution for the random variable Y, the number of heads when three coins are tossed. Use the following random numbers to simulate ten trials of tossing three coins.

0.578   0.890   0.964   0.054   0.172   0.232   0.858   0.585   0.315   0.754

22 Use the random numbers 0.076, 0.345, 0.355, 0.817, 0.934 to simulate five values of the random variable Z where:

$$P(Z = z) = \begin{cases} \dfrac{^{2}C_z\,^{3}C_{3-z}}{^{5}C_3} & \text{for } z = 0, 1, 2 \\ 0 & \text{otherwise} \end{cases}$$

Preparation for Course Assessment

OUTCOME 3
Work with continuous probability distributions

1 A continuous random variable X has the probability density function:

$$f(x) = \begin{cases} \dfrac{1}{k} & 0 \le x \le 3 \\ 0 & \text{otherwise} \end{cases}$$

Find: **a** the value of k
     b the cumulative distribution function $F(x)$.
     c (i) $P(X = 1)$ (ii) $P(X < 1)$ (iii) $P(X \le 1)$ (iv) $P(X \ge 1)$

2 The cumulative distribution function for a continuous random variable X is:

$$F(x) = \begin{cases} 0 & x < 0 \\ x^2 & 0 \le x \le 1 \\ 1 & x > 1 \end{cases}$$

a Find the probability density function $f(x)$ for X.
b Draw sketches of $F(x)$ and $f(x)$.
c Calculate the mean and variance of X.
d Calculate the exact values of the median and quartiles.

3 A continuous random variable X has probability density function:

$$f(x) = \begin{cases} kx(1-x) & 0 \le x \le 1 \\ 0 & \text{otherwise} \end{cases}$$

a Find k and sketch the probability density function of X.
b Write down the mean, median and modal value of X.
c Find the cumulative distribution function $F(x)$ for X.
d Calculate $F\left(\frac{1}{4}\right)$ and hence $P\left(\frac{1}{4} \le X \le \frac{3}{4}\right)$.

4 A continuous random variable W has the cumulative distribution function:

$$F(w) = \begin{cases} 0 & w < 0 \\ \frac{1}{16}(8w - w^2) & 0 \le x \le 4 \\ 1 & w > 4 \end{cases}$$

Find: **a** the exact values of the median and quartiles of W

b $P(1 < W < 3)$ and $P\left(W \ge \frac{3}{2}\right)$

c $f(w)$, the probability density function of W

d the mean and variance of W.

5 The random variable Y has the probability density function:

$$f(y) = \begin{cases} ky^2(2 - y) & 0 \le y \le 2 \\ 0 & \text{otherwise} \end{cases}$$

Calculate: **a** the value of k

b the modal value of Y

c the cumulative distribution function of Y

d the probability that Y takes a value less than its modal value.

6 A random variable X has the cumulative distribution function:

$$F(x) = \begin{cases} 0 & x \le 1 \\ 1 - \dfrac{1}{x^2} & x > 1 \end{cases}$$

Calculate: **a** (**i**) $P(2 \le X \le 3)$ (**ii**) $P(X \ge 4)$

b the exact value of the median

c the probability density function for X.

7 The proportion of incorrectly completed income tax returns received by a certain tax office is modelled by a random variable Z whose probability density function is:

$$f(z) = \begin{cases} kz^3(1 - z) & 0 \le z \le 1 \\ 0 & \text{otherwise} \end{cases}$$

Find: **a** the value of k

b the mean and variance of Z

c the cumulative distribution function for Z

d the probability that (**i**) at most (**ii**) at least 50% of tax returns contain errors.

8 A computer has been programmed to draw sectors in a circle of radius 2 units. The angle between the two radii forming the sector is a random variable, Θ radians, with probability density function:

$$f(\theta) = \begin{cases} k\theta(2\pi - \theta) & 0 \le \theta \le 2\pi \\ 0 & \text{otherwise} \end{cases}$$

a Find the value of k and determine the cumulative distribution function for Θ.

b Find the probability that the computer draws a sector with an area greater than π square units.

c Determine the modal value of Θ.

9 The time (in minutes) between consecutive customers joining the queue in a post office is thought to be a random variable with the cumulative distribution:

$$F(x) = \begin{cases} 0 & x < 0 \\ 0.2x(1 - 0.05x) & 0 \le x \le 10 \\ 1 & x > 10 \end{cases}$$

a Calculate the probability that at least 5 minutes elapses between consecutive arrivals in the queue.

b Calculate the exact value of the median time between consecutive arrivals in the queue.

c Determine the probability density function for X.

d Calculate the mean and variance of X.

10 A cofferdam is built to protect a construction site from flooding during periods of heavy rainfall. The engineer believes the proportion of times the flood water will overflow the dam is a random variable with probability density function:

$$f(x) = \begin{cases} k\dfrac{1 - x}{\sqrt{x}} & 0 \le x \le 1 \\ 0 & \text{otherwise} \end{cases}$$

a Find the value of k and determine the cumulative distribution function for X.

b Calculate the probability that the construction site will be flooded on no more than 4% of occasions when there is heavy rainfall.

Preparation for Course Assessment

OUTCOME 4
Analyse the relationship between two variables

1 The following data show the amount of torque produced by four-stroke motorcycle engines of various sizes:

x: Engine size (cc)	125	250	500	600	750	900
y: Torque (ft lb)	7	15	35	45	55	70

   a Draw a scatter diagram and calculate the product moment correlation coefficient. Hence describe the relationship between the size of engine and the amount of torque produced.

   b It is decided to fit a least squares regression line to these data *which goes through the origin,* i.e. to fit a line of the form $y = bx$ where $b = \dfrac{\Sigma xy}{\Sigma x^2}$. Fit such a line to these data and use it to estimate the torque produced by a 400 cc engine.

2 The amount of a certain chemical dissolved (y) depends on the temperature of the solvent (x) as these data show:

Temperature (°C)	0	10	20	30	50	60
Amount of chemical (g)	6	18	20	33	47	63

   A scatter diagram shows that a linear model is appropriate. Determine the equation of the least squares regression line and use it to estimate the amount of chemical dissolved when the temperature of the solvent is 40 °C.

3 The scatter diagram shows the relationship between the weekly wage (£) and the age (years) for a sample of members of a particular profession.

   a Use the following summary statistics to determine the regression equation and use it to estimate the earnings of someone in this profession aged 35.

   $n = 10$ $\Sigma x = 345$ $\Sigma x^2 = 12\,465$
   $\Sigma xy = 84\,616$ $\Sigma y = 2280$ $\Sigma y^2 = 597\,168$

   b Write down the regression equation that would result if each person received:
   (i) a £50 per week increase   **(ii)** a 50% increase.

4 A newborn baby's gestational age is the number of weeks it has been developing in its mother's womb. The following data records the birth weight (y) and gestational age (x) for 12 baby boys:

Gestational age	40	39	40	36	41	38	35	38	38	39	41	36
Birth weight (g)	3207	3070	3102	2912	3138	3195	2555	2926	2847	3189	3428	2588

   A scatter diagram shows a linear model is appropriate and the following summaries were calculated:

   $\Sigma xy = 1\,393\,876$ $\Sigma x^2 = 17\,753$ $\Sigma y = 36\,157$ $\Sigma y^2 = 109\,680\,525$

a Determine the equation of the least squares regression line and use it to estimate the birth weight of baby boys whose gestational age is 37 weeks.

b Calculate the product moment correlation coefficient and comment.

5 The following data show the weight (x) and the fuel consumption (y) for a sample of cars fitted with diesel engines:

Weight (kg)	1430	990	1130	1353	1120	1080	1040	1325	1380	1300
Miles per gallon	40.3	50.6	43.7	40.2	46.0	52.8	46.5	38.0	32.9	43.4

A linear model is proposed and the following summaries were calculated:

$\Sigma x = 12\ 148$ $\Sigma x^2 = 14\ 984\ 934$ $\Sigma y = 434.4$ $\Sigma y^2 = 19\ 186$

a Calculate Σxy.

b Determine the equation of the least squares regression of fuel consumption on car weight.

c Calculate the expected fuel consumption for a similar car with a weight of 1200 kg.

d Calculate the correlation coefficient and comment.

6 Ten similar laying hens of a certain breed were fed on a diet which differed only in the amount of a supplement which is thought to affect the hardness of their egg shells. The following data were gathered and summaries calculated:

Amount of supplement	0.1	0.3	0.6	0.2	0.2	0.1	0.3	0.6	0.2	0.7
Hardness of shells	0.68	1.05	1.73	0.87	0.90	0.71	1.16	1.63	1.90	1.93

$\Sigma x = 3.3$ $\Sigma x^2 = 1.53$ $\Sigma xy = 4.903$ $\Sigma y = 12.56$ $\Sigma y^2 = 17.966$

a One of the readings is suspected of having been recorded incorrectly. Using a suitable diagram, show which reading you think is an outlier.

b Regress hardness (y) on amount of supplement (x) using summary statistics adjusted for the removal of the outlier you identified in part **a**.

c Estimate the hardness of egg shells for similar hens fed a supplement of 0.5.

7 A class of students were allocated at random to undertake one of two practice tests before they sat the final exam. The marks on the test and final exam are shown for these two groups:

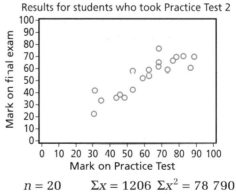

$n = 20$ $\Sigma x = 1220$ $\Sigma x^2 = 80\ 296$	$n = 20$ $\Sigma x = 1206$ $\Sigma x^2 = 78\ 790$
$\Sigma xy = 58\ 219$ $\Sigma y = 943$ $\Sigma y^2 = 47\ 907$	$\Sigma xy = 69\ 820$ $\Sigma y = 1082$ $\Sigma y^2 = 63\ 000$

a Which one of the practice tests is a predictor of student performance on the final exam?

b Calculate the equation of the regression line in this case and use it to estimate the final exam mark for students who get a mark of 60 on the practice test.

Practice Papers

Practice Paper 1

(Non-calculator)

Section 1

Section 2

Practice Paper 2

(Calculator)

Section 1

Section 2

Practice Paper 1

Marks

1 Triangle ABC has an altitude CD. The coordinates of A, B and C are (2, 1), (−2, 11) and (5, 4) respectively.
Find the equation of CD. **(3)**

2 Given $y = \dfrac{x^2 + x}{\sqrt{x}}$, find $\dfrac{dy}{dx}$ **(4)**

3 Find $\displaystyle\int x^3 + \dfrac{1}{2\sqrt{x}}\ dx$ **(4)**

4 The local library has a special stock control policy. At the end of each month they find they have lost 4% of their stock due to *wear and tear*. They consequently add 100 new books to their shelves to start the next month.
   a Form a recurrence relation to model the situation using u_n to represent the number of books on the shelves at the start of the nth month. **(2)**
   b If this policy is maintained, comment on the long-term status of the library's stock. **(2)**

5 The functions f and g are defined on suitable domains by
$$f(x) = \frac{1}{x^2 - 1} \text{ and } g(x) = 3x + 1$$
   a Find an expression for $h(x)$ where $h(x) = f(g(x))$. **(2)**
   b Describe the largest domain for h. **(2)**

6 The equation $(x + 2k)(x - k) = -1$ has real, coincident roots.
Calculate the value(s) of k. **(5)**

7 Two circles, one of radius 3 units and the other of radius 4 units, are concentric. One of the circles has as its equation $x^2 + y^2 - 2x + 4y - 4 = 0$.
Determine the equation of the other circle in the same form. **(4)**

8 Find the exact solutions of the equation
$$4 \sin x° \cos x° = 1, 0 \le x \le 360$$ **(4)**

Section 2

- These questions must be tackled **without** the aid of a calculator.
- Full credit will only be given when the solution contains appropriate working.
- Answers obtained from scale drawings do not receive any credit.
- Answer only the questions appropriate to your course.

PART A: FOR CANDIDATES ATTEMPTING MATHS 3 (H)

Marks

9 Express $\sqrt{3} \sin x° + 3 \cos x°$ in the form $a \sin (x + \theta)°$ where $0 \le \theta \le 360$, leaving a in surd form. **(4)**

10 Calculate the area trapped between the curve $y = x^3$ and $y = x$ in the first quadrant. **(4)**

11 Simplify the following expression using the laws of logarithms.

$$2 \log_2 x + \log_2 4x - 3 \log_2 2x$$ **(5)**

12 $\overrightarrow{AB} = \begin{pmatrix} 3 \\ -4 \\ 12 \end{pmatrix}$ and $\overrightarrow{BC} = \begin{pmatrix} 4 \\ a + 1 \\ 1 \end{pmatrix}$

   a Calculate the magnitude of $\overrightarrow{AB}$. **(2)**

   b For what value of a is $\overrightarrow{BC}$ perpendicular to $\overrightarrow{AB}$? **(3)**

PART B: FOR CANDIDATES ATTEMPTING STATISTICS (H)

Marks

9 Candidates are given an exam in two parts. Performances in the two parts are compared by examining the difference, mark for part 2 – mark for part 1, for each candidate.
The box plot below shows the findings.

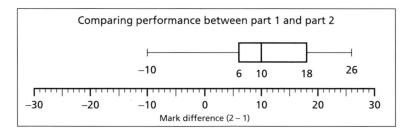

   a Calculate the interquartile range. **(2)**

   b Calculate the range of differences beyond which data are considered outliers. **(2)**

10 When you arrive at a petrol station, the probability of finding a petrol pump free is 0.6. A travelling salesman has to visit the station three times in a week. He said that he found the pump free twice.
   a List the ways over three visits that this can happen. (1)
   b Calculate the probability of it happening. (2)
   c Calculate the probability that, in three visits, you never find the pump free. (2)

11 a Find the value of k so that $f(x) = \begin{cases} \dfrac{k(x+1)}{x^4} & 1 \le x \le 2 \\ 0 & \text{otherwise} \end{cases}$

   could serve as a probability density function of the continuous random variable X. (3)
   b Calculate the mean value of X. (2)

12 A market research firm tries to determine the effect of the cost of a new mobile phone on possible demand. Seven different groups of people were quoted a price and asked if they would buy the phone at that price. The table below records their findings. x represents, in £, the price quoted and y represents the percentage of the group willing to buy at that price, e.g. 51% of the group who were offered the phone at £100 were willing to buy it.

x	100	90	90	80	50	40	40
y	51	52	53	59	77	81	82

A linear relationship between x and y is appropriate.
The following were worked out:

$\Sigma x_i = 490$, $\Sigma y_i = 455$, $S_{xx} = 4000$, $S_{yy} = 1234$, $S_{xy} = -2200$

Calculate the equation of the least squares regression line of y on x. (4)

Practice Paper 2

Marks

1 Relative to a lighthouse in the bay, three fishing
villages have the following coordinates:

    Ashly   (7, 13)
    Belleview (9, −5)
    Collfoot   (−7, −1)

Darkbay is midway between Ashly and
Belleview. Elmbank is also in the bay.

  a Calculate the coordinates of Darkbay. **(1)**

  b A ferry runs between Collfoot and
Darkbay in a straight line. Find the
equation of the line which represents
the route. **(2)**

  c Two underwater cables cross the bay, the
Ashly/Collfoot cable and the Belleview/Elmbank
cable. On the map they appear as straight lines intersecting at right
angles. Calculate the coordinates of the point where the cables cross. **(7)**

2 A function is defined as follows: $f(x) = (x - 3)^2(x + 3);\ x \in R$

  a Find where the graph of this function cuts **(i)** the x-axis   **(ii)** the y-axis. **(3)**

  b Find the stationary points of the function and determine the nature
of each. **(6)**

  c What happens to $f(x)$ as x becomes
    (i) very large and positive
    (ii) very large and negative? **(1)**

  d Sketch the graph of the function. **(2)**

3 Two functions are defined as follows: $f(x) = 2x + k;\ g(x) = 6 - x$

  a **(i)** Show, by finding the relevant formulae, that in general
      $f(g(x)) \neq g(f(x))$. **(3)**
    (ii) Find a value of k such that $f(g(x)) = g(f(x))$. **(1)**

  b Using this value of k, $h(x) = f(f(x))$
    (i) Find an expression for $h(x)$. **(2)**
    (ii) For what value of x does $f(x) = f^{-1}(x)$? **(2)**

4 A spacecraft goes round the planet Phaedra on a
circular orbit with equation $x^2 + y^2 = 13$, centre P.
It wishes to transfer to another orbit around the
planet's moon, Jason. This orbit has equation
$x^2 + y^2 - 24x + 16y + 195 = 0$ and centre J.
To do this it follows a *circular transfer* orbit,
leaving Phaedra's orbit at A and arriving at Jason's
orbit at B. The centre of this circular orbit is T.

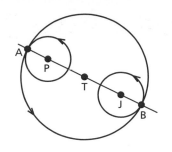

  a State the coordinates of P and J and give the
    radius of the orbit round each point. (3)
  b Find the equation of the line PJ. (2)
  c Find the coordinates of the points A and B. (5)
  d Find the equation of the transfer orbit. (3)

5 The gears on a bike are such that as a wheel goes round once, the pedal
goes round twice. The height of a point P on the wheel is given by the
formula: $f(x) = -3 \cos x°$
The height of a point Q on the pedal is given by $g(x) = 2 \sin 2x°$
Heights are measured in convenient units from the line joining the axles
of the wheels; the time, x, is measured in sixtieths of a second.
The graph shows the situation over six seconds.

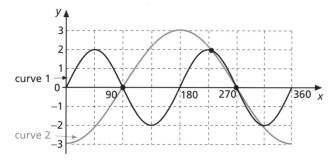

  a Identify which of the curves is associated with the wheel. (Give a reason.) (1)
  b Form an equation and solve it to find the times that P and Q are at the
    same height. (7)
  c Describe the times in this 6 second period when Q is higher than P. (3)

6 Blocks for use underwater are given a special
chemical coating. They are made to a standard
volume of 36 000 cm^3. They are three times as
long as they are wide.

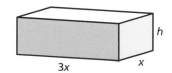

  a Show that the total surface area, S, is given
    by the formula: $S(x) = \dfrac{96\,000}{x} + 6x^2$ (4)
  b The blocks have, in fact, a surface area of 9000 cm^2.
    (i) Form an equation in x. (1)
    (ii) Show that one solution to this equation lies in the region
       $11 \le x \le 12$. (1)
    (iii) Calculate the width of the block correct to 1 decimal place. (4)

7 A lounge chair is to be
cut from foam rubber.

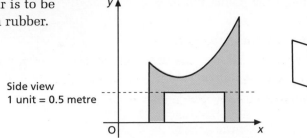

Side view
1 unit = 0.5 metre

The curved edge of the side is given by the equation $f(x) = x^2 - 4x + 6$.
The vertical lines in the diagram have equations $x = 1$, $x = 1.5$, $x = 3.5$, $x = 4$.
The horizontal broken line has equation $y = 1$.
  a Find the shaded area
      (i) in square units   (5)
      (ii) in square metres.   (1)
  b The width of the chair is 0.8 m. Calculate the volume of foam used.   (2)

8 In an experimental greenhouse, the insulation is such that the temperature
drops by 2% a minute.
  a If u_n represents the temperature at the end of the nth minute, write
      down a recurrence relation to model the situation.   (1)
  b If $u_0 = 25$ °C
      (i) calculate u_{10} correct to 1 decimal place   (1)
      (ii) express it as a percentage of u_0 correct to the nearest whole number.   (1)
  c At the end of every 10-minute period, the heaters boost the temperature
      by b°. If v_n represents the temperature at the end of the nth 10-minute
      period, form a recurrence relation to model the situation.   (2)
  d It is desired that the temperature never falls below 18 °C. By considering
      limits, give a reasoned answer for a suitable value for b.   (4)

9 We know there are no real numbers which fit the description: $x = \sqrt{-4}$.
But imagine there was a non-real number, i, which fitted the
description: $i^2 = -1$
Then we would get things like: $i = \sqrt{-1}$
                    and $\sqrt{-4} = \sqrt{(4 \times -1)} = 4 \times \sqrt{-1} = 2i$
                    and $3 + \sqrt{-4} = 3 + 2i$
  a Write an expression involving i for $\sqrt{-25}$.   (1)
  b Multiply the following two non-real numbers together, expressing your
      answer as simply as possible.
          $(3 + 2i)(2 + 3i)$ (3)
  c (i) Simplify the expression $(3 + 2i)(3 - 2i)$.
      (ii) Comment on your answer.   (3)
  d Using the result of part c, or otherwise, simplify the following:
          $$\frac{1 + 2i}{3 + 2i}$$ (4)

Section 2

- *Calculators may be used in this paper.*
- *Full credit will only be given when the solution contains appropriate working.*
- *Answers obtained from scale drawings do not receive any credit.*
- *Answer only the questions appropriate to your course.*

PART A: FOR CANDIDATES ATTEMPTING MATHS 3 (H)

Marks

10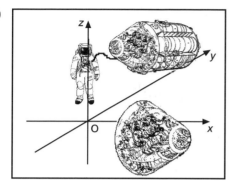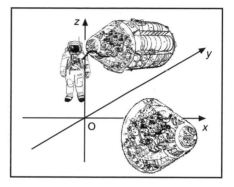

An astronaut is transferring from a larger to a smaller craft.

a Relative to a set of axes, their positions can be given by
Astronaut, A(–2, 3, 5), Small craft, S(–4, 2, 2), and Large craft, L(2, 5, 11).
Prove that, in these positions, the three objects are collinear. **(4)**

b A little later in the maneouvre, the situation has changed.
Astronaut, A(8, 5, 6), Small craft, S(5, 4, 3), and Large craft, L(11, 7, 11).
Calculate, correct to 1 decimal place, the size of the angle SAL. **(5)**

11 The function f is defined by $f(x) = 7 \cos x° + 24 \sin x°$

a Show that $f(x)$ can be expressed in the form $k \cos (x + \theta)°$
where $k > 0$ and $0 \leq \theta \leq 360$. **(4)**

b Hence find, in the interval $0 \leq x \leq 360$, where $f(x) = 12$.
Give your answers correct to 1 decimal place. **(4)**

12 A large holding tank is originally full of gas. It springs a leak. As the
contents escape, they are replaced by air which mixes with the gas left in
the tank. The percentage of gas in the tank after x days can be modelled
by $g(x) = ae^{bx}$ where a and b are constants.

a On day zero the contents are 100% gas. After 1 day the contents are
80% gas. Calculate the values of a and b to 2 decimal places. **(3)**

b What percentage of the tank is gas after 5 days? **(1)**

c Use logarithms to determine when the percentage gas content first
drops below 10%. **(4)**

13 A waveform has the equation $y = 3 \cos\left(2x - \dfrac{\pi}{3}\right)$. It crosses the y-axis at A and the x-axis at B as shown below.

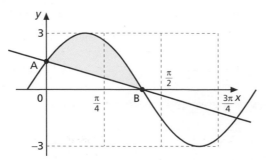

    a Calculate the coordinates of A and B. **(4)**

    b Calculate the shaded area trapped between the wave and the line AB. **(5)**

PART B: FOR CANDIDATES ATTEMPTING STATISTICS (H)

10 A country pottery makes little models for the tourist trade. Each has to be fired three times in a kiln. After each firing, the models go through a quality control inspection. The probability of successfully passing this inspection is 0.9. A model has to pass all three inspections to be classed as *perfect*. Any model which passes two inspections only is classed as a *second*. All the rest are scrapped. Assume the results of each firing are independent.

    a What is the probability that a model will be classed as

       (i) perfect   **(ii)** a second   **(iii)** not perfect? **(4)**

    b A model costs £1 to make. A perfect model sells for £5. A second sells for £2. Calculate the expected profit when 1000 models are made. **(4)**

11 The darts team were auditioning three potential new members, Tom, Dick and Harriet. Each player had ten visits to the board, throwing three darts at each visit. Tom's attempts produced the following scores:

    26   30   100   60   60   26   100   180   22   100

    a Calculate the sample mean and standard deviation of Tom's scores. **(4)**

    b The results of all three are illustrated in the following box plots.

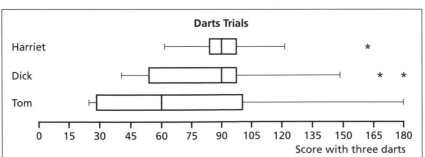

    Compare and contrast each player's potential and possible value to the team. **(3)**

12 A small sheep farm examines its records over the last 10 years. The table shows the size of the flock each year. At the start of 1990 the farm had 100 sheep.

Year	1990	1991	1992	1993	1994	1995	1996	1997	1998	1999
Size	100	90	94	82	87	66	72	75	58	57

If x represents one year's population and y the next year's population then the data can be paired off (100, 90), (90, 94), (94, 82), etc.

The following summary statistics were calculated:

$\Sigma x^2 = 60\ 122$, $\quad \Sigma y^2 = 53\ 371$, $\quad \Sigma xy = 56\ 240$

a **(i)** Determine the equation of the least squares regression line. **(4)**

    (ii) Use it to estimate what would become of a similar flock under similar circumstances the year after there had been 62 sheep. **(1)**

b Calculate the product moment correlation coefficient and comment. **(3)**

13 On a particular stretch of road there are loose chippings. Cars taking the bend on this stretch send the chips flying. The distance, in metres, these chips fly is a random variable, X, with a probability density function:

$$f(x) = \begin{cases} \dfrac{1}{16}\left(13 - x - \dfrac{12}{\sqrt{x}}\right) & 1 \leq x \leq 9 \\ 0 & \text{otherwise} \end{cases}$$

a Calculate **(i)** the mean **(ii)** the variance of X. **(4)**

b Calculate the probability that the next chip will be sent more than 4 metres. **(3)**

Answers

Mathematics 1 (H)

Preparation for Unit Assessment

Outcome 1a Page 2

1 a $y = 2x + 1$ b $y + 3x = 6$
   c $y = 3x + 5$ d $y = 5x - 20$
   e $y + 2x = 2$ f $y + 4x = -17$
   g $2y - x = 5$ h $2y + x = -4$
   i $3y - 2x = 14$

2 $y = 2x - 7$; $y + 3x = 8$; $2y - x = -5$

3 a $m_{AB} = 1$ b $m_{KL} = -1$ c $m_{EF} = 4$
   d $m_{CD} = 2$ e $m_{GH} = -\frac{1}{2}$ f $m_{MN} = -\frac{2}{5}$

4 a $y = 2x + 3$ b $y + 3x = 16$
   c $y + x = -1$ d $y + 2x = -5$
   e $2y + x = 3$ f $3y + 2x = -5$

5 a $5y - x = 7$ b $y + 3x = 11$
   c $y = 5x - 13$ d $y = x - 5$
   e $y + x = -1$ f $3y + x = 1$

6 a $2y - 5x = 11$ b $3y - x = 10$
   c $y = 9x - 14$ d $4y + 3x = -17$
   e $y + 4x = -1$ f $5y - 6x = 8$

Outcome 1b Page 3

1 a 2.75   b −1.19   c 0.268   d −5.67
2 a 0.839   b 11.4   c −0.466   d 0.933
   e −3.73
3 a $\sqrt{3}$ b 1   c $\frac{1}{\sqrt{3}}$

Outcome 1c Page 4

1 a 3   b −2   c $\frac{1}{2}$ d 0
   e −4   f 3   g −5   h 2
   i 3   j $\frac{1}{2}$ k $\frac{2}{3}$ l 2

2 a (i) 2   (ii) $-\frac{1}{2}$ b (i) $\frac{1}{2}$ (ii) −2
   c (i) 0   (ii) undefined   d (i) −1   (ii) 1
   e (i) 1   (ii) −1   f (i) −4   (ii) $\frac{1}{4}$
   g (i) 2   (ii) $-\frac{1}{2}$ h (i) $-\frac{1}{3}$ (ii) 3
   i (i) $-\frac{3}{2}$ (ii) $\frac{2}{3}$

3 a $y = 2x$ b $x + y = 2$
   c $y = -2$ d $y + 3x + 7 = 0$
   e $y = 2x - 6$ f $y = 5x + 16$
4 a $x + y = 3$ b $2y + x = 11$
   c $x = 1$ d $2y = x - 2$
   e $3y + x = 39$ f $y = -2x$
5 a $2y = x + 4$ b $2y = x - 2$
   c $y = -2x + 4$

Outcome 1 Assessment Page 5

1 $y = 3x - 2$
2 $y = -4x + 5$
3 a 0.675   b −0.810
4 a $y = -2x + 3$ b $y = \frac{1}{2}x + \frac{1}{2}$
5 a $y = -3x + 4$ b $y = \frac{1}{3}x + \frac{2}{3}$

Preparation for Unit Assessment

Outcome 2a Page 6

1 a curve displaces 1 to left
   b curve displaces 1 to right
   c reflected in x-axis
   d reflected in y-axis
   e all y-coordinates halved
   f displaces 1 up
2 a displaces 2 to left
   b displaces 3 to right
   c all y-coordinates times by 3
   d reflected in x-axis
   e displaces 1 down
3 a reflected in x-axis
   b displaces 1 to right
   c displaces 2 to left
   d all y-coordinates times by 2
   e displaces 2 down

Outcome 2a Page 7

1 a $2 \sin x$ b $\sin 2x$ c $-\sin 2x$
   d $\sin (x - 60)$
2 a $\frac{1}{2} \cos x$ b $-\cos x$ c $\cos x - 2$
   d $\sin 2x - 1$

Outcome 2b Page 8

1 a–d Sketches
2 a 2   b 4   c 3
3 a (i) 3   (ii) 2   b (i) 4   (ii) 3
   c (i) −1   (ii) 5
4 a–e Sketches
5 a $y = \log_9 x$ b $y = \log_4 x$
   c $y = \log_2 2x$ d $y = \log_{48} 4x$

Outcome 2c Page 9

1 a (i) $2x + 2$ (ii) $x^2 + 2x + 1$ (iii) $x + 4$
     (iv) $2x - 1$
   b (i) $3x^2$ (ii) $x^2 - 1$ (iii) $4x^2 + 1$
     (iv) $\frac{1}{2}x^2$

c (i) $4x^2 - 16x + 16$ (ii) $4x - 12$
   (iii) $x - 2$ (iv) $2x - 1$

2 a (i) $x^2 + 2x + 1$ (ii) $x - 1$
   (iii) $3x + 3$
  b (i) $5 - 2x$ (ii) $2x + 1$
   (iii) $4x^2$
  c (i) $x^2 - 2x + 1$ (ii) $\sqrt{x - 1}$
   (iii) x

3 a (i) $2x + 2$ (ii) $2x + 4$
  b (i) $x^2 - 2x + 1$ (ii) $x^2 - 1$
  c (i) $\sqrt{x + 1}$ (ii) $\sqrt{x} + 1$
  d (i) $\sin 2x$ (ii) $2 \sin x$
  e (i) $1 - 2x$ (ii) $2 - 2x$
  f (i) $3 \cos x$ (ii) $\cos 3x$

4 a $x + 2$ **b** $x + 4$ **c** $4x^2 + 16x + 16$
  d $2x^2 + 4$ **e** $4x + 12$ **f** $\frac{1}{2}x^2$
  g x^4 **h** $\frac{1}{4}x$ **i** $\frac{1}{4}x^2$

5 a (i) $x + 8$ (ii) $3x + 4$ (iii) $3x + 12$ (iv) $9x$
  b (i) $x - 10$ (ii) $2x - 5$ (iii) $2x - 10$ (iv) $4x$
  c (i) $4x$ (ii) $2 - 2x$ (iii) $1 - 2x$ (iv) x
  d (i) x^4 (ii) $x^2 + 4x + 4$ (iii) $x^2 + 2$
   (iv) $x + 4$

Outcome 2 Assessment Page 10

1 a reflect in x axis **b** (i) 3 to right (ii) 4 up
2 a $y = 3 \sin x$ **b** $y = \sin 6x$
3 a $y = -\cos x$ **b** $y = \cos x + 2$
4 a $y = 9^x$ **b** $y = \log_9 x$
5 a $y = \log_7 x$
6 a $9x^2 - 6x + 1$ **b** (i) $\cos\left(\frac{1}{x}\right)$ (ii) $\frac{1}{\cos x}$

Preparation for Unit Assessment

Outcome 3a Page 11

1 a $12x^2$ **b** 1 **c** 2 **d** $4x + 2$

2 a $3x^2 + 2x^{-3}\left(= 3x^2 + \frac{2}{x^3}\right)$
  b $1 - x^{-2}\left(= 1 - \frac{1}{x^2}\right)$ **c** $3 + x^{-2}\left(= 3 + \frac{1}{x^2}\right)$
  d $10x + 3x^{-4}\left(= 10x + \frac{3}{x^4}\right)$

3 a $x^{-2}, -2x^{-3}$ **b** $3x^{-1}, -3x^{-2}$
  c $x^{-3}, -3x^{-4}$ **d** $-3x^{-4}, 12x^{-5}$
  e $-\frac{2}{3}x^{-2}, \frac{4}{3}x^{-3}$ **f** $\frac{1}{4}x^{-1}, -\frac{1}{4}x^{-2}$
  g $\frac{2}{3}x^{-1}, -\frac{2}{3}x^{-2}$

4 a $\frac{1}{2}x^{-\frac{1}{2}}\left(= \frac{1}{2\sqrt{x}}\right)$ **b** $\frac{3}{2}x^{-\frac{1}{2}}\left(= \frac{3}{2\sqrt{x}}\right)$
  c $-x^{-\frac{1}{2}}\left(= -\frac{1}{\sqrt{x}}\right)$ **d** $-\frac{1}{2}x^{-\frac{3}{2}}\left(= -\frac{1}{2(\sqrt{x})^3}\right)$
  e $2x^{-\frac{3}{2}}\left(= \frac{2}{(\sqrt{x})^3}\right)$ **f** $\frac{2}{3}x^{-\frac{3}{2}}\left(= \frac{2}{3(\sqrt{x})^3}\right)$

5 a $2x + 2$ **b** $8x - 4$ **c** $2x - 2$
  d $3x^2 - 2x$ **e** $6x - 6$ **f** $4x + 6$
  g $-2x + 6$ **h** $18x - 12$

6 a $3 + \frac{1}{x^2}$ **b** $2x - \frac{2}{x^2}$ **c** $\frac{1}{2\sqrt{x}} + 3$
  d $\frac{-3}{x^2} - \frac{1}{2\sqrt{x}}$ **e** $\frac{1}{2} + 2x$ **f** $\frac{1}{\sqrt{x}} - \frac{1}{3}$
  g $\frac{2}{5}x - \frac{3}{2\sqrt{x}}$ **h** $-\frac{1}{2(\sqrt{x})^3} + \frac{1}{2\sqrt{x}}$

7 a $-\frac{1}{x^2} - \frac{2}{x^3}$ **b** $1 + \frac{1}{x^2}$ **c** $-\frac{4}{x^3} - \frac{9}{x^4}$
  d $-\frac{5}{x^2}$ **e** 3 **f** $-\frac{2}{x^2} - \frac{1}{2}$
  g $\frac{1}{2\sqrt{x}} - \frac{1}{2(\sqrt{x})^3}$ **h** $\frac{1}{\sqrt{x}} + \frac{1}{2(\sqrt{x})^3}$
  i $-\frac{1}{2(\sqrt{x})^3}$ **j** $1 + \frac{1}{(\sqrt{x})^3}$

Outcome 3b Page 12

1 a (i) 6 (ii) 0 (iii) -4
  b (i) 11 (ii) -7 (iii) 2
  c (i) 20 (ii) -1 (iii) -6
2 a 12 **b** -8 **c** 1
  d 6 **e** -27 **f** 38
  g -20 **h** 4 **i** -12
3 a -2 **b** -3 **c** 3
  d 7 **e** 1 **f** -24
4 a -2 **b** -15 **c** 1
  d $\frac{1}{4}$ **e** -2

Outcome 3c Page 13

1 a (i) $(-3, 71)$ and $(2, -54)$ (ii) $(-3, 71)$ is a maximum stationary point; $(2, -54)$ is a minimum stationary point
  b (i) $(1, -5)$, $(0, 0)$ and $(-2, -32)$
   (ii) $(-2, -32)$ and $(1, -5)$ are both minimum stationary points and $(0, 0)$ is a maximum stationary point

2 a $(1, 0)$ is a maximum stationary point and $(2, -1)$ is a minimum stationary point
  b $\left(1, -\frac{2}{3}\right)$ is a minimum stationary point and $\left(-1, \frac{2}{3}\right)$ is a maximum stationary point
  c $(-3, 7)$ is a maximum stationary point and $(1, -25)$ is a minimum stationary point
  d $(0, 1)$ is a maximum stationary point and $\left(1, \frac{2}{3}\right)$ is a minimum stationary point
  e $(0, 0)$ is a maximum stationary point and $\left(\frac{2}{3}, -\frac{4}{9}\right)$ is a minimum stationary point
  f $(0, -1)$ is a minimum stationary point and $\left(-2, \frac{1}{3}\right)$ is a maximum stationary point
  g $\left(-\frac{1}{2}, -\frac{1}{8}\right)$ is a maximum stationary point and $\left(1, -\frac{7}{2}\right)$ is a minimum stationary point
  h $\left(-4, -\frac{64}{3}\right)$ is a rising point of inflexion

Outcome 3 Assessment Page 14

1 $2x - 2x^{-2}$ **2** $-2x^{-3} + \frac{3}{2}x^{-\frac{3}{2}}$ **3** 3
4 -3 **5** $(3, -23)$, max; $(-1, 9)$, min
6 $(-1, 3)$, max; $(0, 1)$ point of inflexion; $(1, -1)$, min

Outcome 4a Page 15

1 a (i) 250   (ii) 160   (iii) 106
  b (i) 832   (ii) 688   (iii) 499
  c (i) 88   (ii) 46   (iii) 39
  d (i) 30   (ii) 34   (iii) 37.2

2 a $u_{n+1} = \frac{2}{3}u_n + 20$ **b** $u_{n+1} = \frac{3}{4}u_n + 1000$
  c $u_{n+1} = \frac{4}{5}u_n + 80$ **d** $u_{n+1} = 0.9u_n + 600$

3 a $u_{n+1} = 0.2u_n + 3$ where u_n is the number of tonnes of pollutant in the loch at the start of the nth week
  b $u_{n+1} = 0.95u_n + 8$ where u_n is the number of kilometres of 'suitable' roads at the start of the nth month
  c $u_{n+1} = 0.92u_n + 25$ where u_n is the number of undamaged CDs in stock at the start of week n.

Outcome 4b Page 16

1 a 24   **b** 20   **c** 1.25   **d** 15
  e 3000   **f** 28   **g** 90   **h** 40

2 a In the long run 60 fish remain alive
  b In the long run 170 shrubs are blighted

3 a (i) $u_{n+1} = 0.75u_n + 600$ (ii) 2400 tonnes
  b (i) $u_{n+1} = 0.6u_n + 800$
    (ii) 2000 mushrooms

Outcome 4 Assessment Page 17

1 a $u_{n+1} = 0.8u_n + 500$ **b** 2500 litres
2 a $u_{n+1} = 0.85u_n + 18$ **b** 120 cm

Preparation for Course Assessment

Outcome 1 Page 18

1 a $y = \frac{1}{2}x$ **b** $2y - 5x = -8$
  c (2, 1)   **d** 26.9 km

2 Ramp 1: 31.0°; Ramp 2: 35.0°. Ramp 1 is OK but Ramp 2 is not.

3 a $2y - x = 6$ **b** $N\left(-\frac{6}{5}, \frac{12}{5}\right)$ or N(−1.2, 2.4)

4 a M(1, 2)   **b** $y + 2x = -3$
  c $2y - x = 3$ **d** $N\left(-\frac{9}{5}, \frac{3}{5}\right)$ or N(−1.8, 0.6)

5 a AB = AC = 10
  b AB = BC = $\sqrt{125}$ = $5\sqrt{5}$ with B(−7, −1)

6 a $2y - x = 1$ **b** (5, 3)
  c (i) Queen's Road: 26.6°; King's Street: 108.4°
    (ii) 98.1°

7 Angle between supports is 102.5°, 12.5° greater than a right angle; not acceptable.

8 a (i) $5y + 3x = -1$ (ii) $y + 12x = -4$
  b $\left(-\frac{1}{3}, 0\right)$
  c 3rd median: $4y - 9x = 3$; when $x = -\frac{1}{3}$, $y = 0$ then $4y - 9x = 3$

9 a (i) B(3, 5)   (ii) C(7, −3)   **b** 12 unit²

Outcome 2 Page 20

1 a $2\left(x - \frac{3}{2}\right)^2 + \frac{1}{2}$ with $a = 2$, $b = -\frac{3}{2}$ and $c = \frac{1}{2}$
  b Minimum turning point is $\left(\frac{3}{2}, \frac{1}{2}\right)$

2 Sketch; max (330, 3), min (150, −3)

3 a Proof
  b All real numbers apart from 0
  c x

4 $a = 3$, $b = 1$, $c = 2$ and $d = 2$

5 a (i) reflect in x-axis
    (ii) reflect in x-axis and 'raise' by 2
  b All real numbers apart from −1 and 1

6 a/b Sketch; $(0, \sqrt{3})\left(\frac{2\pi}{3}, 0\right)\left(\frac{50}{3}, 0\right)$
  c 2 solutions

7 $a = 2$, $b = 2$ and $c = 2$

8 a $f(x) = 10 - 3(x + 1)^2$ so $a = 10$, $b = 3$ and $c = 1$
  b Maximum value is 10 when $x = -1$

9 a 0
  b $4 \times \left(\frac{\sqrt{3}}{2}\right)^2 - 2 \times \frac{1}{2} - 1 = 4 \times \frac{3}{4} - 1 - 1$
    $= 3 - 1 - 1 = 1 = \sin\frac{\pi}{2}$

10 a $2 + x$ **b** Proof   **c** Proof
  d $x \leq 0$

11 a (i) 2; $x = 0$ or 2π (ii) 0; $x = \pi$
  b (i) 2; $x = \frac{\pi}{2}$ (ii) −2; $x = \frac{3\pi}{2}$
  c (i) $\frac{1}{2}$; $x = \pi$ (ii) $\frac{1}{4}$; $x = 0$ or 2π

12 a Graph 1: $y = 2^{-x}$; Graph 2: $y = -2^{-x}$; Graph 3: $y = -2^x$
  b Graph 4: $y = 2^x - 1$; Graph 5: $y = 2^x - 2$; Graph 6: $y = 2^x + 1$
  c Graph 7: $y = 3^x$; Graph 8: $y = 4^x$ Graph 9: $y = 5^x$

13 a $(\sin\theta + 4)^2 + 2$
  b Maximum: 27 when $\theta = \frac{\pi}{2}$; Minimum: 11 when $\theta = \frac{3\pi}{2}$

14 a $g(x) = (x - 1)^2 + 2$ **b** 3 when $x = \frac{\pi}{2}$

Outcome 3 Page 22

1 a A(0, −1)   **b** 3   **c** B(2, 1)

2 $-\frac{1}{54}$

3 a $a = \frac{20}{x}$ **b** Proof   **c** Proof
  d $x = 6.32$, $a = 3.16$

4 a $\frac{1}{64}$ **b** $\frac{35}{54}$ **c** −28

5 a 56.25 metres (when $x = 75$)
  b 45 metres
  c $h(x) = -0.012x^2 + 1.5x$
  d 46.875 metres (when $x = 62.5$)

6 a 1.7 m/s
  b 5 seconds

7 a x-axis intercepts: $(-3, 0)$, $(2, 0)$;
y-axis intercept: $(0, 12)$

b $\left(-\frac{4}{3}, \frac{500}{27}\right)$ is a maximum and $(2, 0)$ is a minimum

8 a $h = \frac{50}{w}$ **b** Proof

c 9 cm × 18 cm (when $w = 5$, $h = 10$)

Outcome 4 Page 24

1 a $u_3 = v_3 = 7$ **b** $w_1 = 1$

c $-1 <$ multiplier < 1 is only satisfied by sequence u_n. Limit in this case is 6

2 $a = 4$, $b = -5$

3 a $u_3 = 6a^2 + 5a + 5$ **b** $a = \frac{2}{3}$ or $a = -\frac{3}{2}$

c only $a = \frac{2}{3}$ satisfies $-1 <$ multiplier < 1. In this case limit is 15

4 a Tank A: $a_{n+1} = 0.35a_n + 50$;
Tank B: $b_{n+1} = 0.45b_n + 40$;
Tank C: $c_{n+1} = 0.6c_n + 30$.
In each case a_n, b_n or c_n represents the amount of pollutant present at the end of n lots of 24-hour periods (after the adding of the pollutant)

b Tank A contains the most (76.9 litres after the addition of the pollutant) and Tank B the least (72.7 litres)

5 a $u_{n+1} = 0.36u_n + 10$ with $u_0 = 3$ where u_n is the number of units of protein in the blood after n days (and after the injection)

b A limit exists $(-1 <$ multiplier $(0.36) < 1)$. The limit is 15.625 units. Maximum is 15.625 and minimum is 5.625 units

c 12.8 units (from limit = 20 units)

6 a $p_{n+1} = 0.88p_n + 4.9$ where p_n is the pressure in psi after n days (after pumping up)

b After 4 days $(p_4 = 39.1)$

c Limit exists $(-1 <$ multiplier $(0.88) < 1)$. Limit is 40.8 (to 3 significant figures). The course of action is not safe.

d 4.8 units maximum (giving limit = 40)

7 a Enclosure 1: $u_{n+1} = 0.82u_n + 150$;
Enclosure 2: $v_{n+1} = 0.45v_n + 450$;
Enclosure 3: $w_{n+1} = 0.7w_n + 300$.
In each case u_n, v_n or w_n is the number of butterflies after n weeks (after the fresh batch is added)

b Enclosure 1: 833;   Enclosure 2: 818; Enclosure 3: 1000

c Enclosure 1: add 90; Enclosure 2: add 275; Enclosure 3: add 350

d Increases from 500 (after adding the new batch) to 917

Mathematics 2 (H)

Preparation for Unit Assessment

Outcome 1a Page 27

1 2, 4, 8

2 a No remainder on dividing by $x - 2$

b no remainder on dividing by $x + 3$ *or* **a/b** factorise the quadratics

3 a -8 **b** 3   **c** -36 **d** -9

4 a, d, e

5 a $(x - 1)$, $(x + 2)$, $(x + 5)$

b $(x - 2)$, $(x + 2)$, $(2x + 3)$

c $(x + 1)(2x^2 - x + 4)$

d $(x + 3)(x - 3)(3x - 1)$

7 a 1, 2, 3   **b** $-1, -2, 3$

c $-2, 4, \frac{1}{2}$ **d** $1, -2, -3$

8 $2, -2, -3, -\frac{1}{3}$

Outcome 1b Page 28

1 a $1.27, -2.77$ **b** $1.44, 0.232$

c $-0.740, 0.540$ **d** $-0.651, 1.15$

2 a, b, d, e, g, h real; **c, f** not real

3 d, g, h equal roots; **a, b, e** unequal roots

4 a $t \leq 2$ **b** $t = 2$

5 a $p \leq 4$ **b** $p = 4$

6 One point of intersection, i.e. equal roots

7 Discriminant > 0, i.e. two points of intersection

8 a $1 < x < 7$ **b** $x < -1$, $x > 3$

9 $x^2 - 3x - 4 = 0$

10 $y(2) = 5 > 0$, $y(3) = -10 < 0$; $x = 2.46$

Outcome 1 Assessment Page 29

1 a 22   **b** 5   **c** -2

2 a $(x - 2)$, $(x + 2)$, $(x + 1)$

b $(x + 3)$, $(3x^2 - 2x + 1)$

c $(x - 3)$, $(x + 2)$, $(2x - 3)$

3 $x = 2$, $x = -3$, $x = \frac{1}{2}$

4 a, c, d, e have real roots

5 a, c, d, e all have unequal roots

Preparation for Unit Assessment

Outcome 2a Page 30

1 a $\frac{x^3}{3} + c$ **b** $2x^3 + c$ **c** $\frac{x^2}{8} + c$

d $-\frac{x^3}{3} + c$ **e** $-3x^{-1} + c$ **f** $-4x^{-2} + c$

g $-\frac{1}{6}x^{-3} + c$ **h** $-\frac{1}{4x^4} + c$ **i** $-\frac{1}{x^3} + c$

j $-\frac{1}{12x^2} + c$ **k** $\frac{2}{5}x^{\frac{5}{2}} + c$ **l** $8x^{\frac{1}{2}} + c$

2 a $2x^2 + 3x + c$ **b** $2x^3 - \frac{x^2}{2} + c$

c $x^4 - 2x - 3x^{-2} + c$ **d** $-2x^{-1} - 2x^{-2} + c$

e $\frac{x^3}{3} + \frac{1}{2x^2} + c$ **f** $\frac{3}{2}x^{\frac{2}{3}} + \frac{3}{4}x^{\frac{4}{3}} + c$

g $\frac{8}{5}x^{\frac{5}{2}} - 2x^{\frac{3}{2}} + c$ **h** $\frac{x^4}{4} + \frac{3x^2}{2} + c$

i $\frac{1}{2}x^4 + \frac{3}{2}x^{-2} + c$ **j** $\frac{x^6}{6} + \frac{x^2}{2} + c$

k $\frac{x^4}{4} - x + c$ **l** $-x^{-1} - x - \frac{x^3}{3} + c$

3 a $\frac{7}{3}$ **b** 4   **c** $\frac{3}{2}$ **d** $\frac{7}{2}$

e 14   **f** 4   **g** −6   **h** $\frac{33}{8}$

i $\frac{-8}{3}$

4 a $\frac{14}{3}$ **b** $\frac{10}{3}$ **c** $\frac{40}{3}$ **d** −6

Outcome 2b Page 31

1 a $\frac{11}{3}$ **b** 8   **c** $\frac{22}{3}$ **d** $12\frac{2}{3}$

e $50\frac{5}{6}$ **f** $50\frac{5}{6}$ **g** $10\frac{2}{3}$ **h** 4

i 12

2 a $4 + 4 = 8$ **b** $15\frac{3}{4} + 5\frac{1}{3} = 21\frac{1}{12}$

c $6\frac{3}{4}$ **d** $\frac{4}{3}$

Outcome 2c Page 32

1 a 48   **b** $21\frac{1}{3}$ **c** $14\frac{2}{3}$ **d** $\frac{1}{6}$

e 12   **f** 16

2 a 4   **b** 8   **3** A, $\frac{5}{4}$; B, $\frac{3}{4}$

Outcome 2 Assessment Page 33

1 a $\frac{x^4}{4} - \frac{x^3}{3} + c$ **b** $-\frac{1}{x} - \frac{1}{2x^2} + c$

c $\frac{x^3}{3} - x + c$ **d** $\frac{2}{5}x^{\frac{5}{2}} - \frac{x^2}{2} + c$

2 a $\frac{9}{10}$ **b** $\frac{2}{3}$ **c** 3

3 $15\frac{1}{3}$ **4** 8

5 a $\frac{23}{12}$ **b** $\frac{1}{3}$

Preparation for Unit Assessment

Outcome 3a Page 34

1 a $x = 30, 150$ **b** $x = 0, 360$

c $x = \frac{\pi}{3}, \frac{4\pi}{3}$ **d** $x = \frac{4\pi}{3}, \frac{5\pi}{3}$

2 a $x = \frac{3\pi}{4}, \frac{7\pi}{4}$ **b** $x = \frac{7\pi}{6}, \frac{11\pi}{6}$

c $x = 15, 105, 195, 285$
d $x = 75, 105, 255, 285$

e $x = \frac{5\pi}{4}, \frac{7\pi}{4}$ **f** $x = 15, 75, 135$

3 a $x = 36.9, 143.1$ **b** $x = 2.7, 3.6$
c $x = 236.3$
d $x = 0.5, 1.1, 3.6, 4.2$
e $x = 0.6, 2.5, 3.8, 5.7$
f $x = 76.7, 166.7, 256.7, 346.7$

4 a $x = 70$ **b** $x = 50$

c $x = 30, 210$ **d** $x = \frac{\pi}{3}$

e $x = \frac{7\pi}{12}$ **f** $x = \frac{\pi}{2}, \frac{3\pi}{2}$

5 a $x = 96.4, 323.6$ **b** $x = 34.4, 125.6$
c $x = 78.4, 258.4$ **d** $x = 0.7, 3.7$
e $x = 0.7, 4.5$ **f** $x = 1.4, 3.0$

Outcome 3b Page 35

1 a sin P cos Q − cos P sin Q
b cos C cos D − sin C sin D
c cos 3M cos N + sin 3M sin N
d sin A cos 2B + cos A sin 2B

2 a $\cos^2 P - \sin^2 P$ **b** $2 \sin x \cos x$
c $\cos^2 2M - \sin^2 2M$ **d** $2 \sin 2E \cos 2E$

3 a $\frac{56}{65}$ **b** $\frac{33}{65}$ **c** $\frac{63}{65}$ **d** $\frac{16}{65}$

5 a $\frac{16}{65}$ **b** $\frac{63}{65}$ **c** $\frac{120}{169}$ **d** $\frac{-7}{25}$

Outcome 3c Page 36

1 $x = \frac{\pi}{4}, \frac{5\pi}{4}$ **2** $x = 30, 210$

3 a $\cos(x + 40°)$ **b** $x = 26.4, 253.4$

4 a $x = 20, 140$ **b** $x = 55, 235$

c $x = \frac{11\pi}{30}, \frac{31\pi}{30}$

5 own proof

6 a 90, 270   **b** 45, 225

7 a $x = 0, 2\pi$ **b** $x = \frac{4\pi}{3}, \frac{5\pi}{3}$

8 a $x = 45$ **b** $x = \frac{\pi}{6}, \frac{5\pi}{6}, \frac{7\pi}{6}, \frac{11\pi}{6}$

c $x = 15, 75$

Outcome 3 Assessment Page 37

1 a $x = 10, 50$ **b** $x = 1.7, 2.7, 4.3, 5.9$
c $x = 31.7, 121.7, 211.7, 301.2$
d $x = 20, 260$ **e** $x = 1.1$

2 own proof   **3** own proof

4 $\frac{36}{325}$

5 a $\cos(x - 30)$ **b** 60, 360
6 a $\sin(x + 25)$ **b** 20, 110

7 a $\frac{3\pi}{2}$ **b** 210, 330

Preparation for Unit Assessment

Outcome 4a Page 38

1 a $x^2 + y^2 = 1$ **b** $x^2 + y^2 = 16$
c $x^2 + y^2 = 49$

2 $x^2 + y^2 = 100$

3 a $(x - 3)^2 + y^2 = 25$ **b** $(x - 8)^2 + y^2 = 36$
c $(x + 1)^2 + y^2 = 4$ **d** $(x + 4)^2 + y^2 = 1$
e $x^2 + (y - 2)^2 = 9$ **f** $x^2 + (y + 5)^2 = 64$

4 a $(0, 0), 5$ **b** $(6, 0), 4$
c $(-2, 0), \sqrt{5}$ **d** $(0, 7), 6$
e $(9, -1), 3$ **f** $(-4, 5), \sqrt{20}$

5 a $(x - 1)^2 + (y - 2)^2 = 9$
b $(x - 4)^2 + (y + 3)^2 = 4$
c $(x + 2)^2 + (y - 6)^2 = 15$
d $(x + 5)^2 + (y + 5)^2 = 36$

e $(x + 3)^2 + y^2 = 8$
f $(x + 9)^2 + (y + 1)^2 = 400$
6 $(x - 4)^2 + (y + 7)^2 = 25$

Outcome 4b Page 39

1 a 4, (0, 0)   **b**   8, (0, 0)
2 Its radius is zero
3 a (−3, 0)   **b** (−5, 0)   **c** (5, 0)
   d (0, −2)   **e** (0, −4)   **f** (0, 6)
   g $\left(-\frac{5}{2}, 0\right)$ **h** $\left(0, \frac{9}{2}\right)$
4 a 3   **b** 4   **c** $\sqrt{26}$ **d** 2
   e 1   **f** 7   **g** $\frac{3}{2}$ **h** $\frac{5}{2}$
5 a 5, (3, 4)   **b** 5, (2, 5)   **c** 8, (−6, 6)
   d 2, (−1, −3)   **e** $\sqrt{21}$, (5, −4)   **f** 9, (−4, 7)
   g 6, (−2, 5)   **h** 6, $\left(\frac{7}{2}, -\frac{9}{2}\right)$ **i** $\frac{9}{2}$, $\left(-2, \frac{5}{2}\right)$
   j $\frac{5}{2}$, $\left(\frac{3}{2}, -3\right)$

Outcome 4c Page 40

1 a, c All four lines are tangents
   b none of the lines are tangents
2-4 Own proofs
5 a, b, e, g line is a tangent **c, d, f, h** line is not
   a tangent

Outcome 4d Page 41

1 a Sketch of circle with centre the origin and
   radius 5
   b $x = \pm 5$, $y = \pm 5$, plus others
   c (5, 0), (−5, 0), (0, 5), (0, −5)
2 b $-\frac{4}{3}$ **c** $\frac{3}{4}$ **d** $4y - 3x = 25$
   e $-\frac{3}{4}, \frac{4}{3}$, $3y - 4x = -25$
3 $y = 3x + 20$
4 a (2, −3)   **b** −3   **c** $y + 3x = 13$
5 $2y + 3x = 20$
6 a (3, −2)   **b** $y = x + 3$
7 a $y = x - 1$ **b** $y = x + 2$
   c $7y + x + 82 = 0$ **d** $y = 3x$
   e $2y = x - 10$ **f** $2y = x - 8$
   g $2y = x - 7$ **h** $4y = 3x - 28$

Outcome 4 Assessment Page 42

1 a $x^2 + y^2 = 36$ **b** $x^2 + (y - 4)^2 = 16$
   c $(x - 5)^2 + (y + 2)^2 = 9$
2 a 3, (−5, 0)   **b** $\sqrt{50}$, (6, −1)
3 Line is a tangent
4 Line is not a tangent
5 $y + 4x + 1 = 0$
6 $5y = 3x - 8$
7 $x + 3y + 20 = 0$

Preparation for Course Assessment

Outcome 1 Page 43

1 a $(x + 2)$, $(x - 2)$, $(2x - 3)$, $(2x + 1)$
   b $(x + 3)$, $(2x^2 + x + 1)$

c $(2x - 1)$, $(2x + 3)$, $(2x - 3)$
d x, $(x + 1)$, $(x^2 - x + 1)$
2 a $(x - 3)$, $(x + 3)$
   b (−2, 0), (3, 0), (−3, 0), (0, −18)
3 a $p = -13$ **b** $p = 1$
4 a 8   **b** 199   **c** −3   **d** $\frac{5}{8}$ **e** $\frac{13}{4}$
5 $m = -11$, $n = 9$
6 a $x = 2.1$, −0.79   **b** $x = 0.19$, −2.7
   c $x = 0.14$, −3.6
7 a $\frac{1}{3}$, −3   **b** 0.62, −1.6
9 a $k = 4$, −4   **b** $t \geq 4$, $t \leq -4$
10 $m = \frac{1}{5}$ **11** $a = 4$
12 $t \geq \frac{1}{3}$ **13** $0 < m \leq \frac{8}{3}$
14 Own proof   **15** $k = -10$, 6
16 Own proof
17 a They do not touch
18 c There are two points of intersection
19 Own proof
20 a −10, 20
   b (4, −2), (−8, 4); $2y + x = 0$
21 $k = 10$, −10
22 a $c = -2m$ **b** $y = 5x - 10$
23 $k = 3$
24 a $-1 < x < 3$ **b** $x \leq -3$, $x \geq 4$
   c $x < -\frac{1}{2}$ or $x > 2$
25 $-4 < x < 2$
26 $x'' - \frac{1}{2}$, $x \geq 3$
27 a $x < -4$, $x > \frac{1}{2}$ **b** $x \leq -\frac{1}{2}$, $x \geq \frac{2}{3}$
28 a $x^2 - 3x - 4 = 0$ **b** $6x^2 + 7x - 3 = 0$
   c $16x^2 + 8x - 3 = 0$
29 $f(2) < 0$, $f(3) > 0$; $x = 2.77$
30 $x = 1.57$ **31** $x = -0.90$
32 2.12, −1.36
33 a 3 roots   **b** −1.82
34 a $(1 - x)(x - 2)(x - 3)$ **b** 1, 2, 3
   c $0 < x < 1$; $2 < x < 3$

Outcome 2 Page 46

1 a $\frac{x^4}{4}$ $\frac{1}{2x^2}$ | c **b** $x^3 + \frac{1}{2x^4} + c$
   c $x - \frac{1}{9x^3} + c$ **d** $\frac{-1}{2}x - \frac{x}{2} - \frac{3}{8x^2} + c$
   e $\frac{2}{3}x^{\frac{3}{2}} - \frac{3}{2}x^{\frac{4}{3}} + c$ **f** $4x - \frac{4}{7}x^{\frac{7}{4}} + c$
   g $\frac{2}{3}x^{\frac{3}{2}} - \frac{3}{4}x^{\frac{4}{3}} + c$ **h** $2x^{\frac{1}{2}} + \frac{8}{3}x^{\frac{3}{4}} + \frac{9}{4}x^{\frac{2}{3}} + c$
2 a $\frac{4}{3}x^3 - 2x^2 + x + c$ **b** $\frac{x^6}{6} - \frac{2}{3}x^3 + c$
   c $\frac{3}{2}x^2 + 6x + c$ **d** $\frac{x^3}{3} - \frac{x^4}{4} + c$
   e $\frac{2}{7}x^{\frac{7}{2}} + \frac{2}{\sqrt{x}} + c$ **f** $x - \frac{x^2}{2} + c$
   g $-\frac{1}{2x^2} - \frac{2}{x} - 3x + c$
   h $\frac{5}{8}x^{\frac{4}{5}} + \frac{5}{12}x^{\frac{6}{5}} + \frac{5}{16}x^{\frac{8}{5}} + c$

3 a 3   **b** 20   **c** $\frac{11}{36}$ **d** $17\frac{1}{3}$

  e 14   **f** 4   **g** $-10\frac{2}{5}$ **h** $-\frac{1}{6}$

4 The area above the x-axis is equal to the area below the x-axis.

5 a $6\frac{3}{4}$ **b** $3\frac{1}{3}$ **c** $\frac{1}{12}$

6 b 1

7 a $51\frac{1}{5}$ **b** $\frac{5}{2}$ **c** 10

8 a $\frac{8}{3}$ **b** $\frac{9}{2}$

9 a Student's own sketch   **b** $\frac{1}{2}$

10 $41\frac{2}{3}$ **11** $\frac{8}{3}$ **12** $\frac{8}{3}$

13 a 4.5   **b** 36

14 a $\frac{16}{3}$ **b** 0.85

15 a 36, $k = 6\sqrt{2}$ **b** $a = 9$

16 a (i) A(10, 12)   **(ii)** B(10, 10)   **b** $86\frac{2}{3}$

17 $\frac{16}{3} + \frac{81}{4} = 25\frac{7}{12}$

18 a $A = \frac{9}{4}$ **b** $B = \frac{16}{3} - \frac{9}{4} = 3\frac{1}{12}$

19 a 3   **b** 0   **c** -5

20 Own proof

Outcome 3 Page 49

1 a $x = 60, 300$ **b** $x = \frac{\pi}{4}, \frac{5\pi}{4}$

  c $x = 35.8, 126, 216, 306$

  d $x = 0.616, 3.76, 2.53, 5.67$

  e $x = 60, 300$

  f $x = 1.68$

  g $x = 30, 90, 150$

  h $x = 0.554, 2.12, 1.02, 2.59$

  i $x = 30, 60, 120, 150, 210, 240, 300, 330$

  j $x = \frac{\pi}{24}, \frac{7\pi}{24}, \frac{5\pi}{24}, \frac{11\pi}{24}$

2 a Own proof   **b** 11.8°, 78.2°

3 a $x = 30, 150$ **b** $x = 0, \frac{2\pi}{3}, \frac{4\pi}{3}, 2\pi$

  c $x = 0.340, 2.80, 4.71$

  d $x = 26.6, 45, 207, 225$

  e $x = \frac{\pi}{3}, \frac{5\pi}{3}$

  f $x = 0.322, 2.03, 3.46, 5.18$

5 a $\cos x$ **b** 1.16, 5.12

  c 0.29 radians, 2.85 radians

7 a $\frac{56}{65}$ **b** $\frac{-33}{65}$ **c** $\frac{-33}{56}$

8 $\frac{-\sqrt{3}}{2\sqrt{7}}$

9 a $\cos x / \sin x$ **b** $\sqrt{2}$

10 a $\frac{\sqrt{5}}{3}$ **b** $\frac{2}{3}$ **c** $\frac{4\sqrt{5}}{9}$ **d** $\frac{-1}{9}$

  e $-4\sqrt{5}$

11 0

12 a $\frac{120}{169}$ **b** $\frac{119}{169}$ **c** $\frac{5}{\sqrt{26}}$ **d** $\frac{28\,560}{28\,561}$

13 a/b Own proof   **c** $\frac{-33}{65}$

14 a (i) $\frac{1}{\sqrt{5}}$ **(ii)** $\frac{9}{\sqrt{85}}$ **b** $\frac{16}{\sqrt{425}}$ **c** $\frac{13}{\sqrt{425}}$

15 $-\frac{63}{16}$ **16** $\frac{33}{65}$

17 $\frac{33}{65}$ **18** Own proof

19 a (i) $\frac{120}{169}$ **(ii)** $\frac{119}{169}$ **(iii)** $\frac{120}{119}$

  b $\frac{1440}{119}$ **c** PQ $\simeq$ PR

20 a $\frac{1}{\sqrt{2}}$ **b** 135°

21 a 90, 210, 270, 330   **b** 0, 75.5, 180, 285

  c 30, 150, 200, 341   **d** 0.723, 3.14, 5.56

  e 0, 240   **f** 141

22 a Own proof   **b** 210, 330

23 256

24 a 145.4°, 214.6°   **b** 0.35 units

25 When $x = 48.6, 131, 270$

26 Own proof

27 a Own proof   **b** 0.927

Outcome 4 Page 52

1 10, (3, −1)

2 a $x^2 + y^2 = 25$ **b** $(x + 2)^2 + y^2 = 16$

  c $x^2 + (y - 2)^2 = 4$ **d** $(x - 3)^2 + (y + 5)^2 = 1$

3 a 4, (−2, −3)   **b** 4, (1, −5)

  c $\sqrt{40}$, (−4, 4)   **d** $\frac{5}{2}$, $\left(\frac{3}{2}, -2\right)$

4 b and **c.** In both cases $g^2 + f^2 - c < 0$

5 a (1, 3), (4, −6)   **b** (−1, 3), (1, 7)

  c (−1, 3), (3, 1)

6 $(x - 1)^2 + (y + 1)^2 = 25$

7 a (2, 0), (4, 2)   **b** $(x - 3)^2 + (y - 1)^2 = 2$

8 (2, −1)

9 (2, −5)

10 $3y + 7x = 11$

11 a (−2, −4), (4, 2)

  b $y = x + 7, \left(-3\frac{1}{2}, 3\frac{1}{2}\right); y = x - 6, (3, -3)$

12 c does not meet the circle

13 They intersect at two points

14 $y = 2x - 4, y = 2x + 6$

15 a 1, 13

  b Points of contact are (2, 3), (−4, 9); $y + x = 5$

16 $k = \pm 10$

17 $6\sqrt{2}$

18 Own proof

19 The circles touch

20 c $3y = 2x - 8$

  d Area of A is 52π, area of B is 13π

21 a 8 units   **b** $x^2 + y^2 = 121$

22 $x^2 + y^2 + 2x - 20y + 49 = 0$ or

  $x^2 + y^2 - 14x + 4y + 1 = 0$

23 $x^2 + y^2 - 8x + 2y - 8 = 0$

24 $(x + 2)^2 + (y - 3)^2 = 15$

25 a $(x - 4)^2 + y^2 = 2$ **b** $x^2 + (y + 4)^2 = 2$

26 $x^2 + y^2 - \frac{10}{3}x + 8y = 0$

27 b $\left(2, -\frac{4}{3}\right)$

Mathematics 3 (H)

Preparation for Unit Assessment

Outcome 1a Page 56

1 a $\begin{pmatrix} 3 \\ 1 \\ 2 \end{pmatrix}$ **b** $\begin{pmatrix} -2 \\ 3 \\ 1 \end{pmatrix}$ **c** $\begin{pmatrix} -2 \\ -5 \\ 2 \end{pmatrix}$ **d** $\begin{pmatrix} 1 \\ -2 \\ -3 \end{pmatrix}$

2 a $\begin{pmatrix} 0 \\ 1 \\ 2 \end{pmatrix}$ **b** $\begin{pmatrix} -4 \\ 3 \\ -3 \end{pmatrix}$ **c** $\begin{pmatrix} -2 \\ 2 \\ -5 \end{pmatrix}$ **d** $\begin{pmatrix} -2 \\ -3 \\ -1 \end{pmatrix}$

3 a $\begin{pmatrix} 1 \\ 2 \\ 2 \end{pmatrix}\begin{pmatrix} 3 \\ 6 \\ 6 \end{pmatrix}$ parallel **b** $\begin{pmatrix} 2 \\ -1 \\ 4 \end{pmatrix}\begin{pmatrix} 10 \\ -5 \\ 20 \end{pmatrix}$ parallel

c $\begin{pmatrix} 3 \\ 0 \\ -1 \end{pmatrix}\begin{pmatrix} -12 \\ 0 \\ 4 \end{pmatrix}$ parallel

d $\begin{pmatrix} 2 \\ 1 \\ -3 \end{pmatrix}\begin{pmatrix} 6 \\ 3 \\ -8 \end{pmatrix}$ non-parallel

e $\begin{pmatrix} 5 \\ 10 \\ -5 \end{pmatrix}\begin{pmatrix} 3 \\ 6 \\ -3 \end{pmatrix}$ parallel

4 a (i) $\overrightarrow{BC} = 3\overrightarrow{AB}$ (ii) B common (iii) collinear
  b (i) $\overrightarrow{PR} = 2\overrightarrow{PQ}$ (ii) P common (iii) collinear
  c (i) $\overrightarrow{TK} = \frac{3}{2}\overrightarrow{SK}$ (ii) K common (iii) collinear
  d (i) $\overrightarrow{QR} = \frac{5}{2}\overrightarrow{SP}$ (ii) cannot identify
    (iii) parallel
  e (i) $\overrightarrow{FG} = -\frac{5}{4}\overrightarrow{EF}$ (ii) F common (iii) collinear
  f (i) $\overrightarrow{JK} = \frac{1}{2}\overrightarrow{GH}$ (ii) cannot identify
    (iii) parallel

5 a (i) $AB = \begin{pmatrix} 1 \\ 1 \\ 4 \end{pmatrix}$ (ii) $BC = \begin{pmatrix} 6 \\ 2 \\ 8 \end{pmatrix}$ (iii) No

  b (i) $\overrightarrow{DE} = \begin{pmatrix} 1 \\ -1 \\ 1 \end{pmatrix}$ (ii) $\overrightarrow{EF} = \begin{pmatrix} 3 \\ -3 \\ 3 \end{pmatrix}$ (iii) Yes

  c (i) $\overrightarrow{GH} = \begin{pmatrix} 1 \\ 2 \\ 3 \end{pmatrix}$ (ii) $\overrightarrow{HI} = \begin{pmatrix} 1 \\ 2 \\ 2 \end{pmatrix}$ (iii) No

  d (i) $\overrightarrow{JK} = \begin{pmatrix} 6 \\ 9 \\ -3 \end{pmatrix}$ (ii) $\overrightarrow{KL} = \begin{pmatrix} 8 \\ 12 \\ -4 \end{pmatrix}$ (iii) Yes

e (i) $\overrightarrow{MN} = \begin{pmatrix} 2 \\ 8 \\ -6 \end{pmatrix}$ (ii) $\overrightarrow{NP} = \begin{pmatrix} 3 \\ 12 \\ -9 \end{pmatrix}$ (iii) Yes

f (i) $\overrightarrow{QR} = \begin{pmatrix} 1 \\ 1 \\ 1 \end{pmatrix}$ (ii) $\overrightarrow{RS} = \begin{pmatrix} -3 \\ -2 \\ -3 \end{pmatrix}$ (iii) No

Outcome 1b Page 57

1 a $\overrightarrow{AP}:\overrightarrow{PB} = 1:5$ so $5\overrightarrow{AP} = \overrightarrow{PB}$
  b $\overrightarrow{PS}:\overrightarrow{SQ} = 1:4$ so $4\overrightarrow{PS} = \overrightarrow{SQ}$
  c $\overrightarrow{CT}:\overrightarrow{TD} = 2:3$ so $3\overrightarrow{CT} = 2\overrightarrow{TD}$
  d $\overrightarrow{GR}:\overrightarrow{RF} = 3:4$ so $4\overrightarrow{GR} = 3\overrightarrow{RF}$

2 a $3p = b + 2a$ **b** $5p = b + 4a$
  c $5p = 3b + 2a$ **d** $5p = 2b + 3a$
  e $7p = 4b + 3a$ **f** $5p = 4b + a$

3 a $\begin{pmatrix} 2 \\ 2 \\ 1 \end{pmatrix}$ **b** $\begin{pmatrix} 4 \\ 2 \\ 1 \end{pmatrix}$ **c** $\begin{pmatrix} 3 \\ 5 \\ 7 \end{pmatrix}$ **d** $\begin{pmatrix} 4 \\ 6 \\ 7 \end{pmatrix}$

4 a $\begin{pmatrix} 0 \\ 1 \\ 3 \end{pmatrix}$ **b** $\begin{pmatrix} 4 \\ -1 \\ 9 \end{pmatrix}$ **c** $\begin{pmatrix} -7 \\ 4 \\ 9 \end{pmatrix}$

5 a $(-4, 0, 2)$ **b** $(-1, -2, -2)$
  c $(8, -4, -1)$ **d** $(0, 0, 1)$
  e $(-2, 10, 10)$

Outcome 1c Page 59

1 a 12   **b** 6   **c** −2   **d** −7
2 a 13   **b** 17   **c** 89   **d** 145
3 a 14.1   **b** −12.7
4 a, b and **c**
5 a 46.4°   **b** 157.8°   **c** 71.5°   **d** 87.1°
6 a 12.6°   **b** 41.6°   **c** 83.7°   **d** 84.4°

7 a $\overrightarrow{AB} = \begin{pmatrix} 1 \\ -5 \\ -5 \end{pmatrix} \overrightarrow{AC} = \begin{pmatrix} 0 \\ 2 \\ -4 \end{pmatrix}$ **b** 71.8°

  c $\begin{pmatrix} -1 \\ 5 \\ 5 \end{pmatrix}\begin{pmatrix} -1 \\ 7 \\ 1 \end{pmatrix}$ 36.5°

8 a 49.5°   **b** 61.2°   **c** 116.6°

Outcome 1 Assessment Page 61

1 $\overrightarrow{AB} = \begin{pmatrix} 1 \\ -2 \\ 3 \end{pmatrix} \overrightarrow{BC} = \begin{pmatrix} 3 \\ -6 \\ 9 \end{pmatrix}$

  $\overrightarrow{BC} = 3\overrightarrow{AB}$; BC‖AB; B common
2 b
3 $(-2, 5, -6)$
4 $(4, -2, 0)$
5 scalar product = 0

6 $\overrightarrow{AB} = \begin{pmatrix} 4 \\ 6 \\ -8 \end{pmatrix}$ $\overrightarrow{CD} = \begin{pmatrix} 3 \\ 2 \\ 3 \end{pmatrix}$ scalar product = 0

7 $50°$ **8** $41.8°$

Outcome 2a Page 62

1 **a** $\dfrac{\pi}{2}$ **b** $\dfrac{\pi}{3}$ **c** $\dfrac{\pi}{4}$ **d** $\dfrac{\pi}{6}$ **e** $\dfrac{5\pi}{6}$

2 **a** $36°$ **b** $72°$ **c** $30°$ **d** $150°$
   e $120°$

3 **a** $3\cos x$ **b** $5\cos x$ **c** $-2\cos x$
   d $-6\cos x$ **e** $\frac{2}{3}\cos x$

4 **a** $-4\sin x$ **b** $-3\sin x$ **c** $3\sin x$
   d $2\sin x$ **e** $-\frac{3}{4}\sin x$

5 **a** $-2\sin x$ **b** $4\cos x$ **c** $-3\cos x$
   d $5\sin x$

6 **a** $-\sin x + 3\cos x$ **b** $2\cos x + 3\sin x$
   c $-3\sin x - \cos x$ **d** $\cos x + \sin x$

7 **a** (i) $\frac{1}{2}$ (ii) $\frac{\sqrt{3}}{2}$ (iii) $\frac{1}{\sqrt{2}}$
  b (i) $\frac{-\sqrt{3}}{2}$ (ii) $\frac{-1}{2}$ (iii) $\frac{-1}{\sqrt{2}}$
  c (i) $\frac{-3\sqrt{3}}{2}$ (ii) $\frac{-3}{2}$ (iii) -3
  d (i) 1 (ii) 0 (iii) $\sqrt{3}$

8 **a** (i) $1 - \frac{3\sqrt{3}}{2}$ (ii) $\sqrt{3} - \frac{3}{2}$ (iii) 2
  b (i) $\frac{8}{\sqrt{2}}$ (ii) $\frac{(3\sqrt{3}+5)}{2}$ (iii) 3

Outcome 2b Page 63

1 $f(x)$, $g(x)$ respectively:
   a x^3, $x+2$ **b** x^4, $2x-3$
   c x^{-1}, $3x+5$ **d** $3x^2$, $x-1$
   e $4x^5$, $3-2x$ **f** $\frac{5}{x}$, $3x+5$
   g $\sqrt{x}$, $2x-1$ **h** $x^{\frac{1}{2}}$, $3-2x$
   i x^3, $3x^2 + 2x + 5$

2 **a** $8(2x+1)^3$ **b** $15(5x-4)^2$
   c $-30(3-5x)^5$ **d** $-10(4-2x)^4$
   e $-2(x+3)^{-3}$ **f** $-7(7x-2)^{-2}$
   g $3(2-x)^{-4}$ **h** $3(5-3x)^{-2}$
   i $\frac{3}{2}(3x-1)^{-\frac{1}{2}}$ **j** $(2x-1)^{-\frac{1}{2}}$
   k $-(3-2x)^{-\frac{1}{2}}$ **l** $-\frac{1}{2}(1-x)^{-\frac{1}{2}}$
   m $4(x+4)$ **n** $72(6x-1)^3$
   o $6(1-x)^{-4}$ **p** $16(1-4x)^{-2}$
   q $-3(x+4)^{-2}$ **r** $-8(2x+1)^{-2}$
   s $6(1-3x)^{-2}$ **t** $-3(3x-4)^{-2}$
   u $4(2x+2)(x^2+2x+1)^3$
   v $36x(3x^2-4)^2$
   w $4(-1-3x^2)(3-x-x^3)^3$ **x** $-40x^3(4-2x^4)^4$
   y $-(4x-3)(2x^2-3x+1)^{-2}$ **z** $9x^2(2x^3-1)^{\frac{1}{2}}$

3 **a** $\sin x$, $2x+1$ **b** $\cos x$, $3x-1$
   c $\cos x$, $2x+7$ **d** $\sin x$, $4-x$
   e $\sin x$, $3-x^2$ **f** $\cos x$, $3x-1$
   g $\sin x$, $\sqrt{x}$ **h** x^3, $\cos x$
   i x^4, $\sin x$ **j** $\sin x$, $\frac{1}{x}$

4 **a** $3\cos(3x+1)$ **b** $-2\sin(2x-3)$
   c $3\sin(1-3x)$ **d** $-5\cos(2-5x)$
   e $2\cos 2x$ **f** $-4\sin 4x$
   g $-5\sin 5x$ **h** $-3\cos(-3x)$
   i $3\sin^2 x \cos x$ **j** $-4\cos^3 x \sin x$
   k $\frac{1}{2}x^{-\frac{1}{2}}\cos\sqrt{x}$ **l** $3x^3\sin(4-x^3)$
   m $2x\cos(x^2+1)$ **n** $-12x^3\sin(3x^4-1)$
   o $-3x^{-4}\sin(1-x^{-3})$ **p** $3x^{-2}\cos(2-3x^{-1})$
   q $-x^{-2}\cos x^{-1}$ **r** $2x^{-2}\sin 2x^{-1}$
   s $(x^{-2}-1)\sin(x^{-1}+x)$
   t $-(4x+1)\sin(2x^2+x+1)$
   u $4x\cos(2x^2-1)$
   v $(-2-2x)\cos(3-2x-x^2)$
   w $4x^3\sin(1-x^4)$
   x $(2x-5)\cos(x^2-5x-1)$
   y $15x^4\cos(3x^5-2)$

Outcome 2c Page 64

1 **a** $\dfrac{(x+1)^5}{5} + C$ **b** $\dfrac{(x+3)^6}{6} + C$
   c $\dfrac{(x-4)^3}{3} + C$ **d** $\dfrac{(x-5)^4}{4} + C$
   e $-(x+7)^{-1} + C$ **f** $\dfrac{-(x-1)^{-2}}{2} + C$
   g $\dfrac{-(x-5)^{-2}}{2} + C$ **h** $\dfrac{-(x+2)^{-5}}{5} + C$
   i $\dfrac{2(x+3)^{\frac{3}{2}}}{3} + C$ **j** $\dfrac{3(x+4)^{\frac{5}{3}}}{5} + C$
   k $\dfrac{3(x-3)^{\frac{4}{3}}}{4} + C$ **l** $\dfrac{3(x-6)^{\frac{7}{3}}}{7} + C$
   m $\dfrac{3(x+2)^{\frac{4}{3}}}{4} + C$ **n** $\dfrac{5(x-5)^{\frac{8}{5}}}{8} + C$
   o $\dfrac{4(x+1)^{\frac{5}{4}}}{5} + C$ **p** $\dfrac{4(x+3)^{\frac{9}{4}}}{9} + C$
   q $-2(x-2)^{-\frac{1}{2}} + C$ **r** $3(x+8)^{\frac{1}{3}} + C$
   s $2(x-1)^{\frac{1}{2}} + C$ **t** $\dfrac{-3(x-4)^{-\frac{2}{3}}}{2} + C$

2 **a** $\dfrac{(x+2)^5}{5} + C$ **b** $\dfrac{(x+3)^6}{6} + C$
   c $\dfrac{(x-9)^4}{4} + C$ **d** $\dfrac{(x-5)^3}{3} + C$
   e $\dfrac{-(x+1)^{-2}}{2} + C$ **f** $\dfrac{-(x+5)^{-3}}{3} + C$
   g $\dfrac{-(x-7)^{-4}}{4} + C$ **h** $\dfrac{-(x-8)^{-2}}{2} + C$
   i $\dfrac{2(x+1)^{\frac{3}{2}}}{3} + C$ **j** $\dfrac{5(x+4)^{\frac{6}{5}}}{6} + C$

k $\dfrac{4(x-2)^{\frac{7}{4}}}{7} + C$ **l** $\dfrac{2(x-1)^{\frac{7}{2}}}{7} + C$

m $\dfrac{3(x+4)^{\frac{2}{3}}}{2} + C$ **n** $3(x+3)^{\frac{1}{3}} + C$

o $-3(x-5)^{-\frac{1}{3}} + C$ **p** $\dfrac{7(x+6)^{\frac{3}{7}}}{3} + C$

3 a $\dfrac{-(x+1)^{-3}}{3} + C$ **b** $-(x+3)^{-1} + C$

c $\dfrac{-(x-2)^{-2}}{2} + C$ **d** $\dfrac{2(x+2)^{\frac{3}{2}}}{3} + C$

e $\dfrac{2(x-3)^{\frac{3}{2}}}{3} + C$ **f** $\dfrac{2(x+5)^{\frac{3}{2}}}{3} + C$

4 a $-3\cos x + C$ **b** $2\sin x + C$
c $5\sin x + C$ **d** $2\cos x + C$
e $-\sin x + C$ **f** $\frac{1}{2}\sin x + C$
g $-\frac{3}{4}\cos x + C$ **h** $-\frac{4}{5}\cos x + C$
i $-\frac{1}{2}\sin x + C$ **j** $\frac{1}{2}\cos x + C$
5 a $3\sin x + C$ **b** $-2\cos x + C$
c $-7\sin x + C$ **d** $\cos x + C$
e $-\frac{1}{3}\cos x + C$ **f** $\frac{2}{5}\sin x + C$
g $-\frac{1}{4}\sin x + C$ **h** $\frac{1}{6}\cos x + C$

Outcome 2 Assessment Page 65

1 a $-3\sin x$ **b** $2\cos x$
c $\sin x$ **d** $-3\cos x$
2 a $-5\sin x$ **b** $7\cos x$
c $-2\cos x$ **d** $3\sin x$
3 a $\cos x - 2\sin x$ **b** $-2\sin x - 3\cos x$
4 a $3(x+2)^2$ **b** $-3(x-1)^{-4}$
c $4(1+x)^3$ **d** $-1(4+x)^{-2}$

e $\dfrac{(x+3)^{-\frac{1}{2}}}{2}$ **f** $\dfrac{-(3-x)^{-\frac{1}{2}}}{2}$

g $-\dfrac{(2-x)^{-\frac{1}{2}}}{2}$ **h** $\dfrac{-(4+x)^{-\frac{3}{2}}}{2}$

5 a $\cos(x+1)$ **b** $-\sin(x-2)$
c $2\sin x\cos x$ **d** $-3\cos^2 x\sin x$
6 a $\dfrac{(x+2)^4}{4} + C$ **b** $\dfrac{-(x+1)^{-3}}{3} + C$

c $\dfrac{3(x-3)^{\frac{5}{3}}}{5} + C$ **d** $\dfrac{5(x-2)^{\frac{2}{5}}}{2} + C$

7 a $\dfrac{(x+1)^4}{4} + C$ **b** $-(x+1)^{-1} + C$

c $\dfrac{2(x-3)^{\frac{3}{2}}}{3} + C$ **d** $\dfrac{3(x+4)^{\frac{2}{3}}}{2} + C$

8 a $2\sin x + C$ **b** $-3\cos x + C$
c $-5\sin x + C$ **d** $4\cos x + C$

Preparation for Unit Assessment

Outcome 3a Page 66

1 a $\log_a 12$ **b** $\log_a 10$ **c** $\log_a 20$
d $\log_a 6$ **e** $\log_a 14$ **f** $\log_a 9$
g $\log_a 60$ **h** $\log_a 15$
2 a $\log_a 2$ **b** $\log_a 6$ **c** $\log_a 4$
d $\log_a 0.5$ **e** $\log_a 5$ **f** $\log_a 1$
g $\log_a 2$ **h** $\log_a 3$
3 a $\log_a 20$ **b** $\log_a 3$ **c** $\log_a 9$
d $\log_a 30$ **e** $\log_a 1.5$ **f** $\log_a 4.5$
g $\log_a 4$ **h** $\log_a 50$
4 a $2\log_a 5$ **b** $4\log_a 3$ **c** $-3\log_a 8$
d $5\log_a 6$ **e** $13\log_a 4$ **f** $5\log_a 2$
g $5\log_a 8$ **h** $-2\log_a 9$
5 a 2 **b** 2 **c** 3 **d** 5
e 1 **f** 2 **g** 2 **h** 4

Outcome 3b Page 67

1 a $\dfrac{\log_{10} 20}{\log_{10} 5}$ **b** $\dfrac{\log_{10} 21}{\log_{10} 3}$

c $\dfrac{\log_{10} 300}{\log_{10} 7}$ **d** $\dfrac{\log_{10} 30}{\log_{10} 2}$

2 a $\dfrac{\log_e 7776}{\log_e 6} = \dfrac{\log_e 6^5}{\log_e 6} = \dfrac{5\log_e 6}{\log_e 6} = 5$
(or by calculator)

b $\dfrac{\log_e 1024}{\log_e 2} = 10$ **c** $\dfrac{\log_e 4096}{\log_e 4} = 6$

d $\dfrac{\log_e 5}{\log_e 25} = 0.5$

3 a $\dfrac{\log_e 20}{\log_e 5} = 1.86$ **b** $\dfrac{\log_e 12}{\log_e 3} = 2.26$

c $\dfrac{\log_e 429}{\log_e 9} = 2.76$ **d** $\dfrac{\log_e 2}{\log_e 20} = 0.23$

4 a $\dfrac{\log_{10} 100}{\log_{10} 4} = 3.32$ **b** $\dfrac{\log_{10} 90}{\log_{10} 2} = 6.49$

c $\dfrac{\log_{10} 20}{\log_{10} 500} = 0.48$ **d** $\dfrac{\log_{10} 12}{\log_{10} 26} = 0.76$

5 a $10^{1.8}$ **b** $10^{0.35}$ **c** $10^{-1.3}$
6 a e^{24} **b** $e^{2.7}$ **c** $e^{0.6}$
7 a 125.89 **b** 1.70 **c** 24.53
d 90.02
8 a $10^{2.5} = 316.23$ **b** $10^{0.12} = 1.32$
c $10^{1.4} = 25.12$ **d** $10^{0.25} = 1.78$
e $10^{-1.2} = 0.06$ **f** $10^{0.05} = 1.12$
g $10^{-1.5} = 0.03$ **h** $10^{-2.3} = 0.01$
9 a $e^{1.9} = 6.69$ **b** $e^{0.23} = 1.26$
c $e^{-1.26} = 0.28$ **d** $e^{-0.9} = 0.41$

Outcome 3 Assessment Page 68

1 a $\log_a 35$ **b** $\log_a 12$ **c** $\log_a 15$
d $8\log_a 5$ **e** 3 **f** 2
2 3.58 **3** 0.88 **4** $10^{0.28}$

5 $e^{3.14}$ **6** 1380.38   **7** 1.164

8 2.00   **9** 2.83

Preparation for Unit Assessment

Outcome 4a Page 69

1 **a** $r \cos \theta \cos \alpha - r \sin \theta \sin \alpha$

    b $r \cos \theta \cos \alpha + r \sin \theta \sin \alpha$

    c $r \sin \theta \cos \alpha + r \cos \theta \sin \alpha$

    d $r \sin \theta \cos \alpha - r \cos \theta \sin \alpha$

2 **a** $5 \cos \theta \cos \alpha - 5 \sin \theta \sin \alpha$

    b (i) $5 \cos \alpha$ (ii) $-5 \sin \alpha$

    c (i) $3 \sin \theta \cos \alpha - 3 \cos \theta \sin \alpha$; $-3 \sin \alpha$; $3 \cos \alpha$

       (ii) $4 \cos \theta \cos \alpha + 4 \sin \theta \sin \alpha$; $4 \cos \alpha$; $4 \sin \alpha$

3 **a** (i) $2 \sin \alpha$ (ii) $2 \cos \alpha$

    b (i) $2 \cos \alpha$ (ii) $-2 \sin \alpha$

4 **a** $63.4°$ **b** $143.1°$ **c** $233.1°$

    d $323.1°$ **e** $213.7°$ **f** $108.4°$

5 **a** 5   **b** 13   **c** 2.5   **d** 17

6 **a** $17 \cos (\theta - 61.9°)$ **b** $29 \sin (\theta + 43.6°)$

    c $25 \cos (\theta + 343.7°)$ **d** $41 \sin (\theta - 347.3°)$

    e $\sqrt{13} \sin (\theta + 146.3°)$ **f** $5\sqrt{2} \cos (\theta + 8.1°)$

    g $5 \sin (\theta + 233.1°)$

Outcome 4 Assessment Page 70

1 $10 \cos (\theta - 53.1°)$ **2** $13 \sin (\theta + 67.4°)$

3 $26 \cos (\theta + 292.6°)$ **4** $37 \sin (\theta - 288.9°)$

5 $\sqrt{97} \sin (\theta + 156°)$ **6** $\sqrt{29} \cos (\theta + 21.8°)$

7 $68 \sin (\theta + 208.1°)$ **8** $61 \cos (\theta + 100.4°)$

Preparation for Course Assessment

Outcome 1 Page 71

1 **a** $-\boldsymbol{a} + \boldsymbol{b}$ **b** $-\boldsymbol{b} + \boldsymbol{c}$

    c $-\boldsymbol{a} + \boldsymbol{c}$ **d** $-\frac{1}{2}\boldsymbol{a} - \frac{1}{2}\boldsymbol{c} + \boldsymbol{b}$

2 **a** $\begin{pmatrix} 60 \\ 24 \\ 7 \end{pmatrix}$ **b** 65   **c** 21.1, 50.4

    d $\begin{pmatrix} 120 \\ 48 \\ 14 \end{pmatrix}$ $\overrightarrow{RT} = 2\overrightarrow{PQ}$; RT∥PQ

3 $\overrightarrow{AB} = \begin{pmatrix} 10 \\ -5 \\ -10 \end{pmatrix}$ $\overrightarrow{AC} = \begin{pmatrix} 70 \\ -35 \\ -70 \end{pmatrix}$ $\overrightarrow{AC} = 7\overrightarrow{AB}$;

    AC∥AB; A common

4 **a** $\overrightarrow{AB} = \begin{pmatrix} 1 \\ -2 \\ 3 \end{pmatrix}$ $\overrightarrow{AC} = \begin{pmatrix} 2 \\ -4 \\ 6 \end{pmatrix}$ $\overrightarrow{AC} = 2\overrightarrow{AB}$;

    AC∥AB; A common

b (i) $\overrightarrow{CD} = \begin{pmatrix} 2 \\ 3 \\ -1 \end{pmatrix}$ $\overrightarrow{CE} = \begin{pmatrix} 4 \\ 6 \\ 0 \end{pmatrix}$ $\overrightarrow{CD} \neq k\overrightarrow{CE}$;

    non-parallel

    (ii) Move E to (7, 4, 10)

5 $(9, -2, 7)$

6 **a** $(2, 1, 5)$ **b** (i) 28   (ii) 7

7 **a** C(6, 17, 27)   **b** D(9, 26, 42)

8 **a** S(28, 10, 2)   **b** 9:7 externally

9 **a** (i) $\boldsymbol{i} + 2\boldsymbol{j} - 3\boldsymbol{k}$ (ii) $2\boldsymbol{i} - \boldsymbol{j} - 2\boldsymbol{k}$

      (iii) $3\boldsymbol{i} + \boldsymbol{j} - 5\boldsymbol{k}$ (iv) $5\boldsymbol{i} + 5\boldsymbol{j} - 11\boldsymbol{k}$

      (v) $-2\boldsymbol{i} + 11\boldsymbol{j} - 6\boldsymbol{k}$

    b (i) 3.7   (ii) 3   (iii) 5.9   (iv) 13.1   (v) 12.7

10 **a** $x = 8$ **b** $n = 4.5$ $m = 6$

    c $a = 4$

11 **a** $21\boldsymbol{i} + 16\boldsymbol{j} + 12\boldsymbol{k}$ **b** 29

12 **a** $\begin{pmatrix} 9 \\ 24 \\ 32 \end{pmatrix}$ **b** 41   **c** $18.2°$

13 $54.2°$

Outcome 2 Page 74

1 $x + \sqrt{2}y = 7 + \frac{\pi}{4}$

2 **a** $-\frac{\pi}{28} \sin \left(\frac{\pi}{14} \right) x$ **b** $-\frac{\pi}{28}$ **c** waxing

3 **a** $5 \cos x - 12 \sin x$; max when $\tan x = \frac{5}{12}$; max value 13

    b $22.6°$

    c (i) $0°$ to $22.6°$ and $202.6°$ to $360°$

       (ii) $22.6°$ to $202.6°$

4 **a** (i) $2x$ (ii) $x = y^{\frac{1}{2}}$ (iii) $\frac{1}{2}y^{-\frac{1}{2}}$

      (iv) $\frac{1}{2}(x^2)^{-\frac{1}{2}} = \frac{1}{2x}$ (v) $\frac{dy}{dx} = 1 \div \frac{dx}{dy}$

    b (i)-(iii) same conclusion in each case:

      $\frac{dy}{dx} = 1 \div \frac{dx}{dy}$

    c $\frac{dy}{dx} = \frac{1}{\sqrt{(1 - x^2)}}$

5 **a** $V = ah$; $h = \frac{V}{a}$; $= \frac{1000}{(6x - x^2)}$ **b** 3

    c 111.1 cm (1 d.p.)

6 **a** $5 \cos \theta + 12 \sin \theta$ **b** $67.4°$

    c 9.23 units by 13 units

7 **a** $\sqrt{400 - x^2}$

    b $L = x + \sqrt{400 - x^2}$

    c (i) $10\sqrt{2}$ (ii) $20\sqrt{2}$ metres

8 **a** $h = \frac{5r}{3}$ **b** $V = \frac{5\pi r^3}{9}$ **c** $\frac{5\pi r^2}{3}$

    d $\frac{3}{5\pi r^2}$ **e** 0.12 units/second

9 **a** $\dfrac{(4x-3)^4}{16} + C$ **b** $\dfrac{3(2x-1)^{\frac{2}{3}}}{4} + C$

    c $\dfrac{2(3x-4)^{\frac{3}{2}}}{9} + C$

10 **a** $\dfrac{1}{3}$ **b** $-\dfrac{1}{6}$ **c** $\dfrac{1}{2}$ **d** 5

11 **a** $\dfrac{1}{3}$ km   **b** $\dfrac{1}{15}$ km

12 **a** $\dfrac{22}{15}$ square units   **b** 2 square units

    c $\dfrac{8}{15}$ square units

13 **a** (1.0, 4.0)   **b** 14.4 square units

14 **a** $-\dfrac{1}{2} \cos(2x+4) + C$

    b $\dfrac{1}{3} \sin(3x+5) + C$

    c $\dfrac{1}{3} \cos(5-3x) + C$

    d $\dfrac{3}{2} \sin(2x-1) + C$

    e $-\dfrac{1}{2} \cos(2x+4) - \dfrac{1}{3} \sin(3x-1) + C$

    f $\cos(2-5x) + C$

15 **a** 1   **b** 0   **c** $-\dfrac{1}{4}$ **d** $\dfrac{\sqrt{3}}{8}$

    e 0   **f** $\dfrac{1}{3}$ **g** 0

16 **a** own check   **b** 2.782 square unit (3 d.p.)

17 **a** $\dfrac{\pi}{12}, \dfrac{5\pi}{12}, \dfrac{13\pi}{12}, \dfrac{17\pi}{12}$

    b (i) 5.196 square units   (ii) 63.2%

Outcome 3 Page 78

1 **a** 0.68 kg   **b** 0.08 kg
    c after 5.42 minutes
2 **a** 1889 cm^2 **b** 259 cm^2
    c after 1.18 days
3 **a** 0.2   **b** -0.070
    c 0.851   **d** 44.6 °C
4 **a** 1.225   **b** £22 500
    c after 3.42 years
5 **a** $C_{10} = C_0 b^{10} (= 0.5 C_0)$ **b** 0.933
6 **a** (i) 98.7 square units (ii) 138.7 square units
    b 18.3 square units
7 **a** (i) 519 mice (ii) 873 mice
    b 6.19 weeks
8 **a** 10 litres   **b** 9.37 litres
    c 0.59 litre
9 **a** 8000 gallons   **b** 2690 gallons
    c 66.4%
10 **a** 500   **b** 2.97 days
11 **a** 50 000, -0.223 **b** after 7.22 years
12 **a** $10 = ae^b, 20 = ae^{3b}$ **b** 0.347
    c 7.07
    d $K(P) = 7.07e^{0.347P}$; 40.1
13 **a** $9 = 8^x$ **b** $\ln 9 = x \ln 8$
    c 1.057   **d** none
14 1.609

15 **a** $\log_{10} 4000 = \log_{10}(4 \times 1000)$
      $= \log_{10} 4 + \log_{10} 1000 = \log_{10} 4 + \log_{10} 10^3$
      $= \log_{10} 4 + 3 \log_{10} 10$
    b $\log_{10}(4.537 \times 10^{12})$
      $= \log_{10} 4.537 + 12 = 12.657$
16 **a** 6   **b** 100 000
17 **a** $8.32 \times 10^{-7}, 8.32 \times 10^{-9}$ **b** 4.6
18 **a** (i) $100 - 29 \ln 1 = 100$
      (ii) begin with 100%
    b 5.5%   **c** $t = 4.6$, i.e. on the 5th day
19 **a** $a = 10\,000$ **b** $b = 4170$ **c** 7109
    d 7.66 minutes
20 **a** $c = -6.91, k = 0.691$
    b (i) $t = 9.4$; 10th day   (ii) $t = 10.6$; 11th day
    c 201 birds
21 **a** $\log_{10} y = \log_{10}(ab^x) = \log_{10} a + x \log_{10} b$
    b $\log_{10} y = \log_{10}(ax^b) = \log_{10} a + b \log_{10} x$
    c (i) $\ln y = \ln a + bx$
      (ii) $\log_{10} y = \log_{10} a + bx$
22 **a**

x	0	1	2	3	4	5
$\ln y$	2.3	2.2	2.1	2.0	1.9	1.8

    b $p = 2.3; q = 1.8$ **c** $b = -0.1; a = 10$
23 **a** $\log_{10} T = \log_{10} a + t \log_{10} b$
    b $a = 200, b = 0.55$ **c** 3 °C
24 **a** $\log_{10} V = \log_{10} a + b \log_{10} h$
    b $a = 3.8, b = 0.5$ **c** 120 km

Outcome 4 Page 82

1 15.4°, 119.4°
2 **a** $\sqrt{58} \cos(x + 336.8)°$ **b** 72.2, 334.2
3 4 radians, 6 radians
4 **a** $13 \sin(x + 1.97)$
    b 0.30 radians, 5.20 radians
5 **a** $85 \sin(x + 1.42)$ **b** 100
    c 0.154 radians
6 **a** $65 \sin(x + 0.533)$ **b** $\dfrac{1}{65}$
    c 1.04 radians
7 $\dfrac{1}{\sqrt{13}}$, 33.7°
8 **a** $10 \sin \theta + 10 \cos \theta + 10$
    b $10\sqrt{2} \cos(\theta - 45) + 10$
    c (i) 45°   (ii) $10\sqrt{2} + 10$
9 **a** $5 \cos x° + 2 \sin x°$
    b $\sqrt{29} \sin(x + 68.2)°$ **c** $\sqrt{29}$, 21.8°
10 **a** $3 \sin x - \cos x = -1$
    b 0°, 216.8°, 360°   **c** 3, 1.2, 3
11 **a** $\sqrt{89} \cos(x + 212)°$
    b $x = 58°, y = 4.24; x = 238°, y = -4.24$
    c (i) $\sqrt{89}$ (ii) 148°
12 **a** $4.98 \sin(x + 280.4)$ **b** days 104 and 236
    c max 11; min 1
13 **a** $13 \cos(3x - 22.6)°$
    b 43.5°, 91.6°, 163.5°, 211.6°, 283.5°, 331.6°
    c (i) 27   (ii) 1
14 **a** $\sqrt{89} \sin\left(\dfrac{\pi}{12}x - 0.559\right)$ **b** 16.8, 23.5
    c (i) 21.4   (ii) 2.6

Statistics (H)

Preparation for Unit Assessment

Outcome 1a Page 85

1 Median pulse rate for females (approx. 80) greater than for males (approx. 70).
   Pulse rates for females more variable (slightly greater interquartile range).

2 Factory's estimates tend to be greater than those of the calibrating equipment.

3 **a** Cholesterol levels are considerably higher and more variable for these heart attack patients.
   b Cholesterol levels seem to become less over time for most patients, although a few patients experienced an increased cholesterol level.

4 **a** Males median increase in pulse rate (12 bpm) is less than for females (36 bpm). Males increase is more variable (range 50 bpm) than for females (range 33 bpm). Curiously, two males recorded a decrease in pulse rate after exercise. An error?
   b Findings can not be generalised – we do not know how students were selected.

5 **a** Dickens, median 14, IQR 17.5; Herriot, median 10, IQR 8.
   On average the passage by Herriot has shorter sentences of less variable length.
   b No. We do not know if these selected passages are representative.

6 **a** Brand 1, median approx 100 hours; Brand 2, median approx 80 hours; Brand 3, median approx 100 hours, about twice as variable as the other brands.
   b Brand 1 and Brand 3 are similar on average but approx 25% of Brand 3 lasted less than 95 hours. Choose Brand 1.

7 Placebo, median 0.5, IQR 3.5; Drug, median 2.0, IQR 3.0
   Positive values for 'Change' represent an improvement and on average the drug seems to have been effective and reduced pain. Two patients receiving the drug reported no improvement. Negative values for 'Change' represent an increase in pain and one patient on the drug actually reported an increase in pain.
   On average the placebo had very little effect with as many patients reporting an improvement as reported either no change or an increase in pain.
   Only a small number of patients took part in this trial and both groups showed a similar amount of variability.

Outcome 1 Assessment Page 87

1 On average, both groups of teachers felt that including statistics in school maths courses was a good idea (median score about 80 and similar variability with IQR about 20 to 25). However, the two groups responded differently to the statement that statistics was more useful than trigonometry. Apart from two extreme views (one in favour of statistics the other trigonometry), opinions in Group A were very consistent (small IQR about 12) and only partly in agreement (median about 50). In Group B opinions were much more variable (IQR 45) but on average were slightly more in favour of statistics (median 60).
   On average Group B found statistics easier than Group A (median about 30 compared to 50) and Group B was more consistent than Group A (IQR 20 compared to IQR close to 50). Note that more than 25% of Group A scored above 70 and so were very sure they found statistics difficult.

2 **(i)** Cash Flow to Total Debt Ratio: Almost all solvent companies have positive values (median 0.2 approx.) while over 50% of bankrupt companies have negative values (median –0.1 approx.). Both types of company show a similar amount of variability.
   (ii) Net Income to Total Assets Ratio: Solvent companies have positive values of this ratio (median 0.05) and are very consistent in this regard (very small IQR). Almost 75% of bankrupt companies have negative values (median –0.05 approx.) and there is considerably more variability (IQR 4 times greater).
   (iii) Current Assets to Current Liabilities Ratio: Bankrupt companies have consistently lower values (median 1.5, very small IQR) compared to solvent companies (median 2.5, IQR larger).
   (iv) Current Assets to Net Sales Ratio: Very little difference in either the average value or the variability. This ratio would not be helpful in predicting future success in business.
   Ratios **(i)**, **(ii)** and **(iii)** could be helpful for predicting future success although since the boxplots overlap for the two types of company there would be some uncertainty if each ratio was considered in isolation. If these three ratios were considered together it should be possible to predict companies with negative Cash Flow to Total Debt Ratio, negative Net Income to Total Assets Ratio and a Current Assets to Current Liabilities Ratio less than 2 are likely to become bankrupt.

Preparation for Unit Assessment

Outcome 2a Page 88

1 a $S = \{$HHH, HHT, HTH, THH, HTT, THT, TTH, TTT$\}$

b $E = \{$HHH, HHT, HTH, THH$\}$

c $P(E) = \frac{4}{8} = \frac{1}{2}$; $P(\bar{E}) = 1 - \frac{1}{2} = \frac{1}{2}$; $\bar{E}$ is the event 'there are more tails than heads'.

2 a 0.38 **b** 0.05

3 a $\left(\frac{1}{6}\right)^5 = \frac{1}{7776}$ **b** $6 \times \frac{1}{7776} = \frac{1}{1296}$

4 a $0.1 \times 0.1 = 0.01$ **b** $10 \times 0.01 = 0.1$

c $1 - 0.1 = 0.9$

5 a (i) $\frac{5}{12} \times \frac{5}{12} = \frac{25}{144}$ **(ii)** $\frac{5}{12} \times \frac{4}{11} = \frac{5}{33}$

b (i) $\frac{5}{12} \times \frac{7}{12} + \frac{7}{12} \times \frac{5}{12} = \frac{35}{72}$

(ii) $\frac{5}{12} \times \frac{7}{11} + \frac{7}{12} \times \frac{5}{11} = \frac{35}{66}$

6 a $1 - 0.05 = 0.95$

b $3 \times (0.05 \times 0.95 \times 0.95) = 0.135375$

7 a $(0.65)^3 = 0.274625$

b The three customers are acting independently.

8 $1 - (1 - 0.4)(1 - 0.6)(1 - 0.9) = 0.976$

Outcome 2b Page 90

1 a $S = \{$HHH, HHT, HTH, THH, HTT, THT, TTH, TTT$\}$

b $X = \{0, 1, 2, 3\}$ **c** $P(X = 1) = \frac{3}{8}$

d

x	0	1	2	3
$P(X=x)$	$\frac{1}{8}$	$\frac{3}{8}$	$\frac{3}{8}$	$\frac{1}{8}$

2 a

			BLUE			
	1	2	3	4	5	6
1	1, 1	1, 2	1, 3	1, 4	1, 5	1, 6
2	2, 1	2, 2	2, 3	2, 4	2, 5	2, 6
RED 3	3, 1	3, 2	3, 3	3, 4	3, 5	3, 6
4	4, 1	4, 2	4, 3	4, 4	4, 5	4, 6
5	5, 1	5, 2	5, 3	5, 4	5, 5	5, 6
6	6, 1	6, 2	6, 3	6, 4	6, 5	6, 6

b $T = \{2, 3, 4, 5, 6, 7, 8, 9, 10, 11, 12\}$

c $P(T = 7) = \frac{6}{36} = \frac{1}{6}$

d

t	2	3	4	5	6	7	8	9	10	11	12
$P(T=t)$	$\frac{1}{36}$	$\frac{2}{36}$	$\frac{3}{36}$	$\frac{4}{36}$	$\frac{5}{36}$	$\frac{6}{36}$	$\frac{5}{36}$	$\frac{4}{36}$	$\frac{3}{36}$	$\frac{2}{36}$	$\frac{1}{36}$

3

d	1	2	≥ 3
$P(D=d)$	$\frac{18\,564}{20\,000}$	$\frac{826}{20\,000}$	$\frac{610}{20\,000}$

4

y	0	1	2
$P(Y=y)$	$\frac{1}{9}$	$\frac{4}{9}$	$\frac{4}{9}$

5 a and **c** could be. **b** fails, negative probabilities. **d** fails, probabilities total more than 1.

6 a $\frac{1}{15}$ **b** $\frac{8}{7}$ **c** 0.25 **d** $\frac{1}{6}$

7

y	0	1	2
$P(Y=y)$	0.36	0.48	0.16

8

h	0	1	2	3
$P(H=h)$	$\frac{230}{406}$	$\frac{150}{406}$	$\frac{25}{406}$	$\frac{1}{406}$

Independence

Outcome 2c Page 92

1 2, 5, 1

2 0.5, 2.45

3 a

s	1	2	3	4	5	6
$P(S=s)$	$\frac{1}{6}$	$\frac{1}{6}$	$\frac{1}{6}$	$\frac{1}{6}$	$\frac{1}{6}$	$\frac{1}{6}$

b $\frac{7}{2}, \frac{35}{12}$

4 2.35, 0.9275

5 a

z	1	2	3	4
$P(Z=z)$	$\frac{1}{2}$	$\frac{3}{10}$	$\frac{3}{20}$	$\frac{1}{20}$

b $\frac{7}{4}, \frac{63}{80}$

6 a

w	0	1	2
$P(W=w)$	$\frac{3}{28}$	$\frac{15}{28}$	$\frac{10}{28}$

b $\frac{5}{4}, \frac{45}{112}$

Outcome 2d Page 93

1 Let r represent a random number:

r 0.444 0.196 0.358 0.599 0.824 0.902 0.610 0.256

a If $r < 0.5$ then Heads, otherwise Tails

H H H T T T T H

b Score = integer part of $6r + 1$

3 2 3 4 5 6 4 2

2 Let r represent a random number:

$x = 0$ if $0 \leq r < 0.4$; $x = 1$ if $0.4 \leq r < 0.7$; $x = 2$ if $0.7 \leq r < 0.9$; $x = 3$ if $0.9 \leq r < 1$

0.27564 0.81744 0.51909 0.36192 0.45263 0.33212 0.71808 0.24753 0.72644 0.74441

0 2 1 0 1
0 2 0 2 2

3 Let r represent a random number:

$0 \leq r < 0.1 \Rightarrow s = 0$; $0.1 \leq r < 0.2 \Rightarrow s = 1$; $0.2 \leq r < 0.6 \Rightarrow s = 2$; $0.6 \leq r < 0.9 \Rightarrow s = 3$; $0.9 \leq r < 1 \Rightarrow s = 4$.

Suppose your calculator gave:

0.949 0.384 0.885 0.975 0.893 0.079

Number of sales calls per month:

4 2 3 4 3 0

4 Let n represent a random number:

a $w = 1$ if $0 \le n < 0.1$; $\quad w = 2$ if $0.1 \le n < 0.3$;
$w = 3$ if $0.3 \le n < 0.6$; $w = 4$ if $0.6 \le n < 1$

$n =$	0.949	0.457	0.129	0.490	0.510
$w =$	4	3	2	3	3

b $r = 0$ if $0 \le n < 0.5$; $\quad r = 1$ if $0.5 \le n < 0.833$;
$r = 2$ if $0.833 \le n < 1$

$n =$	0.949	0.457	0.129	0.490	0.510
$r =$	2	0	0	0	1

c $t = 0$ if $0 \le n < 0.667$; $\quad t = 1$ if $0.667 \le n < 1$

$n =$	0.949	0.457	0.129	0.490	0.510
$t =$	1	0	0	0	0

d $x = -2$ if $0 \le n < 0.5$; $\quad x = 2$ if $0.5 \le n < 1$

$n =$	0.949	0.457	0.129	0.490	0.510
$x =$	2	-2	-2	-2	2

5 Take pairs of digits to represent the number of the lottery ball. Ignore repeats within a game, 00 and 50. If a pair of digits is a number in the range 51 to 99, subtract 50 to get number of lottery ball.

Game 1:

Pair of digits	35	65	35	36	38	00	56	45	72
Ball number	35	15	–	36	38	–	6	45	22

Game 2:

Pair of digits	30	07	39	51	08	13	99
Ball number	30	07	39	1	8	13	49

Game 3:

Pair of digits	19	48	15	92	96	83	42	13
Ball number	19	48	15	42	46	33	–	13

Outcome 2 Assessment Page 94

1 a $\dfrac{6436}{9977}$ $\qquad$ **b** $\dfrac{7507}{9977}$ $\qquad$ **c** $\dfrac{1239}{9977}$

2 0.6561. Each blood sample is analysed independently.

3 $\dfrac{1}{676}$

4 $\dfrac{4}{7}$

5 a

x	0	1	2	3	4	5
$P(X = x)$	$\dfrac{1}{32}$	$\dfrac{5}{32}$	$\dfrac{10}{32}$	$\dfrac{10}{32}$	$\dfrac{5}{32}$	$\dfrac{1}{32}$

b $E(X) = 2.5$ $\quad$ $Var(X) = 1.25$

6 mean = 2.4, variance = 1.24

7 a $\dfrac{1}{9}$ $\qquad$ **b** mean $= \dfrac{53}{9}$, variance $= \dfrac{152}{81}$

8 $k = 0.1$; mean = 45.5, variance = 8.25

9 Let r be a random number:
$0 \le r < 0.05 \Rightarrow n = 0$; $0.05 \le r < 0.2 \Rightarrow n = 1$;
$0.2 \le r < 0.55 \Rightarrow n = 2$; $0.55 \le r < 0.8 \Rightarrow n = 3$;
$0.8 \le r < 1 \Rightarrow n = 4$

r	0.322	0.161	0.922	0.153	0.664
n	2	1	4	1	3

10 Let r be a random number:
$0 \le r < 0.4 \Rightarrow x = 1$; $0.4 \le r < 0.7 \Rightarrow x = 2$;
$0.7 \le r < 0.9 \Rightarrow x = 3$; $0.9 \le r < 1 \Rightarrow x = 4$

r	0.23740	0.22505	0.07489	0.85986	0.74420
x	1	1	1	3	3

r	0.21744	0.97711	0.36648	0.35620	0.97949
x	1	4	1	1	4

Preparation for Unit Assessment

Outcome 3a Page 96

1 $3x^2 \ge 0$ for $0 \le x \le 1$ and $\displaystyle\int_0^1 3x^2 \, dx = 1$

a 0.125 $\qquad$ **b** 0.875

2

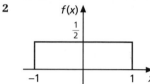

$f(x) \ge 0$ for $-1 \le x \le 1$ and
Area of rectangle $= 2 \times \dfrac{1}{2} = 1$
$P\left(-\dfrac{1}{4} \le X \le \dfrac{1}{2}\right) = \dfrac{3}{4} \times \dfrac{1}{2} = \dfrac{3}{8}$

3

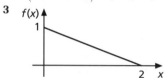

Area $= \dfrac{1}{2} + \dfrac{1}{4} = \dfrac{3}{4}$

$\displaystyle\int_0^1 \left(1 - \dfrac{1}{2}x\right) dx = \dfrac{3}{4}$

4 $P\left(\dfrac{1}{4} \le X \le \dfrac{1}{2}\right) = \displaystyle\int_{\frac{1}{4}}^{\frac{1}{2}} 4x \, dx = \dfrac{3}{8}$;

$P\left(\dfrac{1}{2} \le X \le \dfrac{5}{8}\right) = \displaystyle\int_{\frac{1}{2}}^{\frac{5}{8}} 4(1 - x) \, dx = \dfrac{7}{32}$

$P\left(\dfrac{1}{4} \le X \le \dfrac{5}{8}\right) = \dfrac{19}{32}$

5 a $\dfrac{5}{4}$ $\qquad$ **b** $\dfrac{1}{9}$ $\qquad$ **c** $\dfrac{3}{16}$ $\qquad$ **d** 12

e $\dfrac{5}{24}, \dfrac{7}{36}, \dfrac{3\sqrt{3} - 2\sqrt{2}}{8}; \dfrac{5}{16}$

6 a $k = \dfrac{8}{3}$ $\qquad$ **b** $\displaystyle\int_{1.2}^{1.4} \dfrac{8}{3t^3} \, dt = 0.2457$ to 4 d.p.

Outcome 3b Page 98

1 $\dfrac{2}{3}, \dfrac{1}{2}, \dfrac{1}{18}$

2 a $\dfrac{3}{4}, \dfrac{3}{80}$ $\quad$ **b** $0, \dfrac{1}{3}$ $\quad$ **c** $\dfrac{2}{3}, \dfrac{2}{9}$ $\quad$ **d** $\dfrac{5}{8}, \dfrac{19}{320}$

3 0.75 m, 0.1875 m^2

4 3 minutes, 0.5 minute^2

5 a 2 minutes, 1.8 minutes^2 $\qquad$ **b** $\dfrac{2}{27}$

6 0.5, 0.05, 0.104

7 a $\dfrac{23}{3}$ seconds, $\dfrac{200}{9}$ seconds^2 $\qquad$ **b** $\dfrac{39}{400}$

Outcome 3 Assessment Page 100

1 $f(x) \geq 0$, $\int_5^{10} f(x)\mathrm{d}x = 1$; $P(X > 7.5) = 0.75$

2 $k = -\frac{3}{32}$; $P(3 < X < 5) = \frac{11}{16}$

3 $k = \frac{5}{4}$; $P(T > 3) = \frac{1}{6}$

4 a $\frac{5}{16}$ **b** $E(X) = \frac{2}{5}$; $Var(X) = \frac{1}{25}$

5 a 0.0784 **b** $E(X) = \frac{25}{3}$; $Var(X) = \frac{625}{18}$

6 a $k = \dfrac{1}{2(\sqrt{3} - 1)}$

   b $P(X \geq 2) = \dfrac{\sqrt{3} - \sqrt{2}}{\sqrt{3} - 1} \approx 0.4342$

7 a mean $= 3$, variance $= 1$
   b $P(2 < X < 3) = 0.296$

Preparation for Unit Assessment

Outcome 4a Page 101

1 a $\Sigma xy = 45\,100$
   b $y = 14.8 + 0.0514x$; 27.65 cm

2 a $y = 24.25 + 1.64x$ **b** 171.85 cm

3 a $t = 67.7 - 13.9m$; 56.58 seconds

4 a $y = -4.87 + 0.545x$ **b** 22.38

Outcome 4b Page 103

1

	a	b	c
Σx	26	22	105
Σy	49.7	91	138
Σx^2	176	144	2275
Σy^2	672.47	2139	4030
Σxy	342.3	479	1805
$\bar{x}$	5.2	4.4	17.5
$\bar{y}$	9.94	18.2	23

2 a

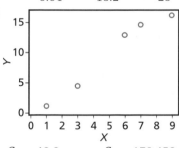

$S_{xx} = 40.8$ $S_{yy} = 178.452$
$S_{xy} = 83.86$ $r = 0.983$

   b

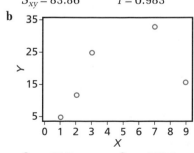

$S_{xx} = 47.2$ $S_{yy} = 482.8$
$S_{xy} = 78.6$ May not be linear.

c

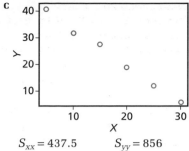

$S_{xx} = 437.5$ $S_{yy} = 856$
$S_{xy} = -610$ $r = -0.997$

3 $r = -0.988$, very strong negative linear relationship

4 $r = 0.671$, moderate positive linear relationship

Outcome 4 Assessment Page 104

1 a Scatter shows a linear model is appropriate
   b $\Sigma x = 369$; $\Sigma y = 813$; $\Sigma xy = 38\,548$;
     $\Sigma x^2 = 17\,539$; $\Sigma y^2 = 84\,929$
   c $S_{xx} = 518.875$ $S_{yy} = 2307.875$
     $S_{xy} = 1048.375$
   d $r = 0.958$; strong positive relationship
   e $y = 8.4 + 2.02x$; 79.1 mm

2 a 1743
   b $y = 22.9 - 0.648x$; 6.7 years
   c $r = -0.981$; strong negative relationship

3 a 1754
   b $r = 0.914$; strong positive relationship
   c $y = -149 + 1.27x$; 79.6 kg

4 a $32\,681$
   b $y = -2.89 + 0.874x$
   c $49.55 \approx 50$ marks
   d $r = 0.943$; strong positive relationship

Preparation for Course Assessment

Outcome 1 Page 105

1 a $Q_1 = 162$, median $= 164$, $Q_3 = 166$
   b lower fence $= 156$, upper fence $= 172$
   c possible outliers 151, 176
   d

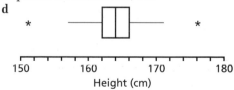

2 a $Q_1 = £111$, median $= £117$, $Q_3 = £132$
     lower fence $= 79.5$, upper fence $= 163.5$,
     possible outlier $= £165$

Return air fares

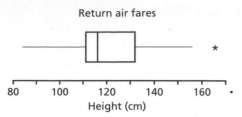

Height (cm)

3 a median = 541.5 pence, semi-interquartile range = 88.5 pence

b $\Sigma x = 4042$, $\Sigma x^2 = 2142668$; $\bar{x} = 505.25$p, $s = 119.79$p

c

	Semi-IQR	s
Breweries	214.0p	261.0p
IT	226.0p	525.3p
Chemicals	189.5p	346.4p

The values for standard deviation are considerably increased because of the influence of a few high prices. This is especially so for the Information and Chemical stocks. Semi-interquartile range is not affected to such a large extent and is a more robust measure of variability.

d Like standard deviation, the mean is strongly influenced by a few large values. The median is a more robust measure of location because it is less affected by the outliers. On average the highest price is paid for Electricity stocks and these also have the least variability. In order of the median price per share we have Electricity highest, followed by Breweries, Information Technology and Chemicals. Except for Electricity the variability in the prices of these stocks is around 200p when judged by the semi-interquartile range which is not greatly influenced by the outliers. There are some very high prices per share paid for three of the Information Technology stocks.

4 Method B results in higher values for the level of mercury in all but six fish.

5 On average Lab 2 and Lab 3 correctly estimated 5 mg per tablet although Lab 3 was much more consistent (less variable). Lab 1 consistently over-estimated the amount of active ingredient per tablet.
The variability of Lab 1 and Lab 3 is approximately the same.

6 There is a strong seasonal pattern – sales highest in 3rd quarter. The seasonal pattern becomes more pronounced over the six years.
There is a clear upward trend – sales are increasing year after year.

7 The scores for pupils at School 1 range from around 25% to 95% at the beginning of S1 and from around 30% to 100% at the end of S3. The scores for pupils at School 2 range from around 45% to 85% at the beginning of S1 and from around 80% to 100% at the end of S3. The results at School 1 are more variable than those at School 2.
On average the pupils at School 2 performed better at the beginning of S1 and much better at the end of S3. Their S3 marks are higher on average and less variable than their S1 scores.
At the end of S3 a large number (12 out of 17) of the pupils at School 1 scored less than any of the pupils at School 2.
On average, pupils at School 1 scored less than pupils at School 2 and made less progress.

Outcome 2 Page 107

1 a 24 **b** 3024 **c** 126 **d** 126
2 a 120 **b** 30 **c** 20 **d** 6720
3 a 10 **b** 56 **c** 35 **d** 924
4 a 1287 **b** $\dfrac{1}{1287}$
c 2598960 **d** $\dfrac{1}{649\,740}$
5 a (i) 120 (ii) 20 (iii) 10 (iv) 96
b $\dfrac{1}{5}$, 0, $\dfrac{3}{5}$, $\dfrac{7}{16}$
6 a $\dfrac{1}{13\,983\,816}$ **b** $\dfrac{6\,096\,454}{13\,983\,816}$
7 a $5 + 4 + 3 + 1 = 13$
b $7 + 3 + 2 + 1 = 13$; $6 + 3 + 2 + 1 = 12$;
$5 + 3 + 2 + 1 = 11$; $6 + 4 + 2 + 1 = 13$;
$5 + 4 + 2 + 1 = 12$; $4 + 3 + 2 + 1 = 10$
$5 + 4 + 3 + 1 = 13$
c 70 **d** $\dfrac{1}{10}$
8 a 0.82 **b** (i) 82 (ii) 12
c $\dfrac{6}{41}$
9 a $\dfrac{1}{10\,000}$ **b** $\dfrac{9997}{10\,000}$ **c** $\dfrac{53}{56}$
10 a $\dfrac{25}{102}$ **b** $\dfrac{4}{17}$ **c** $\dfrac{32}{221}$ **d** $\dfrac{15}{34}$
11 a 0.0018 **b** 0.0499
c (i) 18 (ii) 517
d $\dfrac{18}{517}$
12 a

x	0	1	2	3	4	5
$P(X = x)$	$\dfrac{1}{32}$	$\dfrac{5}{32}$	$\dfrac{10}{32}$	$\dfrac{10}{32}$	$\dfrac{5}{32}$	$\dfrac{1}{32}$

b 2.5 1.25

13

r	0	1	2	3
$P(R = r)$	$\dfrac{10}{56}$	$\dfrac{30}{56}$	$\dfrac{15}{56}$	$\dfrac{1}{56}$

mean = $\dfrac{9}{8}$, variance = $\dfrac{225}{448}$

14 a $\frac{1}{35}$ **b** $\frac{153}{35}$ **c** $\frac{201}{35}$

15 a 0.1 **b** 0.6 **c** 1.0 **d** 1.0

16 a $0.61k^2$ **b** $p(1-p)$

17 a $k = \frac{1}{16}$ **b** $E(X) = 2$, $Var(X) = 1$

18 a

x	0	1	2
P($X = x$)	$\frac{1}{5}$	$\frac{3}{5}$	$\frac{1}{5}$

mean = 1, variance = $\frac{2}{5}$

b

x	0	1	2	3
P($X = x$)	$\frac{27}{64}$	$\frac{27}{64}$	$\frac{9}{64}$	$\frac{1}{64}$

mean = $\frac{3}{4}$, variance = $\frac{9}{16}$

19

x	1	2	3	4
P($X \le x$)	0.1	0.3	0.6	1.0

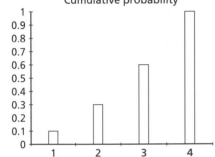

Cumulative probability

20

x	1	2	3	4
P($X \le x$)	$\frac{5}{32}$	$\frac{12}{32}$	$\frac{21}{32}$	$\frac{32}{32}$
P($X = x$)	$\frac{5}{32}$	$\frac{7}{32}$	$\frac{9}{32}$	$\frac{11}{32}$

21

y	0	1	2	3
P($Y \le y$)	0.125	0.500	0.875	1.000

Let r represent the random number:

$0 \le r < 0.125 \Rightarrow y = 0$;

$0.125 \le r < 0.500 \Rightarrow y = 1$;

$0.500 \le r < 0.875 \Rightarrow y = 2$;

$0.875 \le r < 1.000 \Rightarrow y = 3$

r	0.578	0.890	0.964	0.054	0.172
	0.232	0.858	0.585	0.315	0.754
y	2	3	3	0	1
	1	2	2	1	2

22 Let r represent the random number:

$0 \le r < 0.1 \Rightarrow z = 0$; $0.1 \le r < 0.7 \Rightarrow z = 1$;

$0.7 \le r < 1.0 \Rightarrow z = 2$

r	0.076	0.345	0.355	0.817	0.934
z	0	1	1	2	2

Outcome 3 Page 111

1 a 3 **b** $F(x) = \begin{cases} 0 & x < 0 \\ \frac{1}{3}x & 0 \le x \le 3 \\ 1 & x > 3 \end{cases}$

c (i) 0 **(ii)** $\frac{1}{3}$ **(iii)** $\frac{1}{3}$ **(iv)** $\frac{2}{3}$

2 a $f(x) = \begin{cases} 2x & 0 \le x \le 1 \\ 0 & \text{otherwise} \end{cases}$

b

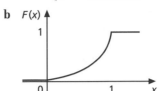

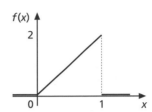

c $E(X) = \frac{2}{3}$, $Var(X) = \frac{1}{18}$

d $Q_1 = \frac{1}{2}$, median $Q_2 = \frac{1}{\sqrt{2}}$ or $\frac{\sqrt{2}}{2}$, $Q_3 = \frac{\sqrt{3}}{2}$

3 a $k = 6$

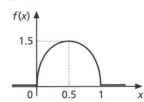

b mean = median = mode = $\frac{1}{2}$

c $F(x) = \begin{cases} 0 & x < 0 \\ 3x^2 - 2x^3 & 0 \le x \le 1 \\ 1 & x > 1 \end{cases}$

d $F\left(\frac{1}{4}\right) = \frac{5}{32}$ $\quad$ $P\left(\frac{1}{4} \le X \le \frac{3}{4}\right) = \frac{11}{16}$

4 a $Q_1 = 4 - 2\sqrt{3}$, $Q_2 = 4 - 2\sqrt{2}$, $Q_3 = 2$

b $P(1 < W < 3) = \frac{1}{2}$, $P\left(W \ge \frac{3}{2}\right) = \frac{25}{64}$

c $f(w) = \begin{cases} \frac{1}{8}(4 - w) & 0 \le w \le 4 \\ 0 & \text{otherwise} \end{cases}$

d $E(W) = \frac{4}{3}$ $\quad$ $Var(W) = \frac{8}{9}$

5 a $k = \frac{3}{4}$

b Show there is a maximum when $y = \frac{4}{3}$

c $F(y) = \begin{cases} 0 & y < 0 \\ \frac{1}{16}y^3(8 - 3y) & 0 \le y \le 2 \\ 1 & y > 1 \end{cases}$ $\quad$ **d** $\frac{16}{27}$

Answers content

6 a (i) $\frac{5}{36}$ **(ii)** $\frac{1}{16}$ **b** $\sqrt{2}$

c $f(x) = \begin{cases} \dfrac{2}{x^3} & x > 1 \\ 0 & \text{otherwise} \end{cases}$

7 a 20   **b** $E(Z) = \frac{2}{3}$, $\text{Var}(Z) = \frac{2}{63}$

c $F(z) = \begin{cases} 0 & z < 0 \\ 5z^4 - 4z^5 & 0 \le z \le 1 \\ 1 & z > 1 \end{cases}$

d (i) $\frac{3}{16}$ **(ii)** $\frac{13}{16}$

8 a $k = \dfrac{3}{4\pi^3}$; $F(\theta) = \begin{cases} 0 & \theta \le 0 \\ \dfrac{3\theta^2}{4\pi^3}\left(\pi - \dfrac{\theta}{3}\right) & 0 < \theta < 2\pi \\ 1 & \theta \ge 2\pi \end{cases}$

b $P(\text{Area} > \pi) = \frac{27}{32}$

c mode $= \pi$

9 a $P(X \ge 5) = 0.25$ **b** median $= 10 - 5\sqrt{2}$

c $f(x) = \begin{cases} 0.2(1 - 0.1x) & 0 \le x \le 10 \\ 0 & \text{otherwise} \end{cases}$

d $E(X) = \frac{10}{3}$, $\text{Var}(X) = \frac{50}{9}$

10 a $k = \frac{3}{4}$, $F(x) = \begin{cases} 0 & x < 0 \\ \dfrac{\sqrt{x}}{2}(3 - x) & 0 \le x \le 1 \\ 1 & x > 1 \end{cases}$

b $P(X \le 0.04) = 0.296$

Outcome 4 Page 114

1 a Almost perfect positive linear relationship; $r = 0.999$
b $y = 0.074431x$; 29.8 ft lb

2 $y = 5.81 + 0.895x$, 41.61 g

3 a $y = -137.3 + 10.6x$, £233.70
b (i) $y = -87.3 + 10.6x$
(ii) $y = -205.95 + 15.9x$

4 a $y = -1323.5 + 112.9x$, 2853.8 g
b 0.862, strong positive relationship

5 a $\Sigma xy = 520\,571$
b $y = 81.6 - 0.0314x$
c 43.9 mpg
d -0.842, strong negative relationship

6 a A scatter diagram shows the reading (0.2, 1.90) is an outlier
b $y = 0.490 + 2.016x$
c 1.498

7 a Test 2 is informative
b $y = 8.634 + 0.754x$, $53.874 \approx 54$ marks

Practice Papers
Paper 1
Section 1 page 117

1 $2x - 5y + 10 = 0$

2 $\dfrac{3\sqrt{x}}{2} + \dfrac{1}{2\sqrt{x}}$

3 $\dfrac{x^4}{4} + \sqrt{x} + c$

4 a $u_{n+1} = 0.96u_n + 100$
b stock will oscillate between 2400 and 2500 books

5 a $\dfrac{1}{(3x + 1)^2 - 1}$
b all real x except $x = 0$

6 $\pm \frac{2}{3}$

7 $x^2 + y^2 - 2x + 4y - 11 = 0$

8 15°, 75°, 195°, 255°.

Section 2 Part A page 118

9 $\sqrt{12} \sin (x + 60)°$

10 $\frac{1}{4}$

11 -1

12 a 13   **b** 5

Section 2 Part B page 118

9 a 12   **b** above 36 and below -12

10 a FFN, FNF, NFF,
b $3 \times 0.6 \times 0.6 \times 0.4 = 0.432$
c $0.4 \times 0.4 \times 0.4 = 0.064$

11 a $\frac{3}{2}$ **b** $\frac{21}{16}$

12 $y = 103.5 - 0.55x$

Paper 2
Section 1 page 120

1 a $(8, 4)$ **b** $y + 1 = \frac{1}{3}(x + 7)$ **c** $(-1, 5)$

2 a (i) $(3, 0), (-3, 0)$ **(ii)** $(0, 27)$
b $(3, 0)$ min; $(-1, 32)$ max
c (i) $f(x)$ gets very large and positive.
(ii) $f(x)$ gets very large and negative.

d

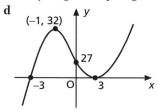

3 a (i) $f(g(x)) = 12 - 2x + k$;
$g(f(x)) = 6 - 2x - k$
(ii) $k = -3$
b (i) $h(x) = 4x - 9$ (ii) $x = 3$
4 a P(0, 0), J(12, –8), $r_P = \sqrt{13}$; $r_J = \sqrt{13}$
b $y = -\frac{2}{3}x$
c A(–3, 2), B(15, –10)
d $(x - 6)^2 + (y + 4)^2 = 117$
5 a curve 2 (amplitude of 3)
b 90°, 270°, 228.6°, 311.4°
c $0 \le t < 1.5,\ 3.8 < t < 4.5,\ 5.19 < t \le 6$
6 a $h = \dfrac{36\,000}{3x^2}$ and $S = 6xh + 2xh + 6x^2$
b (i) $\dfrac{96\,000}{x} + 6x^2 - 9000 = 0$
(ii) $f(11) = 831 > 0,\ f(12) = -272 < 0,$
For some x between 11 and 12,
$f(x) = 0.$
(iii) 11.7
7 a (i) 7 units^2 (ii) 1.75 m^2
b 1.4 m^3
8 a $u_{n+1} = 0.98u_n$
b (i) 20.4 °C (ii) 82%
c $v_{n+1} = 0.82\, v_n + b$
d 3.24
9 a $5i$
b $13i$
c (i) 13 (ii) it is real
d $\dfrac{(7 + 4i)}{13}$

Section 2 Part A page 123

10 a $\overrightarrow{SA} = \begin{pmatrix} 2 \\ 1 \\ 3 \end{pmatrix}$ $\overrightarrow{SL} = \begin{pmatrix} 6 \\ 3 \\ 9 \end{pmatrix}$
$\overrightarrow{SL} = 3\,\overrightarrow{SA} \Rightarrow SL \| SA$
b 165.4°
11 a $25 \cos(x + 286.3)°$
b 12.4, 135.0
12 a $a = 100,\ b = -0.22$
b 33.3%
c $x \ge 10.5$ i.e. during 11th day.
13 A$\left(0, \dfrac{3}{2}\right)$, B$\left(\dfrac{5\pi}{12}, 0\right)$
b $\dfrac{3}{2} + \dfrac{3\sqrt{3}}{4} - \dfrac{5\pi}{16} = 1.82$

Section 2 Part B page 124

10 a (i) 0.729 (ii) 0.243 (iii) 0.271
b £3131
11 a $\bar{x} = 70.4,\ s = 50.3$
b Tom is poorest having a very variable
performance and the lowest median;
Dick has a higher median but is still
fairly inconsistent; Harriet has the
same mean as Dick but is a much
more consistent player.
12 a (i) $y = 18.9 + 0.71x$ (ii) $y = 63$
b 0.71 reasonable positive correlation
13 a (i) $\dfrac{13}{3}$ (ii) $\dfrac{326}{90}$ **b** 0.53

Formulae List

The equation $x^2 + y^2 + 2gx + 2fy + c = 0$ represents a circle centre $(-g, -f)$ and radius $\sqrt{(g^2 + f^2 - c)}$.

The equation $(x - a)^2 + (y - b)^2 = r^2$ represents a circle centre (a, b) and radius r.

Scalar Product: $\mathbf{a.b} = |\mathbf{a}|\,|\mathbf{b}|\cos\theta$ where θ is the angle between $\mathbf{a}$ and $\mathbf{b}$

or

$\mathbf{a.b} = a_1b_1 + a_2b_2 + a_3b_3$ where $\mathbf{a} = \begin{pmatrix} a_1 \\ a_2 \\ a_3 \end{pmatrix}$ and $\mathbf{b} = \begin{pmatrix} b_1 \\ b_2 \\ b_3 \end{pmatrix}$

Trigonometric formulae:

$\sin(A \pm B) = \sin A \cos B \pm \cos A \sin B$

$\cos(A \pm B) = \cos A \cos B \mp \sin A \sin B$

$\cos 2A = \cos^2 A - \sin^2 A$

$\quad\quad\quad = 2\cos^2 A - 1$

$\quad\quad\quad = 1 - 2\sin^2 A$

$\sin 2A = 2\sin A \cos A$

Table of standard derivatives:

$f(x)$	$f'(x)$
$\sin ax$	$a\cos ax$
$\cos ax$	$-a\sin ax$

Table of standard integrals:

$f(x)$	$\int f(x)\,dx$
$\sin ax$	$-\dfrac{1}{a}\cos ax + C$
$\cos ax$	$\dfrac{1}{a}\sin ax + C$

Formulae List

Statistics formulae

Sample standard deviation: $s = \sqrt{\dfrac{\Sigma(x_i - \bar{x})^2}{n - 1}} = \sqrt{\dfrac{\Sigma x_i^2 - \dfrac{(\Sigma x_i)^2}{n}}{n - 1}}$

Sums of squares and products: $S_{xx} = \Sigma(x_i - \bar{x})^2 = \Sigma x_i^2 - \dfrac{(\Sigma x_i)^2}{n}$

$S_{yy} = \Sigma(y_i - \bar{y})^2 = \Sigma y_i^2 - \dfrac{(\Sigma y_i)^2}{n}$

$S_{xy} = \Sigma(x_i - \bar{x})(y_i - \bar{y}) = \Sigma x_i y_i - \dfrac{\Sigma x_i \Sigma y_i}{n}$

Linear regression: The equation of the least squares regression line of y on x is given by $y = \alpha + \beta x$ where estimates for α and β, a and b, are given by

$a = \bar{y} - b\bar{x}$

$b = \dfrac{\Sigma(x_i - \bar{x})(y_i - \bar{y})}{\Sigma(x_i - \bar{x})^2} = \dfrac{S_{xy}}{S_{xx}}$

Product moment correlation coefficient r: $\quad r = \dfrac{\Sigma(x_i - \bar{x})(y_i - \bar{y})}{\sqrt{\Sigma(x_i - \bar{x})^2 \Sigma(y_i - \bar{y})^2}} = \dfrac{S_{xy}}{\sqrt{S_{xx}S_{yy}}}$